RECLAIMING
THE FAMILY

RECLAIMING THE FAMILY

Edited by
Ralph Segalman, Ph.D.

A PWPA Book
St. Paul, Minnesota

Published in the United States of America by
Professors World Peace Academy
2700 University Avenue West
St. Paul, Minnesota 55114

Trade distribution by Paragon House Publishers

A Professors World Peace Academy Book

The Professors World Peace Academy (PWPA) is an international association of professors
and scholars from diverse backgrounds, devoted to issues concerning world peace. PWPA
sustains a program of conferences and publications on topics in peace studies, area and cultural studies, national and international development, education, economics and international
relations.

Library of Congress Cataloging-in-Publication Data

    Reclaiming the Family / edited by Ralph Segalman
          p.   cm.
    Includes bibliographical references
    ISBN: 1-885118-07-4 (Paper)
    1. Family—United States—Congresses. 2. Family policy—United States—
    Congresses.

HQ536.R4327 1998
306.85—dc21

                              98-18742
                                  CIP

TABLE OF CONTENTS

Preface vii

Chapter 1   The Problem of Broken Families in the Western World
             Ralph Segalman 1

Chapter 2   The Family Today
             Ralph Segalman 25

Chapter 3   Family Services in the Modern World: Failure and Betrayal
             David Marsland 71

Chapter 4   The Philistine Trap: Family, Education and Culture
             in the Western World
             Dennis O'Keeffe 95

Chapter 5   Families and Education: Reform from Above or Below
             Geoffrey Partington. 119

Chapter 6   Restoring America's Civil Society Through
             Community-Based Initiatives to Strengthen the Family
             Robert L. Woodson 141

Chapter 7   Programs of Traditional Agencies for Families
             David M. Genders 165

Chapter 8   Signs of Hope in Troubled Times:
             U.S. Programs that Work for Children and Families
             David S. Liederman and Mary Liepold............................ 185

Chapter 9   What Can Be Done to Reclaim the Family
             Ralph Segalman 215

About the Authors 261

Preface

Traditionally, it has been believed that the family is the one fundamental building block of the civil society. It has long been considered that without strong family structures civilization cannot prevail. Where there are weak family structures there will be overwhelming social pathology and possibly chaos. Alternative family structures, usually the products of ideological concerns antagonistic to the traditional family have been tried only to be failures in socialization, and destructive to those involved.

This book is a product of the thinking and analysis of about ten people who have been concerned about the state of the family after fifty years of cultural, economic, social, psychological and legal attacks.

Many other people have helped in the shaping of this book. Thanks are due to my colleague and friend who has helped us in the work of the concluding chapter. Dr. Gordon L. Anderson has been deeply involved and encouraging in the effort. Ruth S. Ancheta has contributed her knowledge about the social/psychological dynamics of young people in different levels of the society. I am particularly grateful to the staff of the Professors World Peace Academy for their help in the production of this work.

Ralph Segalman
Northridge, California
February 1998

Chapter 1

INTRODUCTION: THE PROBLEM OF BROKEN FAMILIES IN THE WESTERN WORLD

Ralph Segalman

In 1965 Daniel P. Moynihan, then an assistant secretary in the Department of Labor of the United States stated that "the one unmistakable lesson in American history is that a country that allows a large number of young men to grow up in broken families, dominated by women, never acquiring any stable relationships to male authority, never acquiring any set of rational expectations about the future—that community asks for and gets chaos. Crime, violence, unrest, disorder—most particularly the furious, unrestrained lashing out at the whole social structure—that is not only to be expected: it is very near to inevitable" (note 1).

Moynihan was referring to black youth in the United States in 1965, but as a result of the dynamics of familly life in the United States, his statement could easily apply to many of the young men in America of every color.

This problem affects families in other countries as well. Norman Dennis (note 2) reported at The World Congress of Families at Prague on March 20, 1997 that "British boys and adolescents have been invited to remain in a state of permanent puerility. Not surprisingly, given

1

the attractions of irresponsibility to all of us, in ever-increasing numbers they have gladly accepted the invitation. Any sociologist before the
1960s would have said that a society that did that would be asking for
trouble. And we've got it."

The problem of non-formation and disintegrated families in the
Western world has been serious since the beginnings of the 1960s. Since
then a number of social changes in the Western world have occurred
which have had a destructive effect on the family as well as on other
important institutions. The matter has progressed to the point that it
has had a serious and deleterious effect on the civilization in which
democratic society operates. Only in the intact family can children be
reared to participate as fully functioning citizens in what we know as
"the free society." Any other formulations for rearing children, whether
it be group institutions or alternative forms of the family structure are
so ineffective in the rearing of children as to require extreme elements
of external social control to maintain order in a functioning society.
Only the two-parent, intact family with an effective mother and father
acting as competent and functioning parents seems to be able to produce the building blocks of a democratic society. David Popenoe states
that a substantial stripping down has occurred in the Western world of
the nuclear family supported by the extended family and the integrated
neighborhood. He believes that "this trend is probably irreversible. For
all of these reasons the two-parent nuclear family is far more important
to children and to society in general than ever before in history" (note 3).

There is an old apocryphal story about a high cliff in a distant city
where many vehicles burst through the railing and fell down the cliff.
Many people were hurt. The city council voted to have an ambulance
always stationed at the foot of the cliff to rescue the victims. Little or no
effort was made to make sure that the railing was rebuilt of such sturdy
material so as to prevent such accidents, and to provide signs on the
road to insure that drivers would be more cautious. The road was not
broadened to make it safer.

This story is parallel to the way in which the crisis in family life has
been dealt with in Western society. For decades, we have had cautionary
advice by scholars like Moynihan who advised that we build stronger

protections against family breakup but to no avail by the society. Instead, our ambulances at the foot of the cliff have been heavy in investments, both human and monetary, to provide succor to the children of divorce and cohabitation, and to the mothers—often unprepared and unable—to care for these fatherless children. We have made mighty efforts to deal with the resulting social pathology at all levels of the society emanating from the products of divorce, desertion, lack of parents (especially fathers) and the eventual violence related to the products of such broken families. As far back as 1959, scholars like von Mering (note 4) have called attention to the growing social distance between fathers and their children and between their mothers and fathers. The causes of this condition and the underlying difficulties in many families by which the father became the "odd man out" in their families were not studied and nothing was done about them. Carlson describes the situation: "The period of 1946-1962 was marked by unusual signs of social renewal. After a steady century-long deterioration in measures of the health of 'The American Family', a remarkable recovery occurred: the marriage rate climbed, the divorce rate fell and the birth rate soared. College educated women were in the vanguard of this change. During these same years, America became again a property-holding people, making family-centered investments. Signs of religious commitment climbed in the 1950s. But in the 1960s, all was different, with divorce rates more than doubling, the rate of first marriages falling, and birth rates collapsing. A broad feeling of conformity gave way to a celebration of the abnormal. Ideologies long dormant in America including feminism, militant atheism, plus the challenges of the new left and the counter-culture made assaults on the existing order. They found a new common energy in the American family."

Von Mering described the problems of the reunited family after World War II. After many months and sometimes years of being away at war, the father returned. Because many of these marriages had been of short duration before the mandatory departure of the husband, the reunited family had to learn or relearn their roles in the reunited family. Many of the wives in these families were accustomed to leading independent lives without having to take their husbands into consideration.

Many lived alone with their children who had not yet met their fathers. Now, the mother-child bond had to make room for father. To be "on her own" in terms of her activities and in the rearing of her child or children was no longer possible. The husbands were used to a setting where their meals were presented on time and where their quarters were provided. This meant that many had to relearn life in a family.

Many marriages failed but new marriages now occurred. The "baby boom" was matched with new jobs, new housing, new training under the GI bill, and with very little time available between fathers and their children. This was a high employment period. Many fathers went to college, studied for careers and also worked on part-time jobs to earn the money needed for the family. Many nevertheless spent time in the recreations associated with men, in a continuance of the kind of "R and R" (Rest and Recreation) they had known in the services.

Many of the wives, now reunited with their husbands who had been so long away, had some difficulty in adjusting as wives and helpmates. Many had been employed and had experienced financial independence. Most had used the military allotments and shared part of the soldier's pay which was sent through military channels. After the return of their soldier-husbands many women resented having to "make room for daddy." Often the children resented that their father had gone away and had left them and it was not easy for them to get to know the new stranger who was now apparently "in charge."

Carlson describes some of the problems of the new or newly reunited family. He indicates that "the burgeoning American suburban model failed to resolve the family problem of the industrial civilization: The divorce of work from the home was a principal source of family deterioration. Suburban homes merely exaggerated this problem. Facing longer commutes, fathers tended to be even more separated from home, and the absent dad became a common memory among many of the children of the baby boom. Mothers meanwhile, found themselves in exaggerated isolation, bored and locked into ill-formed neighborhoods lacking natural and historic bonds. Recruits from the various liberations of the 1960s would come from the adults and children of these very suburbs"(note 5).

Carlson did not mean that these new wives were truly isolated. Their isolation was from the world of employment and from the marketplace in which their husbands were involved. The housewives' world involved many contacts with other new wives who had voluminous discussions over home problems, over how to "handle" their husbands and children, how it "felt" to be in the marriage relationship, and so on. After years of managing her home and children by herself, many of these women were now in a situation where there was a new "Pharaoh" in their "Egypt" who assumed that *he* would make most family decisions, and who expected to be waited on after the long commute to and from his day's work. It was perhaps here that the seeds of the "consciousness raising" of the women's liberation began.

It was during these critical years of suburban childrearing that the shaping of the children's attitudes occurred. It was in this period when the children of the newly established or reestablished middle class were shaped by the mothers, the suburban schools, and the childrearing culture of the time.

That childrearing culture assumed that frustration was bad for children. Children, according to the experts "need to explore their world freely" and with the least restraints possible, if they are to complete their necessary learning without which they might not achieve the adulthood due them. This was the time when the new parents sought to "give their children everything that they hadn't had." Every child was to be "special," an attitude which still persists even into the late 1990s, despite the fact that the substance of the term "special" was never really defined. For this "special" child to be restrained or constrained was unthinkable.

Yet another basic concept was general to the childrearing middle-class atmosphere of the time. The culture of the "Levittown women" and their husbands was inbred with an anti-authoritarianism viewpoint which reflected the natural rejection of the Hitlers, the Tojos, the Stalins and others against whom the military and the homefront had conducted a long war. There was an antiauthoritarian rejection of the rigid rules and regulations of the military and government restraints of the war years. The new suburbanites were antibureaucratic and anti-rules. Thus we had a new "special" generation being reared by parents and with a childcare professional ethos of minimal limits.

During and after the war years many of the new mothers looked to advisors beyond their own mothers, few of whom were geographically available. The new mothers now relied on child care specialists who published at a high level of professionalism, according to von Mering. Child upbringing and intensive mother-child bonding had little room for the father who was now intensely making efforts to establish the family on an economic basis. When the father did find time from work or from building his career, many of the fathers still felt "left out" of the family relationships. Many of the social service agencies reported the occurrence of "Monday Morning Crises" when mothers would come to the agency seeking help after a discordant Sunday when some fathers stayed home, when the father's authority was rejected by the children and when the mother was unprepared to help broaden the access of the family for the father (note 6).

In those families where this problem of "odd man out" was not resolved, the situation often ended in divorce. Many families repressed discussion of the problem as long as the children were young. In many such instances of the "odd man out" these problems appeared again during the children's adolescence and/or after the children were away at college. This was especially serious with inflexible fathers or mothers. "As an unchanging father he found only reproach and denial in store for him," according to von Mering. He tilled the field of depression, anger and rage. In the struggle he (was) a master at work. At home, at best, he receives little love and support in his search to help his sons learn to become men and to help his daughters learn how to relate appropriately to men. In this failure to teach his children through the fatherly role the ground was set for the "revolution" of the 1960s. The lack of integration of the parents and marriage partners in the family led to the weakness of the parent generation in guiding their children to "grow up" and become responsible adults. Many of that generation of children are only now, as middle aged and senior citizens, approaching emotional and social maturation.

Zinsmeister reports that:

Teenagers have been throwing high-blown and moralistic fits of child-ishness since the dawn of time. So what was new about the 60s? What was new was that in the 60s the children were allowed to get away with it. Instead of rebutting their exaggerations and silliness, the adult culture told the kids they were idealists and visionaries. Then suddenly whole bunches of people started growing their hair, inventing their own rules and railing against limits, responsibility and adulthood. (Suddenly) WHAM, many of the grown-ups run-ning the country were dressing, thinking and acting in confused sym-pathy (to the immature ideas and patterns of adolescents) (note 6).

Again, according to Zinsmeister:

So many adults went AWOL when the 60s kids came looking for meaning and direction caused big cultural problems. Throughout history it has been the propensity of the young to rebel and push the limits. It has always been the responsibility of adults to push back. What was new starting in the 1960s was that many adults no longer pushed back. They became intellectually and morally disarmed. When that happened, the 1960s turned into a national nervous breakdown (note 7).

The youth rebellion of the 1960s and its continuing effect on the cul-ture and social order is not alone in the thrust against the traditional family and the civilization. Others have chipped away at the necessary conditions without which family processes cannot proceed. Reiland, and others, described the way in which this has occurred in terms of Magnet's account of the behaviors and patterns of the youth movement still functioning even into the nineties (note 8).

By pushing no fault sex, instant gratification, drug decriminaliza-tion, and the idea that crime is social protest, liberal elites created a cultural revolution whose "most mangled victims" turned out to be the members of the underclass. We add to the list of casualties the children in the culture of divorce and children reared in families where the cul-ture of liberation is still the program of life.

The liberal elites of the continuing insurrections are led by indi-viduals with overlapping membership. Although they are quite secure in their control of the social fabric they are not necessarily satisfied with the conditions they have achieved. Ellen Willis, for example, states in a lead editorial in *The New Yorker* that "this is a society riven by cultural tensions." She lists feminism, sexual freedom and market forces along with other changes with which these elites have been involved over the past four decades. "Despite these changes (we) produced a satisfying alternative to the family" (note 9).

David Gelernter provides a helpful note to an understanding of how the elites have gained control of the contemporary culture and the social structure. He believes that there is an intellectual elite in charge of the culture and describes how it came about and the elements it controls. He indicates that this is not the product of conspiracy at work. Instead the seed for it came about during the huge expansion of the institutions of American higher education from 1945 onwards. In the US this growth was fostered under the financing of the GI Bill of Rights of the government for veterans of World War II. Also, the huge invest-ment of American government in education in the teaching of lan-guages, sciences, and mathematics, were a part of the Cold War struggle in competing with the technology of the USSR. The institutions of higher learning were involved in quick growth requiring new additions to their faculties. As usual, states Gelernter, "the tone was set by the ivy league institutions." Thus the social agenda was developed (note 10).

Gelernter indicates that a takeover at the top was decisive, not only at the higher levels of faculty and administration but it was also carried out by the graduates who became the "ranking politicians and staffers, judges and top lawyers, leading bureaucrats and business, financial and newspapers and entertainment people, prominent clergymen and aca-demics. The supply lines that fed these positions are also the same.... The prestige colleges play a separate role in staffing the elite." Obvi-ously, the universities accepted the other revolutionary movements. "Big changes were made," says Gelernter. Starting in the 1940s, admission and hiring policies were transformed. Intellectuals took over in moving from zero to total control. The 'new class' emerged out of the enormous expansion of higher education and the college educated." Gelernter describes how the students became the shapers of what and how learning was to occur. "These students were angry, intolerant, highly vocal, and case-hardened against logical argument."

Student protest at first was almost entirely directed against the compulsory draft for young men who were not temporarily exempted by reason of their educational enrollment. When the draft requirement was removed, the demands of the students broadened beyond the draft to issues of academic achievement and other requirements for students. By and large, the constraints on issues of educational rigor were so loosened for students that many employers had to install increased employee programs to provide learning which was formerly provided by educational preparation (note 10).

The old elite, says Gelernter, were oriented to rationality, attentive to religious precepts and mores as well as church attendees. They set the rules of behavior which required moral standards. Where moral behavior was violated, it was not set in such blatant form as to become a bad example. They respected authority and expected others to do so also. They were part of the conforming society.

Today, Gelernter states there is a new class of elite intellectuals who continue to see themselves as an "adversary culture." Where the new class finds itself in positions of authority, they give the icons of morality authority but do not change their behavior. And even worse, those who are their political admirers or followers do not condemn such hypocrisy. Instead they express their admiration and support for these accomplishments. Gelernter indicates that "today's elite loathes the notion of rules. They discuss and assess society as if it were a sick patient for which they prescribe. Intellectuals (especially in relation to familial issues and welfare state formulations) go back a century and have lots of prescriptions in store for the obstinate, dim-witted public."

Gelernter observes that "the universities (and their allies in the various liberation movements) have been set for a long time and we cannot change them." He believes that new institutions need establishment. He indicates that these new institutions will have to be built as morally oriented and strong enough to counteract the powerful indoctrination engines of university and grade schools in everyday life. These institutions would have no political agendas. "They would merely promote cant-free history, apolitical art, non-feminist news reporting...the teaching of technique and not self-esteem, moral seriousness, ideology-free language-items that today's elite despises and is attempting to destroy. Their aim would be a modest but steady increase (in the items listed above)." The suggestion of the new institutions Gelernter describes are reflective of the increasing movements of home schooling, the efforts of churches to build on pre-marriage educational programs, the movement to undo no-fault divorce, and the stolid retention of cultural and moral behaviors still to be found in the American mid-west, in many European settings and other western nations.

The retention by the intellectual elite of the controls and shaping of social policy in governmental and foundational circles without an understanding or concern for the purposes and cultural values of institutions involved, deserves some examination. Scarlett offers us the following observation about them: "What economist Friedrich Hayek called 'the fatal conceit' is alive and well: The belief that the experts, armed with good intentions and power, can shape economic and social outcomes." That fatal conceit is not uniquely a 1960s mistake. Hayek wrote about it 30 years earlier. The "new class" made central planning a commonplace, with even local family and neighborhood and even private matters became grist for (federal and other) government controllers. All of these programs now flourish in the hands of the senior '60s activists who now have become lawyers, consultants, politicians, media reporters, university officials and full professors (note 11).

Thus, in much of the Western world, and particularly in the United States, an ill-equipped but powerful intellectual elite sets the agenda and makes the decisions which shape the future of life in the third millennium for the Western world. This condition makes the reclaiming of the family very difficult. The reason this is difficult is that the new class in control of the culture and the society is the product of a generation of rearing in which the inner controls and understanding did not "take." Unlike its predecessors, many in this generation never learned the values and norms necessary for functioning families and for the functional democratic order. The socialization process offered by their parents to the baby-boomer generation was not accepted. Every rule necessary for direction and even traffic-control of the family and society were considered only as "optional" to this generation. For the first time in modern civilized history, many of the new generation did not learn the rules. And they are driving the society and teaching this rule-lessness to the new drivers.

Overview of This Volume

It was in the face of these difficulties that a conference on family life was held by the Professors World Peace Academy at Seoul in August 1995. In the conference there was a panel on reclaiming the family with papers given by David Marsland, Dennis O'Keeffe, Geoffrey Partington, David Genders, Robert Woodson, and Ralph Segalman. An additional paper was solicited after the conference from David S. Liederman and Mary S. Liepold. A second paper by Ralph Segalman has been added in order to cover the additional issues raised by the panelists and others on the subject of reclaiming the family.

David Marsland examines in his paper the services to families in Britain and in the westernized nations generally. He points out that most of these services have been focused on money assistance, despite the obvious observation by many that the problems are not monetary but rather familial and related to inadequate socialization as family and members of the society. He examines the nature and functions of the family. He examines the range and character of family services in modern society and points out how these services, governmental and voluntary, have been subverted beyond their logical purposes. In the process of building a national welfare state, he describes how these agencies have sabotaged local communities and left them helpless in their concern for people with problems in their midst. He examines the effect of what he describes as "mischief-making" by social workers, and their effect on the society. He is particularly disturbed by the prejudice against fathers by many of the agencies which has seriously aggravated the problems of family life. He also shows how theories of Marxism, feminism, collectivism and moral relativism have been used by welfare state entities, agencies, and elements of government in destabilizing the family.

He believes that the family is an indispensable mechanism in the production of autonomous, self-reliant personalities and that if the family is to be allowed to prosper then governmental, and particularly welfare systems, need to be radically transformed. He recommends that divorce needs to be made more difficult and marriage needs to be treated as unique, necessary, special, and permanent. He believes that much needs to be done to encourage and enable local communities in protecting and socially supporting the families in their midst.

Dennis O'Keeffe examines the position of the schools in promoting and encouraging what he describes as the worst aspects of human nature including idleness, selfishness, impatience, aggression and frivolity. He ties the malactivity of the schools to the problem of family dysfunction. The malfunctions and dysfunctions of family, schools, and popular culture are so interconnected as to indicate that if the problem of family dysfunction is to be resolved, it will require decisive changes in the schools. O'Keeffe points to a number of dishonest campaigns in the discussion of family breakdown. One is the myth that the single-parent pathogenic family is caused by poverty rather than by the behavior of men and women in such situations.

O'Keeffe deals with the impact of the contemporary culture, especially in terms of the effect of television, and in terms of popular music. He believes that these are impoverished especially against the backdrop of secondary and higher education. He underlines the failure of mass education as an agency of enculturation and in transmitting the high culture of our civilization.

Being less prepared than they ought, the products of secondary education fall victim at university to "political correctness" and other pathologies. O'Keeffe also points to the decline in civility in public and private life, and a lack of integrity which has increased the difficulty of everyday life. O'Keeffe raises the question: Can we eliminate shame and stigma from social life and still maintain the integrity of family life and all the other institutions which are basic to the society?

Professor Geoffrey Partington confirms that there is general agreement among both radicals and conservatives that the effect of single parent living on children is deleterious. He argues that the capacity of a mother to promote child development is seriously reduced if she carries the whole burden without the support of a husband. Partington believes that a good school education can best be built on a stable family life education. Partington classifies schools as high and low doctrine, in that the latter would have more of the civic moralism and less of the content and substance of religious beliefs taught. He states that he has found in his own research in South Australia that many parents who chose high doctrine schools did so because they viewed these schools as less trendy and more oriented to traditional values.

Partington indicates that where parents have been permitted to choose, they have made rational and logical choices. He indicates that the radical elite intelligencia oppose school choices for parents because it would mean a loss of power for themselves and their allies in the society.

Robert L. Woodson focuses on the causes of family dissolution in low income families and communities and provides a self-help approach toward remedial action. This chapter also provides reports of projects already successfully functioning in terms of "Reclaiming the Family" in their midst.

David S. Liederman and Mary Liston Liepold have written "Signs of Hope in Troubled Times: U.S. Programs that Work for Children and Families." It presents examples which the authors believe are effective in prevention of family dissolution and in family reunification. The common elements of these programs include home visiting, parent education, the use of community recruited family helpers and role models, and the linkage of a wide network of community services. Their focus includes prevention and child protection and support services with the many families which do not require an authoritative response. No sharp line divides the fields of family preservation, family reunification, families in the child adoption process and other services for families. They note the changes confronting many of the services especially as they face the devolution and decentralization of public funding and increased responsibility on the local community, regions and states. These conditions, they believe, may be a problem for local agencies but they may also provide an increased opportunity for local and community autonomy and increased local collaboration of services to families and children.

The remaining chapter by David Genders provides us with a view of child welfare agency work by an agency director, based on his own experience and analysis.

Genders examines the history of child care particularly as it shifted from orphanage to foster care, adoption services, group care programs and family service. He also discusses change in family life during recent decades and describes the need for reorganization of the service program to assume a greater role in integrating rather than segregating family members. He suggests an expansion of the scope and services of transitional residential care. He believes that individual treatment should be tied to family treatment and have an expanded scope to meet the child's and family's natural environment needs. He discusses the child's need for relationships beyond his immediate setting. He discusses family centered group practice, treatment focus of children in care, establishing and strengthening of family ties, and the need for personalization and individualization in family intervention. He discusses the need for family relationships, educational integration in the child's world, and community residential life. The requisite services beyond residential care to the family for preservation or rehabilitation, the need for new services including respite care, emancipation support, after care support and other services are also discussed.

Liederman/Liepold and Genders present examples of programs which are both effective and suitable for the reclamation of the family.

Alternative and Conservative Views

Throughout this book, a normative and legitimate family is defined as two married adults, male and female, with or without children and related adults. Bronislaw Malinowski in his work in *Sex and Repression in Savage Society* stated:

> I know of no single instance in anthropological literature where illegitimate children would enjoy the same social treatment and have the same social status as legitimate ones. The universal postulate of

legitimacy has a great sociological significance. (Both) moral tradition and law decree that a group consisting of a woman and her offspring is not a socially complete unit (notes 13 & 14).

An alternative definition of the modern family has been offered and promoted by many feminist scholars. An example is Claire Rayner who states that "the only real family is the mother and the baby. Everyone else is peripheral." In contrast, we have accepted the conclusion reached by Richard Rector and others that much of the sociopathology and dysfunctionality of society is directly tied to the single parent family and alternative familial versions of childrearing which have been substituted for the traditional two parent family of the past (note 14).

The alternative views of the family focus on one of two distinct models. I have designated them as the "liberal" viewpoint and the "conservative" viewpoint.

The liberal viewpoint puts the responsibility for failure of the family, (and also the failure of the family to develop as in non-marriage, nonacceptance of familial commitment, etc.), on factors beyond the individuals involved. It tends to accept that the causes of family problems and their effects derive from the dysfunctionalities of the social system and from the failures of the state (and the related economy) to provide for the families in the society. This view assumes that if there is "want" (often confused with "need") on anybody's part then the state has to do something about providing for it. Also, if anybody's action or inaction is dysfunctional or has a disastrous result, then the "system" (meaning the government, the legislature, the bureaucracy or the courts) needs to pass a law or make rules or arrange for some change which will relieve the affected persons and their "need." The changes suggested by policy advisors usually demand yet more action by the central government.

Related to the liberal view of people with problems is the inclination to assume that those who have trouble have it through no fault of their own. The corollary is social invention of victimology; treated as if a problem derives from external factors then those who are affected are unfortunate objects of the problem rather than potential "actors" in the resolution of their difficulties. Thus, those who have problems are really not responsible for their own difficulties, and the responsibility for solving these problems rests with society and central government.

Charles Murray has provided an explanation of the two different social policies which have appeared in the United States during recent decades. American social policy toward those who do not do as well as others in the society "underwent a transforming in three large domains: welfare, education and criminal justice. These domains were transformed among the elites who define the perceived wisdom in any given era."

Murray goes on to provide details. "The new wisdom has many elements, but the most fundamental and pervasive was the shift away from a belief in America as the land of opportunity, with the best and fairest system in the world, benign and self-correcting toward on assumption that the American system is deeply flawed and is responsible for the plight of the disadvantaged. Poverty, it was concluded, is caused by the structural feature of capitalism. If a student misbehaves in school or a young man snatches a purse, or a young woman has a baby without a husband, these are expressions of or responses to social conditions beyond their control. Value judgments themselves are inappropriate. Having a baby without a husband is a choice, not a sin and not necessarily a mistake. It is society that must change, not individuals, and to hold people accountable for their behavior is unjust—blaming the victim instead of the society or social, economic, occupational, etc., system" (note 15).

It must be noted that because of the growth in many countries of the welfare state and of welfare state policies, the culture of these societies has been strongly affected even in instances where no governmental financial or service aspects are involved. As a result, the behaviors of those who are recipients of such services and benefits are also strongly reflected at all levels of the society.

Another problem caused by this kind of domain activity is that the central government has neither the effective mechanism for dealing with such problems on a systemic basis nor the knowledge of how to solve the problems of poverty, educational ignorance and crime on the local scene where they occur and where the solutions have to be discovered and applied. The result is that the central governmental departments proceed to work at the problems by the development and installation of multitudinous regulations which are applied from border to border and from each state to each locality and have little or no effect on the problem. Compassion in our time has run amok, and been paid for in the coin of social decay (note 15).

The "orthodox conservative" domain, on the other hand, usually puts much of the responsibility on the individuals who experience the problem. Since problems come to everyone and most people are able to resolve their own difficulties, it is entirely up to each of us to plan the necessary changes to solve those problems. Similarly, if anyone's actions or inaction results in harmful consequences for him or his dependents or others, then that person is expected to learn from his experiences, to accept the consequences and to improve on his actions in the future.

If we were to take one example to indicate how this difference in policy stance reflects on a problem situation, it becomes clearer how the "actors" and "objects" of a problem are affected. Let us consider, for example, a family dissolution. If we are convinced that the family broke up primarily because of too little income, because the father in the home had badly prepared himself in school and in his training, then the issue supposedly becomes clearer (note 16). He was therefore less employable in the current market and so he was unable to adequately carry out his responsibility as a provider. If his lesser employability was due partly to the shortcomings of schooling and training available to him, and also partly due to his lack of effort during schooling and training, one can only arrive at the conclusion that both the liberal and conservative views are both only partly valid. This mixed conclusion would also be valid if there were an interactive process involved; namely that the person's lack of effort in school during training was brought on partly because of inadequacies in the school and training conditions and that he lacked sufficient effort in learning.

If both the system's and the individual's actions are interactive, then neither the liberal formula, nor the conservative formula provides a single means for resolution of the problem. It is also critical in an understanding of the process to emphasize that the examiner's view and conclusions are important in that this view changes or strengthens the way in which the persons affected relate to their problem, and how their children will view their own problems in the future, given the example of their parent. Too many people now view their careers, their marriages, their families and other important aspects of their lives on the basis of how others important to them in the society and in their life-space have rightly or wrongly evaluated their life-actions. An analysis of the social problems of the society, and especially of the problems of the family requires an understanding of individual motivation, learning and activity, and the degree of effective performance of the social system. This also requires our study of those who have succeeded in establishing their family and retention of their family cohesion and an understanding of the way in which their motivation and the social system services have been available or helpful and the degree of interaction between them.

The two views, liberal and conservative, are not mixable because any attempt to offer an interactive explanation has an inappropriate formula for change, either in the persons involved or the system. The interactive explanation requires change in both the individuals and those involved with the problem and in the systems in which they exist. The individuals involved are always to be compared with others in other sectors of the social system where the people are usually encouraged to be more appropriately motivated for success. It is also important to realize that these processes occur in a competitive system in which both successes and failures are to be expected. No one is able to or desirous of determining the degree to which the failure occurs as a result of the individual or the system. The truth will show that a "chicken and egg" process frequently occurs in combination of events and conditions which result in success for some and failure in others. To prevent failures from occurring would require that both strong motivational factors for success would have to be developed in the individuals concerned, combined with multiple available, accessible and visible opportunities for success in the social system.

The almost unalterable liberal viewpoint that we need only to increase the desirable opportunities in order to promote success is matched by a likewise unalterable conservative opinion that we need only to motivate the people concerned by establishing disincentives which divert individuals toward failure.

A conservative position would probably require disincentive laws, regulations and social policies which make divorce, separation and non-marriage unattractive and to encourage incentives which favor establishment and support of family life, especially where there are children. The liberal position would be the converse of these incentives and disincentives. Unfortunately, the views of these opposing positions seem to be cast in concrete. Like two tectonic forces moving independently, frequently in opposition and without allowance for the others, they are uncompromising.

Social Transformation and the Family

In the past, each of these interests had something to gain by establishing and promoting family life. Both men and women were benefitted by the social, economic and political support and encouragement of family life in the society.

What did men get out of family life up to the mid-century point? Men, both married and unmarried, needed to be cared for. Their laundry had to be done, their meals had to be prepared, and their homes had to be maintained. Married men were provided with most of their physical needs and with safe, dependable sex without fear of disease or recrimination. Married men were provided with social and community approval for their involvement in family support. Through their children, married men had part of the fulfillment of their need to leave their mark on the future.

What did women get out of life? From marriage with the right man, women received protection both physical and psychic. With a husband, women gained social and community approval. In marriage women, in part, received fulfillment of their need for leaving their mark on the future through their children and this also satisfied their need to fulfill their biological urge for motherhood. In marriage, women were usually assured of financial support as well as social and cultural enforcement of this function by their spouse. With their husband and children, women had social acceptance in the community. During pregnancy, especially, women benefited from the husband's protection and from the social reinforcement of the expectation of support which was placed on the husband.

Conditions in the society were far different during the two halves of the century. In the first half-century, facilities for the care of unmarried men were sparse. There were fewer inexpensive restaurants and proportionately, far fewer inexpensive room and board facilities. There were few relatively safe opportunities for men's sexual gratification in the first half of the century. The situation in the latter portion of this century is very different for men. Facilities for men at inexpensive rates both in terms of meals, lodging, laundry, and so forth are now much more accessible and available (note 17). Sex is now much more available on a socially related basis. And finally, the current feckless pattern of life-purposes among men and women in the culture of the baby-boom generation provides little stimulation for men and women to seek to leave their marks for the future through children.

Conditions for women have also changed. Beginning with the sixth decade of the century, the government, the legislature, the courts, the welfare system, etcetera became the providers of last resort for women (note 18). The community stigma on women who shared sex with men outside of marriage has disappeared, even in cases where children are involved. With increased employment opportunities, women are no longer as dependent upon men for financial support. Despite the increased availability for sex, and despite the apparent increased occurrence of sexual intercourse between the sexes, the undeclared conflict between the sexes has escalated and has become much more destructive to children. The changes in the lives of men and women have brought on an exchange. More and more women generally are giving up the gentle compassion associated with womanhood, and because of the change in their circumstances, careers and rights pressures, many have replaced compassion with the avarice of men in the competitive world (note 19).

It is fatuous and unreal to argue for a return to the conditions of the past when the family was generally secure and stable in Western nations. It probably is more reasonable and effective to call attention to the issues and problems in the present condition of the family and in the social fabric which are apparent if changes are to be considered in reclaiming the family. Lasswell, in his discussion of "Man, the Social Animal" (note 20) states that a "stable society (requires) a common map of perception, belief and identity." He states that "in such a setting the individual learns from earliest infancy to think, feel, and act in ways that bring positive rather than negative consequences from the social and natural environment. Socialization is the process by which private motivations are channels into acceptable public acts."

Conclusion

If our readers are to benefit from this discussion of issues about the family, then they need to understand that the problem of the family as an institution requires a resolution of the issues related to the perceptions, beliefs and (social, economic, political, etc.) identities of the family and their purposes. Because the family as an institution is so important for the functioning and stability of the society, it becomes necessary to reclaim the family. Accomplishing this requires a bridging of the wide gap between the liberal and conservative positions.

It is because of this wide gap between the fundamental belief systems related to family and societal life that we found it necessary to provide so much material in addition to the chapters provided by the contributors. Because devolution has already begun in many of the welfare policy deliberations of the Western nations, even more understanding of contemporary developments in the family will need to be understood. Devolution can be expected to rapidly shift the nexus of family policies issues toward localities and away from centralized planning.

Without the functioning family as an institution, democratic civilization cannot endure. Without the traditional family format as a model of effective socialization and relationships, family reclamation becomes very remote. Without an effective pattern of mutual commitment for the family on the part of the family partners, democratic civilization cannot endure. Without it the social entity is too unstable, insecure and ineffective in rearing the new generation. Without adequate mutual commitment of the family partners appropriate motivations becomes unattainable. Without a stable model of family life, mutually acceptable in all its parameters (including religion), the society and its political entities will not have new citizens to participate appropriately in an adequately democratic social order. Too many of our liberal idealists have hungered for a social order where everyone dioes their share of work and carries out their responsibilities and where no one took will take more than a fair share and let others go without. Conservative idealists hunger for the same kind of society but they kneo that human nature could not make everyone a good citizen. Some would never behave in a way that a centrally planned society needs. The best we can expect in terms of civilized human behavior can only come out of effective, complete families.

We remind the future that human beings are not 100 percent "good." Too many are not. It takes only a few to make a democratic, civil social order unattainable. A society without an adequate number of effective, functional, participating families will probably still be able to maintain a hold on law and order. Only if it has the right *kind* of families can it expect justice and democracy, as well.

NOTES

1. Moynihan, Daniel P., *The Negro Family in America*, A report of the U.S. Department of Labor, Washington, DC, 1965.
2. Dennis, Norman, Report made at the World Congress of Families, Prague, The Czech Republic, March 19-23, 1997. (Proceedings of the World Congress of 1997 can be secured from The Rockford Institute, Rockford Illinois.) Mr. Dennis is the Leverhulme Fellow Emeritus, University of Newcastle Upon Tyne, England.
3. Popenoe, David, "How to Restore the Nuclear Family in Modern Societies," World Congress of Families, Prague, The Czech Republic, March 22, 1997. The Popenoe paper is available as part of the proceedings of the Congress through The Rockford Institute, Rockford, Illinois.
4. Von Mering, Otto O., "Forms of Fathering in Relationship to Mother-Child Pairs" in *The Significance of the Father*, published by Family Service Association, New York, NY, April 1959.

5. Carlson, Allan, "Toward the Virtuous Economy," Keynote Address at The World Congress of Families, Prague, The Czech Republic, March 22, 1997. Mr. Carlson's paper can be secured at the Congress American Office, care of The Rockford Institute, Rockford, Illinois. Many of these "odd man out" families moved on to separation and divorce. In many of these situations the mothers decided to press for divorce because they believed that they would again have the conditions where the husband was away from home, where they would automatically receive "their money" in a timely manner, and where they would again be fully in charge of their homes and family. Many of them neither understood nor knew how to function as a family partner in their marriage because they had not until then experienced or learned these roles and their purposes. As children, their parents had given them everything they might need except the understanding of how to make an effective family life.

6. Zinsmeister, Karl, "Bird's Eye: Days of Confusion," *The American Enterprise*, Vol. 8, No. 3, May/June 1997, pp. 4,5.

7. *The American Enterprise*, vol. 8, no. 3, May/June 1997: Editorial on the 1960s youth counter-culture, with discussion of William Bennett's "Did the 1980s Rock Rot?" in the same issue.

8. Reiland, Ralph R., "The Sixties and America's Underclass," *The American Enterprise*, vol. 8, no. 3, May/June 1997, pp. 12,13. (Note Reiland reference is in connection with the Magnet, Myron article "The Dream and the Nightmare.")

9. Willis, Ellen, "Down with Compassion: Morality isn't all it's cracked up to be" (Editors "comment") *The New Yorker*, Sept. 30, 1996, pp. 4,5.

10. Gelernter, David, "How the Intellectuals Took Over (and what to do about it)." *Commentary*, vol. 103, no. 3, March 1997, pp. 33-38 and Trout, Paul, "Disengaged Students and the Decline of Academic Standards," *Academic Questions*, vol. 10, no. 2, Spring 1997 and The National Association of Scholars Report, *The Dissolution of General Education, 1914-1973*,NationalAssociation of Scholars, Washington, D.C., 1996.

11. Scarlett, Lynn "Missing the Boat: Was the '60s disdain for Business, Centralization and Conformity Healthy Until it went Awry," *The American Enterprise*, vol. 8, no. 3, May/June 1997, pp. 42-44. The failure of the planned society to operate efficiently is due to the nature of its participants. Unlike competitive society, where the participants are motivated by the market to buy, sell, work and purposefully manage resources appropriately and in a timely fashion, the participants in the planned centralized market have little or no motivations to achieve production, to limit waste of resources and work time, etc.

12. Dench, Geoff, *Transforming Men: Changing Patterns of Dependency and Dominance in Gender Relations*, New Brunswick, New Jersey, Transaction Publishers, 1996.

13. See preface, Morgan, Patricia, *Farewell to the Family Public Policy and Family Breakdown in Britain*, IFA Health Welfare Unit, London, 1995.

14. For a detailed discussion of issues and problems of the western family see: Thomas, Cal, *The Things that Matter Most*, Harper-Collins, New York, 1994, Epilogue pp. 209-219; Popenoe, David, *Disturbing the Nest: Family Change and Decline in Modern Societies*, Aldine, New York, 1988, pp. 238-239; Blankenhorn, David, Steven Bayme and Jean Bethke Elshtain, (Eds), *Rebuilding the Nest: A New Commitment to the American Family*, Family Service of America, Milwaukee, 1990, pp. 39-52, Popenoe, David "The Controversial Truth: Two Parent Families are Better," *New York Times*, Deelle, 1992; Rector, Richard, *Combating Family Disintegration: Crime, Dependence; Welfare and Beyond, Heritage Backgrounder #983*, Heritage Foundation, Washington, DC, April 8, 1994; Wilson, James, "The Moral Sense," Free Press, New York, 1993, chapter 7, pp. 141-164, and Popenoe, David, #15.

15. It is harder to convince one central government entity than to sell the change to hundreds of localities and legislatures, and particularly if that central unit is distant, both geographically and socially from the thousands of political and local interest groups who may object to them. Also, Murray, Charles "The legacy of the 60s" *Commentary*, vol. 94, no 1, July 1992, pp. 23-30; Feder, Don, "Killing Us With Kindness: How Liberal Compassion Hurts," *The Heritage Lectures*, no. 574, The Heritage Foundation, Washington DC, Jan. 13, 1977.

16. It is seldom that a family disruption occurs because of any one such factor. We merely offer this example for demonstration of the differing views of a particular problem.

17. The coin-laundromat is one example. The profusion of inexpensive, fast-food facilities and the growth of the frozen food business and microwaves make this aspect of men's lives much different in the latter part of the century.

18. The welfare system, the increased availability of federal and state facilities for the protection of women's rights, etc., are all examples of these developments.

19. Women's advocacy groups have sought and secured the right to fight alongside men in military attack brigades, units formerly restricted to men.

20. Lasswell, Harold D. "Man, the Social Animal," *Encyclopedia Brittanica* (15th ed.), Propaedia-Outline of Knowledge, Introduction to pt. 5, pp. 280-281, 1975.

Chapter 2

THE FAMILY TODAY

Ralph Segalman

Introduction

There is an old African saying, "When the Bull Elephants fight, the grass always loses." For the natives this can be interpreted as a life threat for the baby elephants who need the new grass for food. This view can also be applied as an analogy for the situation of the family in the contemporary world. It can be paraphrased as "when the adults (parents) fight in divorce, the family (and the children) always lose." And in turn so does the society which is dependent on the products of the family. We will present data which ties the quality of family life and familial childrearing to the degree and depth of productivity, standard of living and democratic order in the first century of life in the second millennium.

In chart 1, we present a comparison of the pre-1960s Western family in the Western world with the contemporary family of the current and family of the future.

It is important in an understanding of the differences to compare the norms of the pre-1960 family with those of the current and currently evolving family of the Western world.

Fleming (note 5) indicates that the American Family system in the past has exhibited five crucial qualities:

CHART 1
The Past and Present
Generations

Function	Pre-1960 Parent Generation	Post-1960 Parent Generation
Procreation	These families produced enough children to replace themselves and more. Most of these children had both parents with at least one part time or full time related adult at home who served as responsible and caring parents. Most of these children were successfully reared as self-sufficient and self reliant contributors to the body politic with sufficient education and vocational training to find places for themselves as productive members of the economy. (1)	This parent generation has fewer children, not enough among the married couples to replace themselves. Many of the children born to this generation live in single parent families. Many are in homes headed by a never-married mother and without a father in contact with the children. Too many of these children have not succeeded in becoming self-sufficient contributors to the body politic, and present problems to the society. (4)
Socialization	Most of this generation adhered to a set of core values lived by them and taught by them to their children. Thus, during those years, few social pathology problems were apparent among their progeny as adults. (4)	Many in this generation of parents relied on television to serve as the family sitter. The failure of the family to monitor and guide their children for a sizable portion of their free time and the failure of the schools to maintain and teach academics of adequate standards has led to a variety of social problems and pathology. (4)
Affection	Steadfast and lasting love and romance were a prominent part of the culture. The relationship of parent to parent and parent to child was apparent in this generation. (3)	Due to many instances of both adult parents employed, parents have little time with children. What does come through is questionable "quality time", where father is absent, mother is often either "over employed" or is on welfare and incapable of providing a father surrogate to adequately protect and monitor the children.

Comments	Demographics from the post 1960 parent generation indicate that only by the admission of immigrants will society have adequate people to participate in the economy. Many of the native born children will be unemployable due to inadequate and ineffective preparation. The degree of depth of unemployability, dependence, social pathologies and problems for the society related to dysfunctionality will be presented in these pages.

- The dominance of family economy.
- The power of religious communities and kin over the family including a strong tie to extended families and community.
- The importance of land and the desire to pass family property over to the next generation.
- The abundance of children.
- The power of intergenerational bonds, which set constraints upon individuals.

The sharing of the family economy between husbands and wives (as women entered the work force), the waning of religious and social communities, the weakening of extended family bonds as employment become geographically dispersed, the waning of the importance of land as agriculture became industrialized, the shrinking of the child population as birth control and abortion became generally available and the increase of social distance between generations occurred as job locations became dispersed. These all strained the structure of the American family system.

With the passing of the rapid economic growth of demand for unskilled labor and mass manufacturing, high real wages for untrained high school graduates leveled off during the postwar years, each entering cohort of graduates of limited education and training, according to Farley could expect less income on which to build and support a new family. This meant delayed or never entered into marriages, delayed childbearing and fewer children (note 5). It became harder and harder to support a family on one income. Along with this came higher taxes and this encouraged low income families to send wives to work.

The above, plus the geographic dispersal of jobs, the loss of communications due to job relocations, the shift away from the family farm and the availability of birth control and abortions all made for a loss of the supporting factors of the family system.

Despite the volume of divorces and the pervasive prevalence of cohabitation in the society Talbot (note 5) sees a hefty support of traditional family life, both in social performance and in attitudinal expression. She cites data which indicate that 90 percent of men and women in the United States, for example, eventually marry. Positive attitudes regarding marriage have held steady at 96 percent for over thirty years. She accepts that almost three-fourths of Americans believe that "marriage is a lifetime commitment that should not be ended except under extreme circumstances."

Family Norms, Past and Present

The norms of the pre-1960 time included the following:

• *Respectable single women were not to bear children.* It was accepted that to conceive a child without a known father was a selfish and unacceptable act. If a child were conceived out of wedlock (a rare occurrence) in a middle-class family and even among many working poor, the family of the young woman would usually quietly arrange for the girl to go away from home for a time until the baby was born, and then the child would usually be put up for adoption away from home. Social workers, and the social work establishment usually agreed with the general consensus that children reared in families without fathers were disadvantaged and "short changed" (note 5). Abortions were illegal and generally considered by the society to be violations against life, in moral and legal terms.

• *The ethos of the time supported the view that youth was a period of preparation for adult life.* Idle young men were considered at risk of falling into antisocial ways and, therefore, were kept busy in learning occupational preparation and in involvement in church and community activities in Boys Clubs, Boy Scout Troops, Junior Civic Clubs and other programs which promoted the moral norms of the society. Moral norms were quite clear. The schools, the homes, the civic organizations, the churches and the social work establishment all taught and confirmed clear differences between right and wrong. There was no room for shadings of morals. Cultural and moral relativism was usually judged to be an acquiescence to evil. The golden rule was accepted as a basis of behavior: "That which is hateful to you, do not do unto others." Only later in the sixties did some church leaders of the left substitute "conditional ethics," which provided them and their followers with "room" for moral violations which were difficult, inconvenient, uncomfortable, with ambivalent values and antagonistic to the basic principles of their religion.

•   *Children knew who they were.* It was reaffirmed by family membership, by social, school, church and youth activities officials, neighborhood leaders and the community authorities. Because children knew who they were and also who their parents were they also knew the meanings and beliefs related to their identity. Children knew that they were responsible to their parents and usually behaved accordingly. The community also knew who they were and knew their parents as responsible for them. The family reputation was important both for children and adults. Its continued acceptance in the society was a critical aspect of social control. Children knew that they were responsible for their actions and the consequences related to their actions.

•   *Knowledge was based upon logic and reality.* Children were taught in school and home that thinking was a quality not available to other species of animals. One major corporation mounted the word "THINK" in large capital letters on all of its thousands of office walls. Everywhere around the world, a clear distinction was made between "thinking," which was a necessary process before actions were taken and their consequences and "feeling," which was considered an entirely different matter. A child in school who confused the two terms would quickly be corrected. In business a customer would frequently be heard to say, "I'm not interested in your feelings; I want to know the facts. When *will* you make delivery?" Feeling was a matter for private issues including family cohesion, courtship, emotional understanding and in psychotherapy.

Along with the reinforced knowledge that children and adults had about their identity and the moral precepts related to it, they also understood that the abstract notions of love, compassion, self esteem and welfare were matters which could not be considered separate and above the basic precepts of ethical behavior. This was particularly reinforced in periodic religious and familial activities. "Feelings" about such abstract concepts as love, etcetera were constrained by the clear boundaries of right and wrong as taught in family, church and school. Excuses were offered by children and adults for violations of ethics, but they were usually examined by family and the society in the light of logic of reasoning rather than feeling. The more recent excuses of "victimhood" used in explanations that "people do bad things because of outside forces or because of their feelings" were not really accepted by general public consensus.

The frequent unity of consensus about right and wrong and the clarity related to the understood meanings of such terms made it possible for the general atmosphere in society to enforce public opinion. There was clear stigmatization of any actions which shortchanged children or destroyed family stability. Social control over unmarried motherhood, irresponsible fatherhood, adultery and infidelity, involved severe shame and social exclusion for these transgressors of established norms. Social control of deviant behavior including homosexuality, gambling, drunkenness and drug abuse, was in place and effective in support of the family as an institution. Public opinion was reinforced by the extended family and friends. Community and public attitudes about the protection of family life was reinforced by the policies of social agencies and private psychotherapy practitioners. Where a social agency or juvenile court judge or practitioner acted contrary to their principles, these would often raise discussion of professional ethics violations (note 6).

Of course there was always deviance in the past. The world was never ideal and devoid of social problems. There were always people who violated the established standard. These norms were both moral and utilitarian and set the standards for a functional society with controllable problems. But today's era is different in that there seems to be little or no headway in movement toward improved social order and improvement of societal functionality. In the views of many this direction of movement is retrogressive and makes for a lessening of effective order.

It must be remembered that the family had a special relationship with the government, in that young men in the family were subject to a draft by the military service until the 1980s when selective service became inactive. Until then men who were not required for family support and who were not actively involved in a program of national importance were subject to be "the first called up." Thus many of the men who were married and who had dependents or were in good standing in an educational program were deferred for military service. For many young men this was a positive thrust to marry and/or to pursue higher education.

The Myth of the "Alternative" Family

Any comparison of family life before the 1960s and contemporary family norms and cultural climate needs to be prefaced with a caveat. The reader needs to understand that more than half of the Western world families adhere to the patterns and structure of the 1960 family counterpart. This fact has been clouded by various claims that the "traditional family is dead" (note 7). This misstatement, tied to the rampant rumor of the "death of the family" has been revealed by Thomas Sowell to be incorrect (note 8). Various "experts" and media reporters have claimed that "half of all marriages end in divorce" and that "the traditional family of two heterosexual adult parents raising their children is now an exception among families in the Western world." Both these claims are wrong and reflect an "ignorance of statistics compounded by gullibility." Sowell states that "to say that half of all marriages end in divorce would be like saying that half the population died last year if the number of deaths were half as large as the number of births." He indicated that married couples outnumber unmarried couples by 54 to 3, and that the proportion of minors in intact families has been found to be over seventy percent. This kind of purposive falsity is the basis of propaganda rather than scientific conclusion (note 9).

It is true, however, that alternative forms of surrogate families amounting to almost 30 percent of households with minor children are a matter of serious concern, especially since over 23 percent of all families with children have a mother as sole adult and head of the "family," and this trend is on the increase.

Thus we have problems of failures of traditional families to be established, to become and remain stable, and to successfully rear their children so that they become ready to take their place in the society as productive citizens and parents as well. These are serious problem for Western society.

Similarly, the belief in the mythical death of the traditional family is also a matter of concern. General acceptance of the myth of the death of the family could have the effect of becoming a self-fulfilling prophesy, based only on fiction. The more the public accepts such propaganda, the more people will cease trying to build on their hopes for a moral, stable and productive life for themselves and their children, and the more the cultural climate will be antagonistic to their purposes. Thus "alternative family" propaganda is actually an act of socially destructive behavior.

The Traditional Intact Family

The traditional intact families, according to a variety of reports, and unlike broken families, usually have clearly defined values (note 5). Many, and especially the working poor, have only a minimum of social support from friends and families, but as has been demonstrated in the past, they can usually build on the limited social resources available to them. The traditional intact family usually values education, believing that it is an important and primary avenue for future security and support for their children. The traditional intact family also values self-sufficiency because only by developing one's own support can one become self-reliant and avoid becoming dependent on anyone else.

Usually, the traditional intact family emphasizes the importance of family cohesion and adults, by example and by direction, make it clear to the children that no one person's comfort or satisfaction is more important than the needs of the entire family. Usually, traditional intact families teach their children both by example and direction that most decisions must be based on a general principle of fairness to all wherever that is possible without endangering the security and health of all.

The tradition of the intact family includes the propensity of pressing its members to conform to community morals and standards. Still another quality of the traditional intact family is related to the concept

of the covenant of marriage rather than the contract. Love for one another and mutual responsibility and support are covenant values ahead
of any measures of "quid-quo-pro," or favor for favor. The cohesion of
the traditional intact family usually has little or no relationship to pren-
uptial agreements. It is seldom that the traditional intact family is found
to be without the support of legal and familial recognition.

How does the traditional family develop the strength and stability
to provide such a secure nest for its children? It needs to be noted that
all over the world, the traditional family and the formal marriage has
been the key to civilization. In the functional family the relationship
between parent and young occurs as part of a familial reference group
made up of both the nuclear family and its extended relatives, friends
and community. Under the sponsorship of the broader group, the child
at first finds himself under the terrifying control of humans whom he
does not understand and who do not understand him. If he's fortunate,
this child perceives that his parent cares about him so much that no
other person matters. This attachment to the child is both biological,
evolutionary and glandular in nature. In addition, this relationship can
be, and usually is reinforced by the external culture and social patterns
of the parent's reference group. If the parent has learned from childhood how to positively relate to his or her own parents, then the emotional as well as the physical bonds to the child will be secure.

Decisions of Family and Workplace Facing Young Women

The situation of the young adult woman is not an easy one in contemporary society. If a young woman has just finished college and faces the
choice of what she should do next, she can either (1) get married, have
children and wait to enter a career after the children are successfully
launched; (2) complete her education and graduate work or occupational training and then get married and take time out to have her
children; (3) she can first launch her career and then only after it is
successfully advanced she can get married and have a family; (4) she can
interrupt her career in order to get married and have a family at a much
earlier age; What are her career prospects, in the face of the competition of

the many other men and women who have not interrupted their careers?

Too few young women realize that they can't "have it all." They cannot responsibly carry out a satisfactory dual life of being full-time mothers to their children, full-time mates to their husbands and at the same time become competitive career women. Something has to give. Many career women end up measuring their quality of life not by the security and stability of their family life and they have only a high salary and financial independence as a measure of their success in life.

Despite the fact that many commentators on modern societies claim that women have proven that it is feasible and possible to be both a dependable mother and a career woman, data reported in the literature (note 5) makes it clear that one or both of the outcomes of the dual track life efforts for men and women are heavily faulted in many cases (note 10). Even the contemporary popular pattern of courtship involving premarital sexual experiences and trial living together presents the young adult woman with a quixotic problem. When is her man of the moment really a serious marital prospect and not a noncommittal waste of her precious youth? For many a young woman, if she spent as much time, thought, and effort in creating a family as she does at building a career, her odds of succeeding at both will have greater possibilities of becoming a success in the long run. Only the highly competent young women with a strong familial extended family and an unusually helpful and uncommonly dependable husband who can be counted upon can really be secure in her prospects for success in both realms.

The Development of the Family Adult

As has been indicated in other references (note 11), the child at first seeks to gain control over the enveloping parent, but failing in this goal, the child instead begins to seek ways to please the parent. In the process the child begins to depend on the parent in many ways. The parent now begins to be able to predict the behavior of the child and thus develops trust in him. What happens in the relationship between mother and child is, of course, a mirror of the trust which develops after marriage between husband and wife. Also, the relationship between father and child develops in a similar manner. Only after trust overcomes mistrust between parent and parent and parent and children, do other socio-emotional interactions occur as described by Erikson (note 12).

It is in this process that the child, and later the adult, builds a cohesive tie to other humans and builds an appropriate identity and morality. Without this complex of sophisticated social responses the child may remain animal like or by default, may develop a strong bond with a childish reference group. This kind of child reference group is usually based on immature and antisocial behavior. Such children coming to adulthood and becoming parents themselves often fail in adequately teaching their own children the norms they need. Much of the hedonism, narcissism and rejection of commitment which characterized the counterculture of the 1960s is now reflected in the family patterns of the 1990s.

Carter (note 12) believes that a stable productive marriage is strongly dependent on the development of the ability to discern the differences between right and wrong and to make the choice of right over wrong, despite the personal costs involved. Carter states that "the integrity of a marriage is measured by how each of the partners conducts his or her part of the marriage day by day."

The Dilemma of the Unprepared Generation

The chances for a marriage to be successful are increased when each of the partners is a graduate of a family where moral integrity was practiced between the partners and between the partners and the children. The didactic expression of parental wishes for the behavior and moral integrity of their children is not enough. It must be linked to the demonstration of the desired behavior by the parents. And the dilemma facing the modern society is that too many children have become physical adults without having internalized the moral integrity which their parent also lacked. They now have the powers of adults but lack the internal controls. *This is equivalent to having a car without brakes.*

Many immigrant families, on the other hand, (especially from Asia), arrive in their new lands with a cultural heritage which rejects dependency beyond the extended family and emphasizes familial integrity and morality. This is a continuation of the experience which the United States found with its previous immigrants from eastern and central Europe in the first half of the twentieth century (note 13).

Fatherless Families

Until now, we have mainly discussed intact and broken families. There is another family model that has increasingly become characteristic of the industrialized world. This is the setting where children are raised by single mothers, and where the children have never really known their fathers. Often, such family constellations are found within the culture of welfare dependency.

Within this culture of welfare dependency the family populations are often without personal direction and without a sense of controlling their own lives. The culture of poverty which strongly influences their lives is a type of "neurotic exemption," first described by Karen Horney, a post Freudian psychoanalyst. Persons with the neurotic exemption are unable to understand that something unfortunate might happen to them as a consequence of their behavior, or they do not realize that they might avert this consequence by changing behavior. Life in the inadequately socialized family is profuse with dangerous and unplanned behavior which may have disastrous consequences in the future. Accompanying the problems produced by welfare dependency is the fact that there are better choices possible for their lives and for the lives of their children. They do not realize that better choices are possible or what they must do to make for better days for their families. They know only their own inadequate childhood socialization. This helps explain why many live for the moment and without planning or direction for the future.

Within this lifestyle there is almost no incentive for children and young, inexperienced adolescents to avoid sexual and other immediate but quite serious gratification experiences. Unless there is someone important to them who is ready and able to explain positive reasons and to enforce disincentive consequences, social damage becomes a natural next step. Literature abounds with the problems of incomplete or failed families and subsequent social pathology. Such failed or incomplete family experience is usually followed by socialization of the children by the intense peer involvement surrounding them and the idleness of television. Children with inadequate parent involvement easily switch to peer group, television and "Nintendo" involvement. This occurs not only in the inner city but also in the suburbs where parental concerns do not effectively reach the children (note 14).

The Messages in the Culture and Their Effect

The messages in the popular culture given to children with de-facto or dejure incompetent or absent parents as reinforced by the peer group and the mass media are very much as follows:

• If you are to become somebody who is anybody, you're supposed to become economically successful so that you can buy all the products displayed in TV or exhibited by the locally successful drug pushers. (But no one tells you about the consequence of getting money by stealing or cheating, or drug selling.)

• If you are to become "somebody who is anybody," you need to be popular, and that means that you have to become sexually active. (But, until recently, few really emphasized the negative consequences of sexual conception and sexually transmitted diseases.) Nor does anyone important to you emphasize the benefits of deferred gratification and explain that happiness is a by-product of achievement.

Another message pervasive in the culture is related to learning. Because many of the schools have down-graded their curriculum, and have lowered the required norms of achievement and often are staffed by inappropriately educated teachers, the children cannot overcome the force of these negative messages. Increasingly at all social class levels, the message of the culture is one of "enjoy your rights and don't worry about what might happen to you tomorrow." Although this problem is most acute in the culture of poverty it is becoming daily more prevalent throughout society.

Girls and Teen Pregnancy

What does a young girl learn when she finds she is now pregnant and she has to consider becoming a mother? If she does go through with having the baby, what are her prospects now? What about her own life? Can she now continue to enjoy the pleasures of an undemanding life or does she now have some responsibilities? She may sit through a series of lectures and demonstrations of baby care. Probably for the first time in her life she now faces responsibility for someone beside herself and she usually has to face it alone. Her position is now, for the first time, making demands on her, full of a stress far beyond her comprehension. Any peer help from her extremely youthful friends will probably be less than adequate.

For the first time in her life she now has to make a choice which has major important consequences for her. Other choices she has made in the past have been cumulative in nature. These occurred in small steps, such as not doing her homework, not paying attention in class, truancy and so forth, each of which did not seem catastrophic in itself. Or, perhaps these were positive choices for her in not making learning and job and work readiness a major direction in her life. This kind of cumulative effect on her future is also brought about by parental inaction, or by parental absence or by other forms of parental ineffectiveness.

Now, facing her hard alternatives for the first time, she has to decide whether to have the child of her pregnancy, following which she will have to either rear the child alone, (if her parents continue to be absent-de facto in her life) or to place the child for adoption. This momentous choice of alternatives is soon compounded by her next ensuing crossroads decision.

If she has the child or even if she aborts it, barring significant changes in her behavior, then it may be only a matter of time until she becomes pregnant again. She thus moves ahead in a life devoid of adult moral and ethical directions. She continues in a world without adult guidance or monitoring, and without direction for the future. She has (whether she knows it or not) made the decision to become a single parent, heading up a family entirely without adult influence with many biological fathers of her children but no real fathers for them. Her schooling and training for employment and real adulthood is now at a dead end.

If she makes the decision to place the child for adoption, then she still has the possibility of going on with her schooling and work training for the future. For this to occur she must firmly adopt lifestyle changes which involve serious study and probably a pattern of abstinence from sexual experiences. If she does not make these changes, then it is only a matter of time before the cycle of this opportunity pattern is repeated.

For most of the young women surrounded by the culture of unresolved adolescence and immaturity, we have bred the nexus of social problems for the immediate future. Even though they are in essence still children, they have become enrolled as purported rearers of children including responsibility they have never had before. And rearing of a child is a life faced with almost interminable decision making. Not having been reared as a child by an effective adult who was really involved in her own life, and never having had concerned adulthood demonstrated to her by an on-the-scene parent, she now has to focus full time on her child. She also has to "catch up" on becoming an employable adult, academically, vocationally and otherwise, as well as managing a new household.

Only a very few of these young mothers escape from this pit of cultural self-perpetuating poverty. In a traditionally intact family, these problems are rarer, because the family and extended family culture provide supports and adult models (note 15).

Inevitably, as the growing young new baby becomes physically more active, first at home and then in school and on the streets, the mother will be tested as to her ability to control and guide the child. This becomes more urgent as the child becomes stronger than the mother, learns how to run faster than she, or learns how to lie to her or how to ignore her. This is a frequent occurrence of preadolescent boys who then enter gangs beyond their young mother's control.

Boys and Gangs

Because there is no active responsible father in the home the young boy usually looks outside the home for his male role models. If he is lucky enough to have such an appropriate male in his life who has the time and energy, and who is really concerned about the boy and accepts enough responsibility for him, this person becomes involved in setting limits for him. Often it is a teacher, or an athletic coach or local priest or minister, but even then, such men are often hindered in these efforts because they lack authority over the child and thus they often experience difficulty in setting limits as well as rewards to establish appropriate constraints. Boys who are lucky enough to have such men in their lives are proportionately few. Most of the boys in such fatherless families escape from the home and its limits quite early in their lives and become eager candidates for the local gang. For these boys, their only available heroes are the successful men of the inner city, most of whom are graduates and alumni of the local gang. These include pimps, drug bosses and pushers, ex-cons and other purveyors of marginal and illegal market services.

Many gangs require their aspirants to carry out some act of antisocial defiance or crime before they are granted membership. The discipline of the gang is strong in terms of enforcing group secrecy, loyalty, masculine supremacy and general antisocial behavior. Not to maintain such attitudes is synonymous with weakness. Status in the group requires evidence of increasing "he-man" activity. As far as family values are concerned, a boy has to show independence from women, from authority, from teachers (especially females), etcetera.

Tied to this stance is the position of the male in relation to women: A He-Man tells women off. A He-Man seduces many women. He fathers many children, especially boys, but he owes their mothers nothing. A He-Man doesn't depend on jobs and employers for his support. He eats when he feels like it at one or another of his "girl friends" homes. If her kids get in his way, he "controls" them. He takes "static" from nobody. He runs his own life. He is "macho." This kind of a young man is often out of control by the time his gang has reared him for the street. He's the biological father of many children but is a responsible parent to none. His life is laid out for him by the gang and the street activity. The moment of decision, such as does occur with girls who face a pregnancy, seems not to occur for such boys. Similarly, the act of dropping out of school, joining the gang, committing his first law violation and seducing (or raping) his first girl seems to come on him naturally. It really is no great decision in his life as long as he has not internalized any constraints installed, monitored and enforced by his parents. The "machismo" stance of men in relation to women is demonstrated by the gang and never unlearned by him as long as he remains unschooled, untaught, and in the adult world, unemployable.

The moral standards of the gang culture, unlike societal standards, are continuously in place in much of the lives of these boys. The surrogate "parental" influence of the occasional Big Brother volunteer, the occasional influential teacher or priest or minister is quite limited in the boys' time/life/space. The influence of the inner-city moral standards of the gang, the streets, the juvenile control agencies and the meta-culture of the schools are all counterproductive to the prosocial moral standards of the mainstream society. The cultural and moral standards of the gangs' inner-city community are generally congruent and frequently symbiotic. The gang culture and influence is further strengthened where the gang has associated with it a female auxiliary where girls of the neighborhood are indoctrinated in the values and roles expected of them in the relationships and interactions between the male and female members.

Children in Middle-class Families

In the suburban middle-class neighborhoods many children are fortunate in having two parents who are really influential in their children lives, who are equipped with mainstream related moral values and who are consciously striving to teach and demonstrate these to their children. In many instances they are ready and able to invest so much of themselves in the lives of their children as to have effected a lasting interactive bond to such a degree as to guide their children in decisions even when the children make decisions in their absence. There the child is acting in a way "as if" his parent is constantly guiding him. Frequently the children of intact families and in families of strong support groups are also able to develop prosocial inner constraints if the influential parents or surrogates were adequately equipped, competent and mature. If, on the other hand, these significant others were equipped with alternative value systems, the children will frequently be equipped with inner constraints which are counterproductive for life in mainstream society.

Even when the parents are able to provide an intact family situation for their children, and when they succeed in creating an effective relationship with their children and even when they commit enough of themselves to help their children develop appropriate inner constraints, they frequently fail in that their children often reflect their parents earlier antisocial action. Even when the parents explain to their children that they may have used destructive drugs in their youth and wish their children would not, the children frequently do as their parent had done rather than as their parents now wish. The time worn request by parents to "do as I say, rather than as I have done" is all too often answered by the children's repeat of the parental action.

The degree to which children will follow the path indicated by their parents involves not only the competence and cooperation of the parents but also the degree of commitment demonstrated by the parents to each other and to the children. The children's behavior is a form of "report card" on their parents as parents.

Children are mainly the product of the balance of the routine parental practices as well as parental urgencies. If the parents both become *de facto* absentees from the life space of their children, then the rearing policies become those of the surrogate caretakers, whether it be relatives, day care vendors or school teachers. If no proactive rearing emanates from these adults; then the shaping of the children's inner capacities and choices will be determined by responsible adults, then the lowest common moral denominators of the peer group can be expected in the shaping of these children.

If children are reared by both parents, then the policies of childrearing are the product of the balance of the parents and other adults who are important to them. If only one parent is involved there is less likelihood of the policies being a result of adult discussion and interaction. If one parent is authoritarian or severely imbued with hedonistic personal interests and if the other parent has been imbued with strong plans and concerns for the children's needs and well-being, it is still quite possible that the children will reared by a balanced relationship of the influence of both parents. There are well-established traditional precepts in family life which most likely will influence the children when both parents and their relatives are involved in the children's rearing. An old Hebrew scholar, Hillel the Elder best described the balance of personality influences when he talked about the balance of selfishness and masochism. He said, "If I am only for myself, who am I? But if I am not for myself, who will be for me?" Thus the child's rearing must include a learning of the balanced relationships of all the parameters of personality.

The boys of middle-class single-parent families who are involved in an extended family or in other activities where men are responsible husbands and fathers may escape the dismal situation of the young men. The middle-class single parent family may have a mother with a full-time job, who also has to manage the family, be a mother to the younger children, a guide to the older children, and even try to rebuild her social and/or sexual life. The reality is often stacked against her in her efforts to keep control of her children. This is especially difficult as the children grow into their teens and come under the increasing influence of their peers. In the case of middle-class children, the situation remains less aggravated as long as there are active and committed adult male authority figures in their extended families, their schools, and in the social milieu of their communities.

The Custodial Mother

If we were to examine the roles of parents after divorce, we would usually find that the mother who lives with her children is trying to maintain family life after the domestic storms of a long drawn out divorce process. The mother often has to begin working again, sometimes after years of having been at home. As mother and homemaker, she now adds to her regular home and child care activities the new responsibilities of finding safe, wholesome day care for the children, at a cost she can afford and at a location not too distant from her home, job and the children's schools. Where before divorce she could spare about forty percent of her disposable time to spend with the children and home, she now has sometimes as little as ten percent of her time for this purpose. Thus her children can expect even less time with her at this period in their lives when children are in crisis because of the divorce trauma and need much more attention and monitoring. The children are now at risk of a variety of potential social-ills. The vast volume of research data on the dismal picture of children from single parent settings bears this out (note 16).

Many of these mothers experience early psychological burnout, high levels of stress, increased difficulty on the job, and a variety of other problems due to both extreme fatigue, internal confusion and difficulties of the situation. Added to this are the problems caused by low child support court orders, low and often late child support payments, and conflict with the ex-husbands regarding payments due, visitation hours, and conditions of visitations, etcetera. Frequently the residual anger between both parents is so great as to fuel continuing and often increasing post-marital conflict in which the custodial mothers utilize custodial control to punish their ex-husbands, and the ex-husbands utilize the timing and payments of spousal and child care support as a means of punishing ex-wives.

The custodial mother has additional constraints and stress in relation to her marital life. If she decides not to date other men and not to seek a new mate then she faces a life ahead which may present her with loneliness and with little or no hope for improvement in her personal life. On the other hand, if she decides to date men this presents her with new problems. One of these is finding time and finding new settings where she can safely come into contact with suitable potential mates without disturbing or harming her children. Another of these is finding the energy and resources for this activity. Will this allow her enough time to spend with the children? And, if she again begins dating, will her ex-husband continue his conflict with her by claiming that she is an unsuitable mother? This is more likely to happen if the boyfriend "lives in" or visits overnight frequently. The mother has other problems in this period following her divorce. In the past she had more available time to take the children to various medical, dental, educational and social activities. If she found any activity difficult to service in the past, she was often able to ask her husband to help or to find relatives and neighbors who could help or she could work out a car-pool with other mothers. Her new situation and work might make such arrangements much more difficult.

Often single custodial mothers resent the activities offered to the children on their day with their father which are frequently more interesting and expensive than anything the custodial mother could provide for them during the week. Finally, many such mothers have often not yet brought themselves emotionally to the point where they truly view their ex-husbands as fit partners for child care even for visitation. This is particularly evident where the father brings the children into contact with his new girlfriend in the present atmosphere of relationships of men and women. Frequently the moral standards of divorced mothers and fathers are strongly at variance with each other and become a strong cause of continuing dissension as the children move in to puberty and adolescence.

The Non-Custodial Father

The newly divorced father also often finds himself in a less than enviable position. His net income may now be larger than that of his ex-wife as has been indicated by the findings of post divorce research. (In note 17, Radosh notes that Weitzman's research indicated a drop in income for women after divorce of 73 percent and a rise in income of 42 percent for men, a difference of 115 percent, but corrected figures by other sociologists found a drop of 27 percent and a rise of 10 percent, making a difference of 47 percent.) The costly divorce process, as well as the cost of setting up a new household for himself, also may have added to his problems. If his wife has remained in the family home with the children, he has to help maintain it. Unless he has already moved in with a new girlfriend, he finds his evenings a solo affair. He has to learn to cook or to get accustomed to eating in restaurants, frequently alone. Depending on the way the divorce process has played out, the father will often find himself cut off from contact with his ex-wife's family, relatives and friends. If he hasn't been cut off he still might find that his contacts with her family and friends are less than warm. In many instances, after a time, both partners in a divorce may find themselves "dropped" by people who are used to social patterns of couples in friendship. Unlike his ex-wife, he may not have a group of divorced fathers he can depend upon for emotional and social support, as is often the case with divorced women who are able to find women's support groups. Where his ex-wife may find herself overloaded with meaningful activities and with keeping the home and children together, the ex-husband-father has much less involvement in the home and in the children's lives. Thus his chances of finding meaning in his new life are more limited. Both partners in a divorce often have increased distrust of each other, and both often believe the other has beaten them in the divorce conflict.

Christina Hoff Sommers (note 18) describes the origins and consequences of the covert war between the genders. (This is promoted by various women's organizations, via legislative lobbying, sexual harassment suits and other actions on the one hand, and by the unorganized but de facto resistance of men to women's emancipation by informal interactions with women.) This chronic conflict between divorced women and men starting with grievances about inadequate, missing, or late child and spousal support by women and grievances about deprivation of visitation rights by fathers has resulted in many children being raised by mothers who are in a constant state of anger at their fathers. This result, deliberate or inadvertent is produced by the effect of the children's reflecting of the emotions of the only parent available to them.

Often the divorced partners will act in relation to their former partners in ways which may be emotionally gratifying for them at the moment but destructive to the children and even themselves in the long run. This kind of lifelong war between two parents after the divorce, and often between three or more parents if one of them remarries, causes severe damage to the children's view of what a good father and mother should do, and even worse damage to the children's view of the role of husbands and wives and family life in general. Often children come out of such child raising with an element of hostility in relation to the opposite sex and the world in general and promote it on to the next generation. Child development analysts indicate that it is quite common for children of divorce to believe that the family war is their fault. This is an especially frequent result where the ex-parents no longer talk to each other and where the children have to absorb the assignment of having to be the "go-between." Where this happens, often the child begins to believe that he or she is responsible for anything negative which occurs in relation to the absent parent.

The non-custodial father usually has more time to plan his visiting time with the children. Because he has more money and probably more energy for this activity he can often get tickets for some sport or entertainment program which he believes may interest the children. Because he has so little time with the children he feels himself pressed to be a giving and permissive father—one who feels that if he says "no" to the children that they may decide not to go with him the next time he has visiting privileges. The mother with a grudge against her ex-husband may seek to make life less enjoyable for him and may seek to influence the children to refuse visits. Even if she has no influence in this regard, her ex-husband will often suspect that this is the case. In the event that the children seem eager to go with their father the mother will often believe that their eagerness is caused by his use of unfair tactics—perhaps in his saying "yes" for many things which she has had to refuse them. She may not know how to deal with this problem in regard to the children. The struggle over conditions of paternal visits and the conflict over spousal and child support most frequently result in a continued loosening of paternal child bonds often at a time when the children most need their father and mother united in their care, guidance and presence.

In an atmosphere of frequent conflict between their parents, many children learn how to manipulate their parents for their own whims, and when this happens the children are often bewildered and then terrified because neither of their parents are providing them the rational guidance and limits they need if they are to internalize the social controls of citizenship. The stability which children associated with the condition of united parental policies is thereby missing. This lack of parental unanimity has other serious effects. We frequently observe that children of traditional cohesive parents know what kind of behavior their parents want from them, what their parents want them to get out of their school, church and other out of home experiences, and what their parents see as priorities in the use of their time. In intact families the parents and children usually have many experiences out of the home at visits to museums, in children's learning enrichment centers, in assemblies of the families and with outside "company" where much non-academic but necessary learning occurs. That's because intact families have parents with more disposable time and resources which they may use in building their children's experiences.

Myths of Divorce

The myth that divorce is better than the situation of children with parents engaged in long drawn-out familial conflict has been dispelled. The conclusions on this question have been reported by many researchers. Following are a number of myths about the consequences of divorce and informal marital coupling (note 19):

• Myth: *Living together before marriage leads to longer, lasting marriages.* The facts are that couples who lived together before marriage are 60 percent more likely to be divorced after eight years.

• Myth: *Those who divorce learn from the bad experience and marry much more wisely the second time.* The reality is that those who were previously divorced are more likely to be divorced again.

• Myth: *Divorce is better for children.* The outcomes for children in high conflict intact families more closely resembles those for children in low conflict families than those for children in divorced families. Divorce only aggravates the conflict. Talbot (note 19) provides a review of the literature which bears this out.

• Myth: *Divorce makes a clean break from conflicts so that everyone can settle down and rebuild their lives.* According to data for outcomes in divorced families, the facts are otherwise. Conflict increase between ex-partners is a frequent outcome.

- Myth: *Children prefer it if their fighting parents split up.* The findings are that when children are asked their preferences, they always say they want their parents, above all, to stay together (note 19).

The Legacy of the Single Parent Family

We would be remiss if we did not make it clear that there is a distinction between the situation of the children in the post-divorce single parent family and that of the children in the never-married family, and especially in the never-married families on welfare. Talbot (note16) makes the point that the situation of children of a working divorced mother is far better than the children of a never-married welfare mother especially where the mother has had little education and may probably be estranged from her relatives and friends. Maynard and Gargy (note16) have provided strong and detailed data findings on the state of adolescent motherhood and social pathology in their report on *Kids Having Kids*.

For the last half century scholars and researchers have studied the fruit of the one-parent family, as compared to the products of the two parent family (note 16). Children raised in a single parent family, when compared with the children raised in a two parent family, with income and other important factors controlled, indicate that children in single parent families are

- twice as likely to exhibit antisocial behavior;
- between 25 to 50 percent more likely to manifest behaviors of anxiety, depression, hyperactivity or dependence;
- two to three times more likely to need psychiatric care;
- more likely to indulge in suicidal behavior;
- more likely, as adolescents, to begin sexual activities at an earlier age;
- as teenagers, more likely to have a child out of wedlock;
- as children are likely to abuse drugs;
- when tested, more likely to have lower scores on IQ tests and other tests of mentality;

- three or more times likely to fail and repeat a year in grade school;
- are found to be likely to pass on the same problems they have to their children in the next generation;
- less likely to establish a stable married life when they become adults;
- female children, more likely, if they do marry as adults, to be among ninety-two percent that will be divorced;
- three times as likely to become dependent on welfare as adults;
- more likely to become involved in crime, especially if they are raised in a neighborhood where other single parent families live;
- four times as likely to be expelled or suspended from school;
- likely to have less education the longer the children experience life in a single parent family (regardless of income);
- less likely to be able to delay gratification, to control impulses (and thus less able to choose and persist in life goals);
- likely to have a weaker sense of right and wrong;
- as adults, more likely to be involved in child abuse and neglect; and
- as single parent families associated with violent crime and burglary in significantly greater percentages.

How does a divorced family become a single-parent family? How does a divorced family become a single-parent family? Discussion of the divorced family is incomplete without consideration of the issue of child and spousal support. Because so many divorced mothers often use these payments as the only measure of fatherhood in their discussion of the divorced husband (frequently within the hearing of the children) the children and friends or relatives in time begin to consider the role of fathers as limited only to financial support. And, in time, the divorced father begins to accept this role as their only function for him. After a time, this often becomes a self-fulfilling prophecy and his relationship with the children finally dwindles into nothing.

This pattern of dealing with divorced husbands on the part of divorced mothers is understandable. What is not clear is why it is that the state and federal policies toward divorced fathers is so reflective and often punitive even when the fathers' financial support of the children is adequate and timely. This policy, in its effect on fathers, is counterproductive of the governmental policies which seek to strengthen the father's influence in the lives of their children.

The Legacy of Non-Married Adults

What is the legacy from the lifestyle of the non-married? According to William R. Maddox (note 20) research indicates that:

1. life expectancy is more adversely affected by being unmarried than to be poor, overweight or having heart disease. Divorced males are twice as likely to die prematurely from hypertension, four times as likely to die prematurely from throat cancer, twice as likely to die prematurely from cardiovascular disease, and seven times more likely to die prematurely from pneumonia. Being divorced and a nonsmoker is only slightly less dangerous than smoking a pack or more each day and staying married.
2. women in cohabiting unions (unmarried) are twice as likely to be victims of domestic violence than married women. Cohabiting women are three times more likely to be clinically depressed than married women and have a rate of depression twice as high as other single women. Married people report significantly higher physical and emotional satisfaction with their sex lives than singles (cohabiting or otherwise).

The reasons for these findings are quite clear. Marriage provides individuals with a network of help and support, so necessary when a person in under stress or is ill. It discourages high risk behaviors and encourages savings and earnings.. The benefits are not automatic for all marriages. Lasting marriages are the result of efforts by both partners to work at making them good. The lifetime commitment encourages constructive interaction, compromise and mutual sensitivity. Lifetime commitments, according to Maddox, make it possible for the partners to enjoy intimacy because they need not worry about the other person leaving. This freedom from anxiety about ultimate rejection makes it possible for the parental pair to provide the maximizing level of security to each of them and to their children as well as to strengthen the maximal "united front" in setting the standards for their children's care.

Similarly, the middle class elite who perpetuate a life style based on a lack of commitment, who promote the concept of sexual freedom, and who promote the expression of rights for individuals without commensurate responsibilities can probably expect an absence of the benefits which marriage and family life brings to adults. The image of the older divorced woman whose children are now gone can probably look forward to a future alone. She may have some career benefits but these, too, are often quite fragile as retirement becomes imminent. The position of the male adult, divorced one or more times and out of contact with the children he sired but never really "fathered" or committed himself to, is usually similarly dismal. Erikson named the later "ages of man" quite effectively in calling them "generativity versus ego-stagnation" and "integrity versus despair." It is his view that each of us reaches beyond our delimited lives by extending ourselves throughout notable deeds and through commitment to our children in our influence on them. If all we have achieved in life adds up to little in either route, ego-stagnation and despair, then the life of immediate gratification may turn out to be dismal in the long run.

The noncommittal life style found among the unmarried is not a new phenomenon. In the pre World War II days there was an old drunkards song found among the young adults in the United States. It was sung by what were then called the "family slackers", who were faced with almost universal social criticism. The words of the song went as follows: "I don't want to get married, I'm having too much fun: I don't want to be bothered by any single one."

The history of humanity is replete with reports of "family slackers." The irresponsible behavior in Sodom and Gomorrah in biblical times was rejected by the religious and civilized people of the world. After centuries of rejection of such behavior where this life style was repressed, it was reinvented and rationalized by the counter cultural generation in the 1960s.

How Does Family Help Create a Democratic Society?

In order to understand how this process is made possible it is necessary to consider the role of internal controls installed by the family and its usefulness in the civilization.

We have indicated that we cannot have a peaceful democratic civilization unless most of its citizens have internalized an understanding of right and wrong and are guided by it. This does not mean that all citizens will be conformist in motivation; merely that all citizens will have in common a series of understandings sufficient to provide a consensus of agreement on most matters important to all.

How is the sense of social responsibility developed in the individual? Among babies, the unreasoning (and unreasonable) demand for unlimited attention and caretaking, based on the baby's delusion that he alone exists and that all others are at his service, is usually resolved when cries for unreasonable services are not answered. When the child discovers that he is, in fact, at the mercy of his caretakers, the baby finally arrives at the conclusion that if he cannot control these powerful caretakers upon whom his survival depends, then he must join them. He not only learns to smile at these "giants" around him but also learns to behave in ways which will charm and satisfy them. Thus he begins to behave in ways which the caretakers can predict and they soon learn to provide him with services and attention which he can predict. This kind of mutual confidence based on the behavior of the other is what Erikson had labeled "trust." (note 21) This kind of behavior is actually a positive fact of evolutionary development.

Thus, trust cannot develop until the baby give up his earlier misconception that he is the center of his world and that he is in control of it. Only with learned dependence upon others, and with fear of abandonment (according to Karen Horney) can he learn to subordinate himself to others and thus to develop the elementary relationship of respect for others. Without the power and stable handling by the parent of the child and without the respect of the child for the parent, the larger social entities of the democratic society would be impossible. If we are to try to plan for a resolution of social dysfunction in society we first need to move toward a rational job description of the ideal (or totally goal-directed) parent.

Eight Qualities of Effective Parents

If the parent is to be an effective parent, able to help the child to achieve maximum functionality both for himself and in his relationship with others and the society, the parent would have to have the following qualities as perceived by the child:

• The parent would have to be perceived by the child as important in and *in strong control of the major factors in the child's life.* (Thus the absent father or mother, or the parent who is only infrequently seen by the child hardly qualifies as an active parent.) Mitscherlich, Blitstein and Bettleheim have concluded that a precursor of mutual respect between parent and child is the matter of the maternal and paternal active involvement. A parent who cannot gain access to the child for any meaningful space of time is hardly one who can become what social psychologists define as a "significant other." (note 22)

• The parent has to be perceived by the child as a *competent person* in his dealings with the societal mainstream. An unemployable parent, a parent constantly in trouble with the law, a parent who can't stand up as a protector and provider for the family can only be seen by the child as an inactive or failed significant other. A parent who has been driven out of the family by divorce and is perceived by the child as helpless or weak may achieve sympathy from the child, but that parent will probably not be perceived as a true person of authority for him or her. A surrogate father in the form of a stepfather or "Mama's current boyfriend" can hardly make it as a realistic significant other of the child unless his supervision and authority over the child is truly shared with the biological parent and unless that person is truly motivated by strong paternal feeling. Far too often, the surrogate father does gain authority by brute force over the child.

• The parent has to be perceived by the child as *consistent in his or her demands, expectations, rewards, constraints and supports,* even and especially when the child seeks to test the degree to which the parent will act with concern for the child. Early childhood has been described by Adorno as a period when strength is especially admired and weakness is disdained. Thus, the parent who allows himself to be manipulated by the child disappoints the child. If this issue is not resolved in early childhood, testing of authority in the person's life probably will continue indefinitely.

• The parent has to be perceived by the child as holding the view that *the child is both an object and an actor in the child's life space.* In other words the parent has to allow the child to be shaped by the forces of the family and school as well as to participate in the shaping of others. A child treated as an object tends to develop an institutional personality; a child who is permitted to dominate others without being shaped by them tends to become a permanent anarchist, "a rebel without a cause, " constantly testing the authority around him. Functional personality is, of course, one which interacts the most with others in his or her life space.

• The parent, if he is to be effective, must be perceived by the child as a *rational, planning, goal-oriented person,* especially in terms of his expectations for the child. If the parent is inconsistent, irrational, disorganized and impulse-oriented, and if the child accepts the parent as a role model, the child will generally play out his life in a dysfunctional manner. Thus, persons who are themselves unable to perform as members of the society in mainstream activities will probably fail as effective parents as well.

• The parent must be perceived by the child as *seeking the child's success* in life rather than as seeking the reverse. Many parents consciously want their children to succeed but unconsciously act in ways which operate counter to this goal. This may occur when the parent is excessively gratified by the caretaker role (which occurs with younger children) and unconsciously fears the loss of this role as the child becomes emancipated. The pattern of parental supervision in such instances may take the form of the "self-fulfilling prophesy" (note 22).

- Another obvious requirement for an effective parent would be that the child perceive the parent as *active and regularly present in his child's life* and activities. The relationship has to be interactive to be effective. A child cannot be guided merely by parental directives, written or oral. A parent who is not present in the child's life over the bulk of his or her waking time may convince himself or herself that he is really devoting himself to the child's development, but the facts are that children who are not under parental or equivalent surrogate monitoring and caring supervision usually find others to influence their personalities and their ultimate life determinations. (note 23)

- The final requirement for a truly effective parent is one of *realistic humility*. One parent alone cannot expect to succeed in becoming a fully effective and significant influence over a child. Each human adult is faulted by blind spots, inadequacies, occasional lapses of emotional control and displays of primitive behavior. Those who enter into the experience of parenting without an understanding of their own limits and inadequacies, or who consistently underestimate the requirements of parenting can probably expect to fail. For a child to have a fair chance of succeeding in the world, he or she needs full-time parenting by more than one parent, from parents who can provide a variety of life experiences and skills, from parents who can "spell" each other over difficult periods and from parents who can interact with one another in shaping the socialization of their children.

A parent who fails to be accepted by the child for whatever reason, whether having been perceived the "loser" in a destructive divorce experience, or because of inconsistency in relation to the child will probably end up exerting little or no influence on the child. Mitscherlich indicates that "children's competition with the father" (or other surrogate as compared with the fully-accepting "other surrogate", namely the mother) "leads to incorporation of the father's values." If the father is oriented to the mainstream world of employment and is in active participation in society, then the child will develop and achieve and secure entry in to the world of work, self-reliance and social responsibility. In Mitscherlich's opinion, lack of such an interaction with a parent involved in the mainstream society makes the child's entry into the mainstream unlikely. The need for a child to have two different parents, at least one who provides an interaction which motivates the child's learning of the mainstream values and life pattern is critical. This view faults the position of marriage counselors and therapists of the 1960s and the 1970s who held that divorce was preferable to a marriage with strong familial psychological conflict. The child apparently benefits more from a variety of views of the family and the world than he does from a less stormy one-sided approach to life which prepares him only in the isolated and protected atmosphere and leaves him unprepared to interact successfully with the real world. If the child in the one-parent family has no one other than his mother (and/or grandmother who is most likely a product of the same life patterns as the mother) then the child has little possibility of learning and internalizing the values and skills of the mainstream. Without them self-reliance, social responsibility, and the opportunity to enter into mainstream activity may not occur. With an absent father and a mother who is perceived by the child as powerless or less than competent in mainstream life and less important, knowledgeable and powerful than other adults, the child most probably will fall under the control and the influence of his peer group.

Parenting is a two fold activity in that we teach our children about the world and about themselves both by directing the children and by acting out our own lives on the family stage before them. Whether in the home, in the neighborhood and community, at our world and among our friends, we are all on the stage of our children's perception and imagination, and our children learn their parts, meanings, and purposes from observance of parents. The more effective we are as parents and adults, the more our children aspire to accept us as models in the shaping of their lives. Thus, as parents we need not only to tell our children about the important values of honesty, cooperation, work, justice, fair play, fidelity, integrity but also we need to shape our own behavior with that of others as they perceive it. It matters little how much we tell our children about the important of fidelity if we demonstrate the opposite in our daily activities.

Fundamental to the process of socialization is the concept of the shaping of "as if" behavior in the child. The child, by imitation, by observing, and by aligning himself to parental activities, eventually develops an understanding of what the parent is seeking to do, why he is doing what he does, and how what he does is related to the activities of other adults in the society. The child soon develops an understanding of what his parents would not do and why. His youth allows for him to play at the same activities "as if" he were his parent, and this play involves a variety of activities related to learning the skills and roles of daily living, related to various work settings and opportunities, and related to various situations in daily life where the child learns to choose pathways or life-patterns, as if he were his parent. In terms of the ethical aspects of "as if" behavior, the child does this by putting himself into his parents position. He asks himself, "What would I do if I were my father or mother faced with this problem?" The successfully socialized child tends to begin with the golden rule - in that he develops sympathy or empathy with others - and avoids behavior which he now knows to be "wrong" and engages in behavior which he believes his parents would consider "right."

But what happens with the child who never developed the basic respect which opens up his relations with this parent? Or the child who did not achieve the sense of "trust" in his parents and whose parent(s) did not achieve a sense of "trust" in him? This child is not able to go on to learn the necessary stance of relationships to develop the skills and roles required for further learning needed in the increasingly complex society. Such a child may shape his life on self interest, hedonism, and perhaps narcissism and dysfunctional antisocial behavior. Such persons become a costly drain on social and economic resources.

Without effective parents, everyone suffers.

The Environment of the Family

The effectiveness of the family is not merely a matter of parental effort alone. Much also depends on the environment in which the family functions. The environment of families in the pre-1960 generation differed greatly from the post-1960 generation. We have outlined that difference in the chart labeled "Then and Now: The Environment" which follows in the notes on pages 63-69.

Talbot (note 26) has examined the factors which have affected the family over the years. She believes that two factors were critically important in bringing about the change. The lives of men, women, and children were all strongly affected by the reentry of women into the workforce in the developed countries in the past 30 years and the unprecedented increase of the number of women working out of the home during the same period. Women in the Western nations were no longer dependent on their husbands for financial support. Women now became independent and the terms of a marriage became a matter for equitable negotiation between its partners and husbands, probably for the first time in modern history, could no longer dominate the parameters of family life. Marriage became more of a partnership than ever before.

It is important to study the basic trends in social, economic, and psychological thinking which influenced those who shaped the policies of marriage and the family in the latter part of the century. John G. West, Jr. indicates that there has been a "debunking of traditional concepts of God and men represented by Karl Marx, Charles Darwin and Sigmund Freud. Out of these considerations there has occurred a denial of personal responsibility, Social Darwinism, coercive utopianism (ranging from welfare policy, health care policy, etc.) moral relativism, denial of human responsibility and other belief systems. With these beliefs as a foundation, the revision of family concepts were reshaped in the intellectual realms of academic, governmental and the professional worlds.

The basic interests of these social policy intellectuals as they related to the family are important to consider.

The functional family is known to be an engine of inequality in that it promotes the best interests, especially the best economic interests of its children in rearing them for self-sufficiency. The intellectual class, as noted herewith has as its foundation the elimination of inequality in the society. These social policy leaders promote the state's support of children. Their solution is to promote government involvement in the lives of children with the goal of social equality. The fact that some families do very well in child rearing and enhancement is not important to these social planners. What is important to them is that all children must have government services so that no child will fail and equality will prevail. Unfortunately, government services actually provide services which are usually associated with family destruction rather than children's achievement.

NOTES

1. This is apparent from employment and economic productivity data of the time, allowing for cyclical market adjustments.
2. This is apparent from public statistics about crime, and other social deviance. It should be noted that, despite the turbulent changes which occurred after the industrial revolution and during a series of wars and other disturbances, the economy and its work force was relatively able to make adjustments to technological changes constantly underway during these times.
3. The role of romance was high in the literature of the time. There was relatively less familial strife evident in the reports of the society of that time, as compared with the degree of familial disturbance now evident in divorce reports and police reports of marital disturbances.
4. This conclusion is based on contemporary birth statistics and other demographic data.
5. Blankenhorn, David, *Fatherless America: Confronting Our Most Urgent Social Problem*, Basic Books, NY, 1995; Farley, Reynolds, "America in Decline? New Evidence About Social and Economic Trends." *L.S.A. Magazine*, University of Michigan, Ann Arbor, vol. 20, no. 2, Spring 1977, pp. 18-23, p. 23; Fleming, Thomas "The Truth About Patria Potestas," *The Family in America*, Rockford Institute, Rockford, Il, Vol 10, No 11, Nov 1996, pp. 2-7; Furstenberg, Frank D, and Andrew J. Cherlin, *Divided Families: What Happens to Children When Parents Part*, Harvard University Press, Cambridge, 1996; Larson, David, Hames P. Sawyers and Susan S. Larson, *The Costly Consequences of Divorce: Assessing the Clinical, Economic and Public Health Impact of Marital Disruption in the United States, (Report)* National Institute for Health Care Research, Rockville MD, 1996; McLanahan, Sara and Gary Sanderfur, *Growing Up with a Single Parent: What Helps, What Hurts*, Harvard University Press, Cambridge, MA, 1996; Rector, Robert, "Combating Family Disintegration, Crime and Dependence and Beyond," *Backgrounder Report #983*, Heritage Foundation, Washington DC, April 8, 1994; Stone, Brad Lowell, "Statist Communitarianism and Civil Society," *The Intercollegiate Review*, vol 32, no. 2, Spring 1997, pp 9-18; Talbot, Margaret,

"Love, American Style: What Alarmists About Divorce Don't Get About Idealism in America," *New Republic*, April 14, 1997, pp. 30-38.

6. It is not our intention to provide the data on the expanding degree of familial breakdown evident in the society and its tie to social breakdown and disorder. This has been amply presented in great detail in many sources some of which we have already listed.

7. Skolnick, Arlene, *The Embattled Paradise: The American Family in an Age of Uncertainty*, Basic Books, New York, 1991.

8. Sowell, Thomas, *The Vision of the Anointed*, Basic Books, New York, 1995, pp. 58-59.

9. Goebbels, Paul Joseph (1897-1945) see listing in *Concise Columbia Encyclopedia*, Columbia University Press, NY 1995. His use of the self-fulfilling (false) prophesy included the encouragement of not-yet-fully conquered nations not to struggle.

10. Informal interviews with recruitment officers at university placement meetings have indicated that many of these new groups emphasize that those seeking the fast track in their careers must necessarily devote most of their post-college and training years to their work and that this leaves little time for personal activities, let alone time for the building of a family. The early work years in medicine, law, accountancy and business administration, for example, are becoming increasingly known for their heavy demands on the time of the beginning professional on the fast track.

11. Segalman, Ralph, *Dynamics of Social Behavior and Development*, University Press of America, Washington, DC 1978.

12. Erikson, Eric H., "Identity and the Life Cycle; Selected Papers", *Psychological Issues*, vol. 1, no. 1, International Universities Press, 1959; Carter, Stephen L., *Integrity*, Basic Books, New York, 1996.

13. Glazar, Nathan and Daniel Moynihan, *Beyond the Melting Pot*, MET Press, Cambridge Mass, 1992; Kristol, Irving: "Welfare: The Best of Intentions; the Worst of Results" *Atlantic Monthly*, 228 (2); 45-47, 1971; Yoest, Charmaine Crouse, "Font of Virtue; Spring of Wealth: How the Strong Family Sustains a Prosperous Society" *The World and I*, August 1994.

14. This culture of living with little or no meaning and life-purpose has always permeated the life-style of many of the children of the affluent. It has been described by some social-psychologists as "existential nausea." The surprising aspect of this problem is that this life-pattern has spread to increasingly greater portions of the middle class, as well as in the culture of the inner city.

15. Boys learn the fatherly role of responsibility for the family and fathering of children from men who are involved in their lives. They have difficulty accepting such roles from their young mothers because of the psychological need to differentiate themselves from femininity. They are also diverted from goals appropriate to fatherhood by the anti-social male models of the drug and sex

culture on television and in the recreational street life of cities.

16. Elkind, David, *Ties That Stress: The New Family Imbalance*, Harvard University Press, Cambridge, MA, 1996; Furstenberg, Frank F. Jr. And Andrew Cherlin, *Divided Families, What Happens to Children when Parents Part*, Harvard University Press, Cambridge, MA, 1996; Maynard, Rebecca A. and Eileen M. Gargy, "Adolescent Motherhood: Implications for the Juvenile Justice System." O.J.J.D.P. (Office of Juvenile Justice and Delinquency Prevention) U.S. Dept. of Justice, Fact Sheet 50, January 1997; Maynard, Rebecca A. and Eileen M. Gargy, *Kids Having Kids: A Robin Hood Foundation Special Report on the costs of Adolescent Childbearing*, Catalyst Foundation, New York, NY, 1977; McLanahan, Sara and Gary Sanderfur, *Growing Up with a Single Parent: What Helps, What Hurts*, Harvard University Press, Cambridge, MA, 1996; Rector, Robert, "Combating Family Disintegration, Crime and Dependence and Beyond," *Backgrounder Report #983*, Heritage Foundation, Washington DC, Apr. 8, 1994; Talbot, Margaret, "Love, American Style: What Alarmists About Divorce Don't Get About Idealism in America," *New Republic*, April 14, 1997, pp. 30-38.

17. Radosh, Ronald, "Downtrodden Dads", *Heterodoxy*, Center for the Study of Popular Culture, Los Angeles, CA, Vol. 4, No. 5 & 6, May/June 1996, pp. 1, 18, 19, 20, 21.

18. Sommers, Christine Hoff, "Feminism Is Not the Story of their Lives", *Heterodoxy*, Center for the Study of Popular Culture, Los Angeles, CA, Vol. 4, No. 5 & 6, May/June 1996, pp. 7 & 8.

19. This data is derived from a report "Five Myths About Divorce" by MACF c/o <steven@abbott.demon.co.uk>. His sources include as follows: Central Statistical Office CD-ROM Social Trends, University of Exeter, Exeter Family Study 1994, and the Center for Family Research, Cambridge University, 1994; Talbot, Margaret, "Love, American Style: What Alarmists About Divorce Don't Get About Idealism in America," *New Republic*, April 14, 1997, pp. 30-38.

20. Maddox, William R. Jr., "Marital Bliss", *The American Enterprise*, May/June 1996, pp. 45 - 46.

21. Erikson, Eric, *Childhood and Society*, W.W. Norton and Sons, NY, 1950.

22. Mitscherlich, A., *Society without the Father*, Schoken, NY, 1970, p. 283; Blitstein, Dorothy, *Human Social Development, Psychological Roots and Social Consequences*, NY, College and University Press 1972, p. 195; Bettleheim, Bruno, *Love is Not Enough*, Glencoe, Ill, Free Press 1972; Lewin, Kurt, *Field Theory in Social Science*, Harper, NY, 1951.

23. Bronfenbrenner, Urie, "Children and Families: The Future?", *Transaction: Society*, vol. 18, no. 2, Jan/Feb 1981.

24. The changed meaning of marriage as understood in the pre 1960' and the post 1960s eras requires an understanding of the difference between a contract and a covenant. Before the 1960s marriage was, in reality, a covenant. The pre-1960s tradition was

Chart II
The Environment and the Family

Item	Before 1960s	After the 1960s
Taxes	Generally low taxes, most low income families exempt.	High taxes in the 1970s and very much higher in the 1980s and 1990s on broad range of income
Marriage Penalty or Regard in relation to tax structure	Generally there was a "Marriage Reward," especially in terms of dependent deductions.	A Marriage Penalty. It is cheaper to remain single than to marry.
Government support Provisions	Governmental relationships with the family were relatively benign.	Bureaucratic government growth in scope and in depth serves to repress familial establishment. Cohabitation occurs but this practice lacks long-range stability.
Welfare support of traditional intact family	W.P.A. jobs for unemployed fathers: (head of families) AFDC available only to families where father is dead or disabled.	Welfare is available to families where father has deserted, divorced, and is unavailable or otherwise non-supporting. Thus there is a defacto government entitlement for unmarried motherhood.
Divorce (law)	Generally unavailable except where fault could be proven. Most couples understood marriage to be relatively permanent under the law (note 24).	No-Fault divorce has opened wide the temporary nature of marriage (note 24).
Definition of Marriage as understood by family and community	Marriage and family life were usually understood to be a matter of a covenant which is broader than a contract and much more binding on the couple, and their relatives (note 27).	Marriage is now considered by many as a matter of an open contract: effective on its contractees only as long as both are willing to continue (note 24).
Divorce (social conditions)	Divorce and separation were discouraged by strong social stigma in our community.	Divorce is not stigmatized in the society and is considered "a private affair."
Unmarried sexual relations	Usually stigmatized by family and community.	No longer stigmatized. Sexual freedom now socially considered a right protected by individual privacy.
Unmarried "coupling" and adult sexual freedom	Stigmatized by most. Children of such arrangements usually stigmatized by most in the society environment.	No longer stigmatized. Now it is considered a "right" among consenting adults. Restriction of such arrangements of couples in many states is now illegal. (Example: discrimcrimination of the unmarried as tenants is now usually prohibited.)

Item	Before 1960s	After the 1960s
Sexual coupling involving minors	Sexual intercourse with minors by adults was firmly penalized as statutory rape. Sexual coupling by or with minors was harshly dealt with by juvenile authorities as a serious violation by both parties and called to their parent's attention.	Statutory rape occurs now quite frequently between unrelated as well as related men with minors in homes. The head of household in such instances is usually the mother of the minor. Criminal charges of such statutory rapes are infrequent. Sexual relations between minors is usually not penalized or restricted by authorities.
Cultural setting for family life	Out of wedlock pregnancy was firmly stigmatized by most levels of society and the extended family's effort to enforce this was encouraged in the community.	The new "politically correct" culture now makes individual motherhood out of wedlock a matter of a woman's rights and protected by a woman's right to privacy even among minors
"Choice" in Self-Development and Social Responsibility	Good conduct, schooling and preparing for adult self-sufficiency was emphasized in the community, in the religious institutions and in the youth-serving agencies. There was usually a close social distance between these institutions and the parent of the children they served.	A young women's right to "choose" in terms of abortions makes for a "de-facto" right of non-minors to have sex with persons of their choice. The "right " of a minor to choose an abortion or contraceptive without consulting parents creates a "de-facto" right of minors to have sex with persons of their own choice without permission of parents.
Children's use of peer opinions and actions on parents	The argument by children to parents to allow something "because everybody's doing it" was generally ineffective because "everybody was not doing it" in those times. Parents were usually less socially distant and had the time and opportunity to consult each other. Children's group activities were usually led by adults in community responsibility. Children were generally kept within the norms appropriate for their growth and development. Thus, there was effective guidance of parents and their surrogates over children.	With both parents employed and with less time available for parent contact with children the children frequently become involved in activities inappropriate for their growth and development. Thus, the family is much less able to guide, monitor and control their children.

Item	Before 1960s	After the 1960s
Choice in the medium of communication and control	Parental control was generally established by parental modeling; children usually had an opportunity to view how their parents behaved with others. Parents were able to guide their children with cognitive rules which were clear and understandable to the children.	The counterculture generation emphasized youth autonomy and resistance to authority. This generation became the current parent generation. It is difficult for this generation to have the skills to teach respect for their authority under these circumstances. Also, this generation put a heavy emphasis on "feeling" rather than"thinking" or cognition as a communication mechanism. Rules are hard to express via "emphatic" mechanism without the ability to demonstrate to their children by their own behavior in adherence to sets of rules, standards and norms. It becomes almost impossible to guide and steer one's children into self-sufficient and responsible life patterns. "How can you tell me not to do something, when I've seen you do it or you've told me that you used to do it all the time?", is a common response by some children.
Virtues, values and norms	The norms, virtues, and values taught to children by their parents were reinforced by the community institutions with which the child had contact. These were in the curriculum of the schools. Teachers acted out these moral positions in their lives and the classes. These were also in the teachings of the local religious institutions and in the ethos of the Boy Scouts, Girl Scouts, community centers, boys and girls clubs, the YMCA and YWCA, and various civic associations where the children saw demonstrated the appropriate socially acceptable behaviors.	Youth groups rules and programs are so-called "value free" or "moral relativism" emphasis no longer proposes the ideals of self-sufficiency and responsibility with consequences for one's acts and behavior. In such circumstances, parental guidance of children becomes very difficult.

Item	Before 1960s	After the 1960s
Psychotherapy, Social Services and Psychiatry	Until the 1950s most social services, psychiatry and psychotherapy programs and professions were disposed to promote family cohesion and stability. Responsibility of the family member to the family group was encouraged by these services. Most of these practitioners were grounded in the social-developmental understanding of the importance of the family for the normative rearing of children and promoted the stability of the family for the appropriate rearing of the children.	Beginning with the 1960s a number of changes occurred in these professions. One change was the growth of private practitioners in these services, which was increased with the expansion of health insurances into mental health services. Another was the entry of the counterculture generation into these services. Many of the protesting students graduated into these programs. Both of these developments brought a new policy which promoted the rights of the individual client whose interests were promoted against authority. This authority usually was found to be the family by these practitioners at all levels, including at the highest level of social policy shaping. Another change which occurred was the misconception that divorce was preferable for the children in a family rather than to live in a conflict-ridden family. Only in recent decades has research made it clear that children in conflict-ridden families are generally more able to cope, and that their circumstances in such a family, especially under therapy is far better than life in a father-absent family. It is difficult for a generation promoting radical individualism, radical equalitarianism and presenting challenges to all authority and validity to become the teaching, mediating, corrective and stabilizing professions for effectively socializing and guiding the next generation.

Item	Before 1960s	After the 1960s
Child Care	Most child care was done in the home by the mother. When mother was absent or ill, care was given by a relative who visited in the home or took the children to her house in the neighborhood. Much care was given by older siblings. Many parents with children lived in an extended family where care was always available from relatives. Where child care was arranged for with non-relative, the parents usually knew the child-care giver who lived in the same community or neighborhood (note 26).	Because families are now smaller and because employment locations are now often very distant from where relatives live, much less care is available with relatives and close friends. The new parent generation is often made up of two employed parents. Often there is no one available at home for child care. The result is that children are usually cared for by employees in the home or in day-care centers or schools. Because most parents are now both employed, children now begin to use day-care at an earlier age than did their parents, and many may not have achieved the degree of close bonding with parents and degree of basic learning of relationship with them. The child-care of the current generation has a quality which is much less personal and truly caring than their parents had (note 26).
Parental Preparation	The pre-1950s generation was usually taught parenting by their parents both didactically and by demonstration. When a child care problem occurred or a question arose, grandparents served as consultants and problem solvers.	The post 1960 generation has usually been either socially or physically distant (or both) from their own parents, during the process of becoming parents themselves. They are often alone in the process. At many times, only one parent may be at home when questions arise on how to handle medical, psychological, social, etc., problems. Answers have to come either from books, specialist professionals (doctors, social workers), or acquaintances. Often problems occur when the parent is called at work by the child or by the child care given or the school. There is too little parental time available to work problems out with children and to monitor and guide the children.

Item	Before 1960s	After the 1960s
Pressures on parent in relation to children	With the availability of familial surrogates, the parent or surrogate was not pressed by many other critical matters besides the concerns of the children.	The only available parent is frequently the mother. All too frequently the parent is pressed by a dichotomy of concerns—one relating to her career and the other relating to the needs of the children. In such instances, the issue in relation to the job or career is quite substantive and therefore surgent. The child's needs are often unclear and the temptation to put off the matter for later action is too great. In such circumstances, damage to the child's development may occur.
Physical environment	This generation had a relatively crime-free life. This made it possible to allow children at an appropriate age to go out of the home without fear of damage and with the belief that the neighborhood was generally benign or even helpful to the child's development.	With the increase in crime and delinquency, and with the increased depersonalization of neighborhoods and communities, children now require care in carefully chosen and assured settings. The finding of child care which meets the security and quality requirements of parents becomes more difficult and costly. The lack of safe activity outside the home for the children with and without their parents increases the tension of current family life. Those children not adequately monitored in their disposable time by their parents or surrogates usually end up in the control of their peers or government authorities.
Activities in the home	Home activities included reading, games, social discussions, family sports, music and singing, etc. The only recreation in the home which was external in nature was the radio. The children and parents did not have as much disposable time for recreation because many of the home chores were still very labor intensive and had to be carried out the parents and children.	Because both parents are employed there is little time for such home oriented activities as games, family singing, family sports and encouraged reading. What little time parents have is required for operating the various home appliances in the maintenance of the home. The result is that the children , without parental monitoring who have much disposable time, end up under the influence of their peers, under the domination of the lowest common moral denominator. Thus, many of these children become adults in the physical sense, but lack the elements to become responsible adults in terms of self-sufficiency and social citizen ship and responsibility.

Item	Before 1960s	After the 1960s
The "metaculture" of the family.	There was an extensive "metaculture" in literature, song, art, and in popular discussion around the belief-concept of eternal love associated with its continued fulfilment through the medium of the family and related courtship activities. Without marriage, sexual interaction was viewed as lust, and unworthy of being called "love." This view was held by the intellectual and "approved" levels of the society. "Romance" meant much more than the sexual interchange in that era.	What was viewed as lust is now considered part of a person's rights if mutual consent is given. The "metaculture" of courtship has been stripped of much of its meaning to the point that a third or fourth date becomes a sexual tryout. Thus, except among the very naive and the traditional, love has become lust. Allan Bloom has said that there is much lamenting about the collapse of the family, but practically no attempt to restore the romantic rituals that underlay it (note 26). He said we witness a strange inversion. On the one hand the endeavor to turn the social contract into a less calculating and more feeling connection among its members; on the other hand the endeavor to turn the erotic relationship into a contractual one. Bloom also refers to the relationship in the open marriage contract as promiscuous. Thus Bloom indicates that instead of love and romance in which the partners have been "uplifted," the partners now "use" each other without obligation or true concern for the partner.

that the definition that of the family, including agreement by which the marriage establishes that family, is a covenant rather than a contract. A contract is an agreement between two or more participants but a covenant is an agreement between two eligible adult people, male and female, who make a solemn oath before the accepted religious community and civil authority to create and support the family. If a marriage is based only on a mere contract, it frequently fails the family. Only a strongly held covenant insures cultural conscription of men as fathers of their children. Whether it is a covenant or only a contract depends on the understanding of the partners. The post-1960s era understanding of marriage is not even a contract under the interpretation of no-fault divorce which is in effect in most states and jurisdictions. Under such law either partner can secure a divorce without agreement of the other principal partner. Thus, marriage under such circumstances is not even a contract, which is dissolvable only with the agreement of all partners. Definitions of the covenant and contract as interpreted above can be located as follows: Covenant: *Microsoft Encarta Encyclopedia 1993-1995*, derived from Funk and Wagnalls,, and from the *Concise Columbia Encyclopedia*, Columbia University Press, 1995, New York. Contract (or "Union") as listed in the *Dictionary of the English Language*, Houghton-Mufflin, 1992. Because the post-1960 meaning of marriage is often one in which the partners are free to engage in extra-marital sexual relationships, the contemporary marriage contract would really be more aptly described as, an "Open Marriage Contract."

25. Care with a non-relative is clearly unlike care by a parent in that the parent is usually motivated by a natural love of the child and/or by the generally understood responsibility of the parent for the child and his best interests, which is usually enforced by local government and by social approval or stigma.

26. Bloom, Allan, *Love and Friendship*, Simon and Schuster, NY, 1993, pp. 15, 513, 515; Talbot, Margaret, "Love, American Style: What Alarmists About Divorce Don't Get About Idealism in America," *New Republic*, April 14, 1997, pp. 30-38; West, John G, Jr., "The Death of Materialism and the Renewal of Culture," *The Intercollegiate Review*, vol. 31, no. 2, Spring 1996, pp. 3-5.

Chapter 3

FAMILY SERVICES IN THE MODERN WORLD: FAILURE AND BETRAYAL

David Marsland

Introduction: The Nature and Functions of the Family

It is not possible to assess the effects and effectiveness of services provided for the family in modernized societies without first specifying clearly the structural composition and the social functions of the family. Evaluation of the family, as with any other social institution, is impossible unless evaluators know what it is they are evaluating, and against what operational criteria.

Throughout humanity's historical and civilizational experience, the family has been characterized by constants and by variations. Modern enemies of the family, including many leading sociologists, tend to understate the essential constants (e.g. Coontz, 1992). These are:

- Permanent union of a man and a woman in caring partnership;
- Civic and ritual authorization and recognition of such partnerships;
- Restriction of legitimate procreation of children to such partnerships;
- Protection of the rights and responsibility of married partners to the rearing of their children.

Variations in this structure and these functions over and above and around these crucial constants have been, in what are classified by Parsons (1996) as "primitive" societies, quite extensive and substantial. Variability in family structures and functions is considerably reduced in "archaic" societies, and especially at the evolutionary stage of (in Parsonian terms) "intermediate societies," under the influence of the great religions.

As modernization has continued and accelerated in the contemporary world on the basis of developments in the "seed-bed societies" of Israel and Greece, the constants in family structure and functions have become more and more emphasized. Variation is now chiefly restricted to the persistence of polygamy (mainly in societies least affected by modernization), and especially in the extent of authority and responsibility allowed to the extended family in its dealings with the nucleus.

Neither serial marriage, such as has become increasingly common in the West in recent years, nor mere cohabitation, can properly be treated as variants in family structure. They represent, rather, failures of the family, and challenges to its normative significance and social effectiveness. We should view the institutionalization of concubinage among aristocratic and pseudo-aristocratic elites and in some particular societies such as France, in the same light.

Certainly we cannot properly follow some Scandinavian countries and the European Commission (Conradi, 1995) in construing partnerships between same-sex partners as marriages. Nor can they constitute, in any coherent moral or sociological sense of the concept, families at all (Toledano, 1995). In relation to all these issues, the criticism of the UN's 1995 World Women's Conference working document by the Papal spokesman Joaquim Navarro is apposite. He charges it with "almost consciously forgetting the family" as a result of its exaggerated concern with sexual freedom (*Korea World,* August 27, 1995; see also, for exemplification of this dangerous trend, Sallie and Leslie, 1994).

In short, what we have to assess is the extent to which our family services are succeeding in maintaining and strengthening the special symbolic status of the family, the permanence of marriage, the legitimate status of children, and the effectiveness of childrearing (Shinkoskey,

1995), On my reading of the evidence, their failure on all four fronts is so grave as to constitute rank betrayal of their responsibilities. Moreover, these multiple derelictions are such as to constitute a challenge to the ultimate and essential social function of the family—its role as the key buffer and bulwark of freedom between the individual and the power of large-scale bureaucratic organizations, in particular the state. In this light, I argue here that radical reform of family service agencies is essential urgently.

The Range and Character of Family Services in Modern Societies

Precious and essential though the independence of the family from the illegitimate pressures of large-scale organization is, its autonomy cannot amount to complete self-sufficiency. In particular, some families may require assistance from time to time in the face of inevitable strains and problems. It is in this context that a range of family services has been developed in all modern societies, designed to alleviate family problems. (Arp et al., 1993; McKenry and Price, 1994).

The range of these services is extensive and continually expanding. Particular examples are examined in other chapters of this book. They vary along—and can be classified in terms of—at least the following dimensions:

- Mode of assistance: Money, assistance in kind, information, advice and counseling, or a combination.
- Targets of assistance: The family as a whole, children, young people, mothers.
- Scope of assistance: General problems, marital problems, income deficiency, housing, educational problems, delinquency/criminality, etc.
- Rhythm of assistance: Emergency, reactive or developmental proactive.
- Scale of operations: Local, regional, or national.
- Sponsorship of assistance: Voluntary (resting on various ideologies) or state.

The combination of variations along all of these dimensions makes for a very diverse and complex picture. Such diversity is positively valuable, allowing as it does for trial-and-error experimentation and gradual pragmatic evolutionary development.

In the United States and in some European countries such as Switzerland, the maintenance of diversity seems to be secure (Segalman and Marsland, 1989). In general, however, not least in the United Kingdom, there has been a clear, general trend since the war towards a single type of family service, excluding all the other alternatives in my taxonomy. This is national, state-provided, and focused primarily on money assistance.

Such services are increasingly incorporated within a comprehensive welfare state, comprising indeed one of the welfare state's central elements. As such, they typically evince the characteristic weaknesses of state welfare: bureaucracy, paternalism, and pseudo-professionalism (Marsland, 1995 [1]). They subject families to modern social work's usual ideological and operational vices: bias against incentives and sanctions; utopian concepts of human nature; distrust of discretionary judgments about varied individual cases and situations; susceptibility to bizarre theories (Lightfoot, 1995); and incapacity to understand the role of self-reliance and moral principles in successful living (Anderson and Kaplan, 1992).

Subversion of Voluntary and Charitable Services

More and worse threats to the family are posed by the character of modern family services than can be adequately addressed in a short chapter. I content myself here with a brief analysis of six of the worst. These are: the subversion of voluntary and charitable initiatives; sabotage of the local community; mischief-making social workers; destructive prejudice against fatherhood; bizarre concepts propagated by the intellectuals; and state intrusiveness.

Even if the development of large-scale state welfare during the twentieth century was inevitable, which is doubtful (Seldon, 1994), there was certainly no necessity whatsoever that it should have been the state itself which took on the responsibility of delivering it (Leat, 1993 [2]). On the grounds of its bureaucratic inefficiency, its corruption by collectivist ideology, its monopolistic incompatibility with competition, and its amenability to political interference, the state should be excluded entirely from any role in the delivery of welfare services, including those provided for the family.

The state's role should be restricted to the provision of funding and, through arms-length agencies, the regulation of delivery by companies, mutual associations, and voluntary agencies. These latter—chosen on the basis of competitive tendering by price and quality—should be entirely responsible for the delivery of services. Compared with state agencies they are likely to be less bureaucratic, more resistant to political interference and control, happy with competition, and committed to individualist rather than collectivist principles. As such, they are better attuned to the proper objectives and fundamental mission of genuine family services—restoring those in need of help to self-reliance (Yarrow and Lawton Smith, 1993; O'Keeffe, 1994). On this last crucial point, however, there is a serious problem.

Transferring the delivery of family assistance from state agencies to companies and voluntary organizations should certainly improve substantially the quality of the service provided and reduce significantly the current absurd level of waste and fraud (Leat, 1993). We shall also need, however, a program of development and monitoring for the voluntary sector, which over recent decades has itself—including even the churches (Davies et al., 1995)—been damagingly influenced by the normalization of the hand-out culture.

For example, there are few British agencies in the field of homelessness which are more widely respected by the public than "Crisis." Making efficient use of volunteers, it has for twenty-five years provided food, clothing, warmth, and comfort for single homeless people. Yet even "Crisis" has turned increasingly to campaigning and to that species of research whose primary use is as an instrument of campaigning persuasion.

Thus "Falling Out: a Research Study of Homeless Ex-Service People" (Randall and Brown, 1994), comprises a glossy brochure reporting a re-analysis of an old Department of Environment study and a survey of an entirely inadequate "sample" of just 73 people. As genuine research in any strict sense of the term, it seems highly unlikely that it would have been published in any academic or professional journal.

Yet its sponsors saw fit to publish it for sale, and to accede to the active dissemination of its "findings" in the media. The aim seems to have been primarily to focus the public's attention on allegations about the inadequacy of help made available to people leaving the Armed Services, and to lay a basis for claims to Ministry of Defense housing stock for the homeless. This is certainly partisan, if not quite actually political, campaigning of the sort which has increasingly distracted many charities claiming to work on behalf of families from their proper purposes in recent years.

Provided that the voluntary agencies can be "disinfected," as it were, to clear them of these recent accretions of collectivist habits and inclinations which are alien to their traditional and proper ethos, they should play a central role along with commercial organizations in a competitive network of welfare delivery on behalf of families (Allen and Leat, 1994). There seems little doubt that such a system would serve its clients more efficiently, more effectively, and more humanely than even the best state agencies are managing currently (Yarrow, 1994). Most countries make more use of voluntary agencies in the provision of welfare, especially family welfare, than we do in the UK. The Swiss above all maintain a serious commitment to the voluntary principle which produces real success in practical terms and might serve usefully as an exemplar for other countries as they move away from their current overdependence on state agencies (International Expert Meeting, 1989):

> There is a powerful consensus in Switzerland that it is better to promote (and finance) private organizations than to extend public welfare services. We think that the state should not take over these responsibilities from society. In Switzerland, family, neighborhood, associations, private institutions and the church have their function in this sphere, and they are supported by the state in this role. (Declaration of the Swiss Delegation).

Sabotage of the Local Community

The Welfare State does much of its damage because it is state-wide, surveying blindly and controlling ineffectively the behavior of its clients across the nation from the distant vantage point of the capital city and civil service headquarters. The problems it seeks to address are individual, particular, and local. The remedies which are most likely to work require intimate local knowledge about the culture of particular housing estates and specific streets, about the condition of local labor markets, about the reputations of this family and that. The Welfare State denies itself the benefit of all this essential local understanding by its centralized administration and by its reliance on over-generalized criteria of rights and needs.

When Ralph Segalman and I emphasized the importance of localism in effective welfare provision in our book *Cradle to Grave* (1989), pointing to its crucial role in Switzerland, this provoked more criticism than almost any other aspect of our analysis. Experts on welfare apparently take it entirely for granted that to allow even the slightest degree of local discretion involves a contradiction of the whole spirit of the Welfare State, and condemnation of the disadvantaged to mean-spirited exploitation by provincial and small-town burghers.

Since 1989 there has been some acknowledgment of the value of localism in welfare provision, including some overdue recognition of the fact that we might learn more from the Swiss than from those paragons of welfare, the Dutch and the Scandinavians. Thus, in a recent article, Norman Macrae (1994) says:

> Switzerland does not have a national welfare state. Some 3,000 local communes are responsible for deciding on benefits for their poor. Intriguingly, they have just about Europe's lowest rate of unemployed, lowest rate of welfare dependency, and lowest number of people genuinely poor. The communities decide which of their poorest to chivvy into jobs, and to which of their deserving local poor they should give generous and diverse aid.

Localization of welfare is in the cards in the United States too, as a report by Irwin Stelzer (1994) which interprets recent developments as "the culmination of the Reagan revolution's attempt to scupper the Welfare State introduced by Franklin Roosevelt at the depth of the Great Depression in 1932," quite clearly suggests:

> The welfare system, too, is unlikely to survive in its present form. For one thing, rather than attempt to 'micro-manage' these programs from Washington, the Republicans intend to hand over broadly defined block grants to the states, and let the local folk devise programs best suited to their specific areas. The goal is to encourage experiments, with everything from workfare to, dare I say it, orphanages. Indeed, the Clinton administration was forced, on persistent congressional questioning, to concede that even its milder plan for welfare reform—cobbled together in a hasty effort to offer something by way of competition with the Republicans' more radical plan—will include orphanages, derisively dismissed as cruel, Dickensian institutions by the now-ignored First Lady.

Even in Britain, where the Welfare State is bigger, more all-enveloping, and more centralized than anywhere else in the Free World, and where belief in the necessity of mandarin planning from national headquarters is a matter of cross-party faith, there are signs of tentative interest in the benefits of localized welfare. Demanding, in a speech in January 1995, bigger savings in the £85 billion budget of his Department, Peter Lilley, Secretary of State for Social Security, stated that he did not "conclude that the whole benefit system should be localized, but whenever changes are made in future, I will consider cautiously whether some greater degree of localization could bring improvements." He went on:

> Britain has one of the most centralized and uniform benefit systems in the world. This has many advantages: economies of scale, avoiding disparities and inequities, and preventing internal benefit tourism. But it means local provision cannot be tailored to local circumstances. It becomes harder to bring local knowledge to bear on the delivery of benefits. It is harder to mobilize local pride to generate positive alternatives to welfare dependency....There could be advantages in some circumstances in devolving responsibility to a local level.

It is perhaps not altogether surprising that an important official statement by the Cabinet Minister explicitly responsible for the core services of the Welfare State should cling to the old-established faith in economies of scale and bureaucratic equity, despite mounting evidence about the excess costs inflicted by scale and the extent of fraud encouraged by over- regulation (Bishop et al., 1995). This aside, however, Mr Lilley's statement is a remarkable acknowledgment of the advantages of localism, which promises serious attention to one of the major sources of inefficiency in the Welfare State.

He went as far as citing, with some degree of approval, the Swiss system. He pointed out —again with approval—the localist discretion already available in the UK in relation to housing benefits and community care, and he identified accurately a key advantage of localism—the scope for experimentation and testing which it allows. Above all, his reference to the mobilization of local pride in creating positive alternatives to dependency represents a very important step forward in public and official appreciation of the communitarian commitment and energy of which the disadvantaged have been robbed during four decades of centralized, homogenized welfare (Shrimsley, 1995).

Reformed family services should be localized at least to Borough and District Authority level, and perhaps to some even more intimate scale. The closer the relationship between those helping and those helped, the more likely it is that judgments of need will be made accurately, that appropriate discretion will be brought to bear in the determination of the assistance offered, and that monitoring and control of clients' responses will be effective.

Hysterical responses to recent official attention to the possible benefits of localizing welfare (Charlesworth, 1995) are a measure of its potential positive role in genuinely radical reform, rather than an indication of real difficulties with the proposal. Modernized and reformed family services should be thoroughly localized. Real help starts with friends and with neighbors.

Mischief-making Social Workers

Aside from and on top of the influence of the structure and ethos of the whole state welfare system, the personnel of state welfare, and especially social workers, play a significant role on their own account in creating dependency, and thus in stripping the family of its capacity for self-reliant autonomy. In a reformed system of family service we would be better not to use social workers, as such, at all. Highly trained specialist social workers may perhaps still have valuable work to do in significant numbers in the health, education, housing, and employment sectors of a mainstream, privatized welfare system, where they would be subject to normal market disciplines. In programs of special assistance for families, however, the dangerous temptations of social work should be avoided altogether.

Their first line personnel should be simply welfare workers, and as far as possible volunteers rather than full-time "professionals." Moreover, their training needs to be transformed as radically as the communist systems of training for teachers in the former German Democratic Republic and the Czech Republic. There should be a decisive shift away from the current emphasis on "rights" to education in the practical skills required to help people to help themselves and to inculcation of values appropriate in a free society.

Useful reforms are currently underway in the UK, led by the new Chairman of the Central Council for Education and Training in Social Work, Jeffrey Greenwood, but they do not go anywhere near far enough (CCETSW, 1991 and 1995, and a press release on requisite "competencies" issued on March 1, 1994). *The Times* (September 10, 1994) has it right: "There is now little or no public support for the social orthodoxies of the 1960s which still hold sway in social work training ....."

The prevailing attitudes of social workers, in particular their simplistic and exaggerated conception of rights and their impertinently antidemocratic commitment to "liberating" their clients from "oppression," are a major impediment to genuine welfare. They do nothing but harm to families.

More particularly, the social work profession is using its central role in established family services (both in local authority Social Services Departments and in voluntary agencies) to damage the family in the following ways:

- By advocating the rights of unmarried mothers and delinquent fathers at the cost of their responsibilities;
- By encouraging disadvantaged families to demand extended rights to state financial assistance instead of helping them to find practical routes towards self-reliance;
- By orchestrating campaigns for speciously defined rights of children and young people, and thus subverting the authority of parents;
- By over-emphasizing the normalcy of divorce and cohabitation, and thus contributing to the notion that permanent marriage is passé and unnecessary.

In short, the impact on family functioning of the key personnel of family services as currently organized is almost wholly negative and destructive.

Prejudice Against Fatherhood

Apparently we have to rely on a Democratic President of the United States for honesty about young, lone parents and welfare. "We will say to teenagers," Mr Clinton said recently:

> ...if you have a child out of wedlock, we will no longer give you a check to set up a separate household....We want families to stay together...People who bring children into the world cannot and must not walk away from them.

Britain, by contrast, has become so much a haven of fraudulent welfare-speak that even allegedly right-wing Ministers respond to the shameless demands of Lone Parents Incorporated in the fawning, honeyed tones of ideological surrender. In yielding thus cravenly to the campaigning bluster of collectivist ideologues, we are denying commonsense, betraying rational political principles, and subverting the family (Berger and Berger, 1983; Davies, 1993).

These enemies of the family have become more and more powerful in recent years, and are now out of control. It seems to have occurred to none of the supporters of what one might call, according to taste, either "modernized domestic arrangements" or "the continuing decay of the family" that the reason for the reduced rate of marriage, and for fewer divorced women re-marrying may be the forfeiture of benefits and housing costs involved.

Yet the damage done to the family by welfare is admitted even by its supporters—and without the slightest trace of regret. For example, a correspondent writing to the *Sunday Times* to criticize Charles Murray's latest examination of the underclass (May 29, 1994) calmly suggests that "...couples do not get married for the sound economic reason that with children their social security and housing entitlements improve if they stay single with separate addresses."

Again, the Director of the National Council for One Parent Families, Susan Slipman, was able to take it entirely for granted that the Broadcasting Complaints Commission would back her in her criticism of a penetrating BBC Panorama investigation ("Babies on Benefit") of "young never-married mothers." Yet, as the distinguished *Observer* journalist Melanie Philips has established (September 11, 1994 [2]), the case is arguable:

> Ms. Slipman is understood to have claimed to the Commission that she was only interested in fairness and balance. Phooey. Her allegations against Panorama simply don't stand up to serious scrutiny. Some of them misrepresented what the program actually said and she apparently retracted them in subsequent correspondence with the Commission. Her allegations formed a nit-picking miasma which ranged from the misleading to the bizarre. She claimed that the program had failed to distinguish adequately between young never-married and the majority of lone parents. False. It did so on a number of occasions. She accused it of giving prominence to right wing or "predictable" opinion, naming among others Professor A. H. Halsey. Halsey is, of course, the renowned ethical socialist; but since his thought-crime is to have pointed out some home truths about family breakdown, who cares about a little detail like that?

We should all care—but those claiming to represent one-parent families won the argument.

Young lone parents need a home: but they are better off in a supervised institution in the countryside than in a flat of their own in the inner city. They need money: but the father of their child or children should be paying up, as should their current boyfriends—who trade in their tens of thousands on the credulity of social workers to obtain free lodging.

They need, above all, wise adult support and training: but of this we provide, out of deference to their spurious rights, almost nothing. As a recent report (Whelan, 1994) has conclusively demonstrated, child abuse is concentrated overwhelmingly among single parents—particularly those involved in casual serial relationships. The risk of fatal abuse is almost twenty times greater from cohabiting than from married parents!

According to Whelan, summarizing the findings of the four-decade, nation-wide National Child Development Study, which provides the most trustworthy longitudinal data available anywhere: "At every stage at which the follow-up interviews have been conducted it has been found that children from broken or incomplete homes do significantly worse than the children of intact homes by every indicator of educational and social status" (see also Carlson and Christenson, 1988). As Dennis and Erdos (1992) put it, making the connection between family decay and welfare: "Young men who are invited to remain in a state of permanent puerility will predictably behave in an anti-social fashion." Fatherhood must be restored (Blankenhorn 1995).

Tom Sackville, junior Health Minister in the British government, should be allowed the last word on this crucial topic, since he spoke so wisely on it that his words won him an award for Political Incorrectness in the Guardian (November 9, 1993).

> We have to expect people to see that there needs to be a contract between a father and mother to stay together to bring up the child they created....The existence of a very comprehensive benefits and free housing system has reinforced the conclusion that anyone can have a baby at any time, regardless of their means and of the circumstances in which they can bring up their babies.

Trahison des clercs

As Digby Anderson has demonstrated in a new and valuable analysis of the preconditions of civility (1995, chapter 3), the post-war world has been increasingly dominated by what he calls "outlandish and socially damaging ideas". These include mistaken concepts of the family and family functioning, of which Brannen and O'Brien's *Childhood and Parenthood* (1995) provides an exotic recent collection. They also include broader theories, such as Marxism, feminism, collectivism and moral relativism, which directly and indirectly damage the family when they are adopted by family services personnel, local politicians, legislators and the media.

Consider, for example, the continuing resistance among academics to Ralph Segalman's delineation of the key principle of effective social functioning, including, not least, effective family functioning: loss of autonomy and consequent descent into dependence, is socially produced by the absence of effective controls; it can be restored only by the determined application of alternative controls. On the basis of extensive research—some his own and some by other experts, including Erik Erikson (1956 and 1968)—he has traced these destructive and re-constructive processes in detail. He lays bare the process of decay in the power and valency of the family, the neighborhood, and the school which generates dependency, and the structures of influence by systems of welfare which either (organized badly) reinforce dependency, or (organized well) restore control, facilitate thereby self-control, and establish self-reliant autonomy.

Reformed family services must be shaped by the commonsensical and truthful understandings and principles which Segalman and others are seeking to retrieve from the wreckage of individual and family life produced by the utopian heresies of modern educational and welfare theory. Yet resistance continues, finding its justification in ill-founded contempt for the accumulated wisdom and knowledge we have about the family—the best source of real welfare there is (Segalman and Himelson, 1994).

It is no accident that Alva Myrdal, co-founder with her husband Gunnar of the intellectual infrastructure of the Swedish Welfare State, viewed "the modern, miniature family" as "an abnormal situation for a child," and sought to displace it with "apartment houses with a single nursery and a single kitchen for the entire building," that is, collectivist and socialist provision designed to iron out individual quirks (Carlson, 1988).

By contrast David Popenoe's advice (1988), grounded in carefully collected evidence rather than derived from utopian fancies, has rather less fashionable, rather more radical, implications for the way we order welfare:

> Social science research is almost never conclusive. There are always methodological difficulties and stones left unturned. Yet in decades of work as a social scientist, I know of few other bodies of data in which the weight of evidence is so decisively on one side of the issue: for children, two parent-families are preferable to single-parent and step-families.

The family is the indispensable mechanism in the production of autonomous, self-reliant personalities, capable of resisting the blandishments of welfare dependency. It is only in the context of loving support and rational discipline which the family offers—provided it is intact and functioning effectively—that children can be reliably socialized into the values and skills which social autonomy requires (Segalman and Marsland, 1989, pp.121-124).

Family services must therefore avoid at all costs weakening the family as an institution, seek wherever possible to repair families under strain, and in all aspects of their work with dependent clients strive to reproduce the subtle mix of care and discipline which distinguishes families and other natural, spontaneous systems from the empty bureaucratic structures of state welfare. To this endeavor, the mistaken theories of mainstream social scientists, particularly sociologists, offer nothing that is helpful and much that is thoroughly destructive (Marsland, 1988 [2], 1992, and 1993).

State Intrusiveness

All of the weaknesses in family services which I have examined are either amplified, or to a significant extent actually occasioned, by the accelerating domination of welfare as a whole by the state (Marsland, 1988). None of the reforms of family services I have proposed are likely to succeed unless the welfare system as a whole is radically transformed (Marsland, 1995 [1]). The deficiencies of the Welfare State are manifest.

First, the whole concept of the "Welfare State" is philosophically incoherent. There is no agreement about its purposes. It means all things to all men, and nothing rationally justifiable to anyone (Barry, 1990). This inevitably produces hopeless confusions in practice, notably by social workers in their dealings with the family.

Second, the forward march of economic progress has led to a massive improvement in standards of living. Prosperity makes the bloated system of universal state welfare provision entirely unnecessary. Some people need help, but most don't (Berger, 1987; Marsland, 1995 [2]). Unnecessary handouts simply serve to discourage the commitment of families to saving and self-reliance.

Third, the costs of the Welfare State have escalated to such an extent that they threaten national bankruptcy. Public expenditure on welfare goes up year by year in real terms, even though genuine need for it declines year by year in parallel (Marsland, 1995 [2]). The result, as far as families are concerned, is reduced scope to practice genuine self-reliance and family autonomy out of their own financial and moral resources.

Fourth, the Welfare State is almost wholly ineffective. Its monopoly power, its bureaucratic character, and its incapacity to take account of the varied needs of different people, leads to routine failure to help those who genuinely need special support. It squanders the billions of pounds which it costs every year on third-rate services delivered to the wrong people, in inappropriate ways, to little useful effect (Green, 1982; Marsland, 1988). The inefficiency of state-provided welfare, compared with what the market, voluntary agencies and charities can manage, ensures that those families which most need help are deprived of the guidance and practical assistance they deserve.

Finally, and worst of all, the Welfare State does enormous harm to its supposed prime beneficiaries—the vulnerable, the disadvantaged and the unfortunate. By generating dependency it makes of perfectly normal, capable people who happen to be in temporary difficulty, a fractious, subjugated underclass of welfare dependents. The Welfare State thus cripples the enterprising, self-reliant spirit of individual men and women and lays a depth-charge of explosive resentment under the foundations of free societies (Segalman and Marsland, 1989; Murray, 1990; Marsland, 1995 [1]). This effect is steadily destroying the family root and branch, first in the inner city, now increasingly in the suburbs, and bit by bit in hitherto salubrious towns and neighborhoods as well. In its dependency-generating function, the Welfare State is an organized instrument of annihilation for the family as an institution.

Reform, then, is essential if we are to prevent general social collapse and inhibit the continuing decay of the family (Rector, 1992). Radical change is required on two fronts (Marsland, 1995 [2]).

First, the prosperous majority should be encouraged to opt into independent market or mutual provision of all the services we have been deceitfully schooled by collectivists into defining as "welfare" (West, 1990). Second, the small, temporary, and changing minority who genuinely cannot manage self-reliance should be provided with effective assistance in a quite different spirit from the sentimental, rights-oriented approach to which we have become habituated.

With the large majority of the population catered to by the disestablishment of state welfare, an effective program of special assistance will need to be organized for the minority of people who are temporarily incapable of self-help. This might appropriately be called the National Special Assistance Program in order to symbolize unambiguously its mission of providing help for those in real and unusual need. It is in this context that a radically restructured system of family services, organized along the lines outlined in preceding pages, should operate. Its first principle and absolute priority should be the restoration and preservation of individual self-reliance and family autonomy.

Conclusion: Counter-productive Family Services

Established family services are clearly working much less than adequately. They are to a significant extent positively counterproductive (Peery, 1991).

I do not need to rehearse the saddening facts about the escalating rate of divorce, about the increasing scale of illegitimacy, about the problematic impact of generalized step-parenthood, or about the sabotage of parental authority by enemies of the family (Dennis and Erdos, 1993; Morgan, 1995). Nor do I need to emphasize the crucial role played by properly functioning families in civilizing children's natural barbarity, and in socializing them to the disciplines and ambitions of the world of work (Dennis, 1993).

Instead I limit myself in concluding to describing some of the results of a recent large-scale nationwide survey on morals and morality, in which I was involved, commissioned by the *Daily Express* from ICM (March, 1994). The family is where, if anywhere, morals are learned, and where, therefore, the necessary psychological infrastructure of freedom is laid down. What do the British feel about its role?

Only 40 percent apparently believe that marriage is for life regardless, while slightly more, at 42 percent, feel you should stay married only as long as you love the other person. Nearly a fifth—an extraordinarily high proportion, I think—say that marriage is out of date and living together is just as good. The youngest age group 18-24 are nearly twice as likely as 35-50 year aids to take this "realistic" or "cynical" view of marriage.

In the same vein, less than a third of the sample believe that parents of children should be married, and nearly a quarter believe that marriage is "not at all necessary" for parents of children. These are patently disastrous trends in attitudes as far as the survival and strength of the family is concerned.

In this context, it might seem encouraging that a majority—if only of 63 percent—believe it is very important for a child to have mum living at home with them. But this relatively positive finding is more than somewhat diminished by the fact that less than half—only 42 percent—think it is very important for dad to be there too!

Family structure aside (Ballard, 1995), there seems to be a considerable weakening in the extent of guidance and control which parents exert. Barely half of parents check that their children have done their homework. Not many more than this claim to listen to them reading when they are young and learning. And only about four in ten control their television viewing, barely a quarter in social classes D and E. Less than half of all parents insist on a set bed-time for young children. Despite longstanding criticisms by southern Europeans and Asians, with their rather different assumptions and structures, of British attitudes to the family, this precious institution has for many hundreds of years been a central value-focus of British culture, disseminated throughout all levels of society. It does now seem to be in a state of incipient decay.

We seem intent on making divorce ever easier. We seem, if we may judge from the Children Act of 1989—a reform, extraordinarily enough, introduced not by communitarian hippies of the left but by a Conservative Government—to be as overattentive to rights and as neglectful of duties as ever we were in the long destructive years of the 1960s (Ryan, 1994).

Indeed, as the ongoing debacle over the Child Support Agency farcically demonstrates, we seem incapable of attempting rational family reform without blundering into ever sillier problems. Worst of all, we seem quite hopeless at addressing the issue of the so-called one-parent family—a wonderful contradiction in terms—and of reforming the welfare provisions which are normalizing mother-only households as a successfully competitive alternative to real families (Marsland, 1995 [2]).

The family, then, is under threat by the enemies of freedom. The wreckers of the traditional family—referred to with condescending contempt in a new sociology textbook as "the cereal packet family"—are enemies of the British people and all the people of the Free World, and we should fight them hard. This struggle is all the more difficult because, as my analysis suggests, these are to a large extent "enemies within." It is those who organize, manage and staff our established family services who are the family's chief enemies, actively impeding its essential purposes as specified above.

Thus, they do not believe that marriage is unique and special, or that it should be permanent. By their actions (for example, in relation to the tax and benefits equation) and their advice they encourage vagabond cohabitation and the stigmatization of family respectability. They are averse in principle to any distinction between legitimate and illegitimate children. They encourage women to acquire children like consumer commodities and men to procreate at random. They are contemptuous of the rights of parents to rear their own children, and eager to seize the family's childrearing responsibilities and transfer them wholesale to the state. They know that the family is the crucial bulwark of freedom, and precisely for that reason make it their primary business to sabotage its functioning. On all these counts, root and branch reform of family services across the board is essential (Carlson, 1995).

REFERENCES

Allen, I. and Leat, D. (1994), "The Future of Social Services: Accountability, Planning, and the Market" (Policy Studies Institute).

Anderson, D. ed. (1995), *This Will Hurt: The Restoration of Virtue and Civic Order* (Social Affairs Unit).

Anderson, G. L. and Kaplan, M. A. eds. (1992), *Morality and Religion*, Paragon House.

Arp, C. S. et al. (1993) "Family Enrichment: Programmes to Foster Healthy Family Development" (United Nations, Occasional Paper no. 8).

Ballard, C. A. (1995), "Prodigal Dad: How We Bring Fathers Home to Their Children," (Policy Review, Winter, pages 66-70).

Barry, N. (1990) *Welfare*, Open University Press.

Berger, B. and Berger P. (1983) *The War Over the Family*, (Hutchinson).

Berger, P. (1987) *The Capitalist Revolution*, (Gower).

Bishop, M. et al. (1995) *The Regulatory Challenge*, Oxford University Press.

Blankenhorn, D. (1995) *Fatherless America: Confronting our most Urgent Social Problem*, Basic Books.

Brannen, J. and O'Brien, M. eds. (1995) *Childhood and Parenthood* (Institute of Education, London).

Carlson, A. (1994) *Family Questions*, Transaction Books.

Carlson, A. (1995) "Preserving the Family for the New Millennium: a Policy Agenda" (*Family in America*, vol 9, no. 3).

Carlson, A. and Christenson, (1988) "Of Two Minds: the Educational and Cultural Effects of Family Dissolution" (Family in America, Vol 2, No 8).

Central Council for Education and Training in Social Work (1991) Rules and Requirements for the Diploma in Social Work (Paper 30, 2nd Edition, CCETSW).

Central Council for Education and Training in Social Work (1995) The Statement of Requirements for Qualification in Social Work (Revised).

Charlesworth, L. (1995) "The Poor Laws by a Modern Tory Name", (*Independent*, January 19). Conradi, P. (1995) EC Gays Push for Marriage Perks (*Sunday Times*, August 13).

Coontz, S. (1992) *The Way We Never Were: American Families and the Nostalgia Trap*, Basic Books.

Davies, J. ed. (1993) *The Family: is it Just Another Lifestyle Choice?* (Institute of Economic Affairs).

Davies, J. et al (1995) The Churches and the Family (*Salisbury Review*, vol. 13, no. 4).

Dennis, N. and Erdos, G. (1992, revised 1993) *Families Without Fatherhood* (Institute of Economic Affairs).

Dennis, N. (1994) *Rising Crime and the Dismembered Family* (Institute of Economic Affairs).

Erikson, E. H. (1956) *Childhood and Society* (Norton).

Erikson, E. H. ed. (1968) *Identity: Youth and Crisis* (Faber).

Green, D. G. (1982) *The Welfare State: for Rich or for Poor?* (Institute of Economic Affairs).

Leat, D. (1993) *Managing Across Sectors: Similarities and Differences between For-Profit and Voluntary Non-Profit Organizations* (Centre for Voluntary Sector Management, City University).

Leat, D. (1993 [2]) *The Development of Community Care by the Independent Sector* (Policy Studies Institute).

Lightfoot, L. (1995) "Ruling on Child Abuse Brings Parents Despair" (*Sunday Times*, July 30).

McKenry, P. C. and Price S. J. (1994) *Families and Change: Coping with Stressful Events* (Sage).

Macrae, N. (1994) "Is Newt Giving the Right a Bad Name" (*Sunday Times*, January 15).

Macrae, N. (1995) "America Gets Sensible About Welfare" (*Sunday Times*, February 5).

Marsland, D. (1988) *Seeds of Bankruptcy: Sociological Bias against Business and Freedom* (Claridge Press).

Marsland, D. (1988 [2]) "The Welfare State as Producer Monopoly" (*Salisbury Review*, vol 6, no 4).

Marsland, D. (1992) *Fact and Fancy in Social Analysis* (Libertarian Alliance).

Marsland, D. (1993) *Deadly Embrace: the Socialist Appropriation of Sociology*, (Libertarian Alliance).

Marsland, D. (1995 [1]) *Self-Reliance: Reforming Welfare in Advanced Societies* (Transaction Publishers).

Marsland, D. (1995 [2]) *Welfare or Welfare State?* (Macmillan).

Morgan, P. (1995) *Farewell to the Family: Public Policy and Family Breakdown in Britain and the USA* (Institute of Economic Affairs).

Murray, C. (1984) *Losing Ground: American Social Policy 1950-1980* (Basic Books).

Murray, C. (1990) *The Emerging British Underclass* (Institute of Economic Affairs).

Murray, C. (1994) *The Underclass: the Crisis Deepens* (Institute of Economic Affairs).

O'Keeffe, D. (1994) "Charity and the State" (Economic Affairs, vol. 14, no. 5).

Parsons, T. (1966) *Societies: Evolutionary and Comparative Perspectives* (Prentice Hall).

Peery, J. C. (1991) "Children at Risk: the Case against Day Care" (*Family in America*, vol. 5, no. 2).

Popenoe, D. (1988) *Disturbing the Nest: Family Change and Decline in Modern Society* (Aldine de Gruyter).

Randall, G, and Brown, S. (1994) *Falling Out: a Research Study of Homeless Ex-Service People* (Crisis).

Rector, R. (1992) "Requiem for the War on Poverty: Rethinking Welfare after the Los Angeles Riots" (Policy Review, No 61, Summer).

Ryan, M. (1994) *The Children Act 1989: Putting it into Practice* (Ashgate Publishing).

Segalman, R. (1978) *Dynamics of Social Behavior and Development* (University Press of America).

Segalman, R. (1986) *The Swiss Way of Welfare* (Praeger).

Segalman, R. (1994) "The Underclass Revisited: Causes and Solutions," Chapter 5 in D. Marsland ed., *Work and Employment in Liberal Democratic Societies*, PWPA Books.

Segalman, R. and Basu, A. (1981) *Poverty in America* (Greenwood).

Segalman, R. and Marsland, D. (1989) *Cradle to Grave: Comparative Perspectives on the State of Welfare* (Macmillan).

Segalman, R. and Himelson A. (1994) "The Family: Past, Present and Future" from *The Future of the Family*, PWPA Books.

Seldon, A. ed (1994) "Welfare: the Lost Century" (Special Issue, vol 14, no 5, of *Economic Affairs*).

Shinkoskey, R. K. (1995) "Deep Roots in Thinning Soil: the Ten Commandments in American Law and Family Life" (Family in America, Vol 9, No 4).

Shrimsley, R. (1995) "Lilley Studies Plan for Local Benefit Levels" (*Daily Telegraph*, January 10).

Sallie, D. L. and Leslie L. A. (1994) *Feminist Research on Families and Relationships* (Sage).

Stelzer, I (1994) "Runaway Welfare Costs Stoke Fears of Inflation" (*Sunday Times*, August 28).

Stelzer, I. (1995) "Clinton Swept to the Right by Republican Tidal Wave" (*Sunday Times*, January 15).

Tolerant, R. de (1995) "Tyranny of Gay Liberation" (*Freedom Today*, vol. 20, no. 4).

West, E. G. (1990) "Restoring Family Autonomy in Education" (*Chronicles*, October, Pages 16-21).

Whelan, R. (1994) *Broken Homes and Battered Children* (Family Education Trust).

Yarrow, G. (1994) "The Friendly Societies" (Economic Affairs, vol. 14, no. 5).

Yarrow, G. and Lawton Smith, H. (1993) "Social Security and Friendly Societies: Options for the Future" (National Conference of Friendly Societies).

Chapter 4

THE PHILISTINE TRAP:
FAMILY, EDUCATION AND CULTURE
IN WESTERN SOCIETY

Dennis O'Keeffe

Introduction

There is a widespread intellectual and moral crisis in the free societies of predominantly European background. I mention these particular free societies advisedly, recognizing that the new Oriental capitalist societies seem, at least to date, much less plagued with the problems I will be treating. Whether this is an abiding cultural difference between "East" and "West," or on the contrary merely a question of different positions on a trajectory of universal tendency, is not something which can be gone into here, certainly not at any length.

There is nothing new in the proposition that societies of advanced Western type are at present in fundamental crisis. This view has recently been most powerfully put by the group of American and British academics assembled in Digby Anderson's new reader,[1] as it was in his earlier volume, to which I contributed a long essay on the moral crisis in education.[2] My general thinking on problems of the welfare state coincides with that of David Marsland[3] and Charles Murray[4] and many other British and American scholars. My thought on education echoes that of the French philosopher, Philippe Nemo.[5]

The reference points of this essay are mainly British and American. All the same, a very similar argument could be made for the rest of Europe and for Canada and Australia. In all these countries both the major private institution of society (the family) and society's major public institution (the school) are in great distress. All these advanced countries are burdened, moreover, with mass cultures of grotesque character, incorporating and encouraging all the worst features of modern family and school life, all their shortcomings and adverse aspects. It is the fatal trap in which family, school and culture are ensnared and the way in which the ensnarement is promoted and maintained by the state, which will occupy the bulk of this chapter.

The thesis can be put clearly: the interlocking effects of family breakdown, bad schooling and a moronising mass culture, are encouraged by the activities, legislative and fiscal, of the modern state, whose essential tendency, administrative and ideological, is towards socialist hypertrophy.

Malfunctions and Dysfunctions

In sociology, shortcomings and adverse features of institutions are often explained in the alternative vocabulary of "malfunctions" and "dysfunctions." These terms meet, unlike many in sociology, the exacting criteria of a genuinely useful subject: they convey their meanings more compendiously than existing standard vocabulary. I bow to the rule that a social scientist should always use ordinary words unless the alternative specialist vocabulary is better. In this case I hold that it is. To demonstrate that this is the case, I will try to bring out the sense of these words (malfunction and dysfunction) in the first instance in relation to school.

Sociologists often allege that modern education systems tend to be dysfunctional in many respects. Geoffrey Partington put it to me more than a decade ago that we could mount at least a *prima facie* case that our educational arrangements are dysfunctional.[6] The word is ugly but rather powerful. Dr. Partington was referring to things which should not be done, things seen by most people as objectively invalid and improper. Obvious educational examples include the promotion through the formal or informal curriculum of lies, envy, idleness, self-pity, promiscuity, hatred, cruelty, greed and so on. Examples are seen in books by Kilpatrick,[7] O'Keeffe,[8] and Kramer.[9]

I am straightforwardly conflating public opinion and objective morality here. I trust public opinion because it so often coincides with the objective moral beliefs which I too hold. I also believe with Digby Anderson that there has been too much probing, too much debate, on issues of fundamental social and moral importance, and that a period of renewed silence and of argumentative foreclosure would be most welcome.[10] The public think it wrong for children to experiment sexually at any early age and are also opposed to teenagers taking drugs; the public are right and we should stop pressing adolescents to debate these fundamentals.

Dysfunctions go beyond malfunctions, the latter merely signifying the inadequate performance of what ought to be done. For example, schools and colleges ought to transmit knowledge, skills and morals. If they do not do so, or at least not adequtely, they are malfunctioning.

The exact relationship between malfunctions and dysfunctions, in school or anywhere else, is problematic. At the moral level, malfunctions may be thought of as shortfalls in the work of moral agencies. A school may be thought of as malfunctioning when it is marked by failure to restrain or modify the ills and derangements inherent in human nature. Traditional education has typically thought of moral transmission as a process whereby human nature is repressed, brought under control, made acceptable. Schools, families or churches, etcetera, which fail to achieve this with their charges, may be held to be malfunctioning, morally.

There is a kind of oddity involved in our needing to spell any of this out. Half a century ago the discussion would have been largely incomprehensible. It is probably the case that most Americans or Britons over the age of 50, experienced a moral formation under precisely the set of assumptions indicated above.

I associate progressive education, so-called, by contrast, with the view that education should seek to give expression to the appetites and fancies of children. I take this to be an aberrant and unsustainable philosophical psychology for which we will be atoning for half a century to come, even if we abandon and repudiate it now, which is by no means certain. Progressive education at school, and its running mate, progressive parenting, are inherently dysfunctional. They seem to me to glory in, promote and encourage, some of the worst aspects of human nature: idleness, selfishness, impatience, aggression and frivolity.

At the margin it will often be hard to determine whether any particular objectionable behavior reflects malfunctions or dysfunctions. If a child is selfish, greedy, aggressive, has he or she not had these aspects of human nature tamed, in which case the experience has malfunctioned? Or, alternatively, has the experience been such as directly to encourage this morally unacceptable outcome, in which case the experience has been dysfunctional?

Schools: Malfunctional and Dysfunctional

It is now an international commonplace that schools often malfunction. The evidence is overwhelming in the form of massive illiteracy, innumeracy and general ignorance. Our educational institutions are widely seen as not doing what they ought satisfactorily. It will be interesting to see if the public in societies like the USA and Great Britain, also come widely to perceive the schools and colleges as doing things which they should not be doing.

At any rate, the evidence of the moral failure of schools is irrefutable, though I would be the first to admit that parents often hypocritically look to the school for the imposition of standards and discipline which they themselves are not willing or able to provide. Be that as it may, the failure of school to maintain an adequate moral formation is witnessed in the crisis of criminality, especially juvenile criminality in the Anglophone world. Criminality is also evidence of family dysfunction, by definition, and the issue is now beginning to seem not whether but why these failures should be happening.

It seems probable that if the public has not already spotted the dysfunctions, as well as the more obvious malfunctions, it soon will. It must now be starting to sink in that the crisis is worse than a matter of mere deficits. Gross sins of commission are also happening. The young are being subjected to immoral, antisocial and even antinomian subject matter during their school and university experience. Educational institutions—by common consent—should not teach the two sexes or the various races and people of different cultures to hate each other. Nor should they teach majority populations that their history and culture are uniquely or invariably criminal or blameworthy. If they do, they are dysfunctional.[11]

It is easier to get an empirical handle on the terrifying incidence of mass illiteracy and innumeracy in the American and British populations today than it is to chart their moral pathology. Yet there is little doubt that moral shortfalls and pathologies do accompany those of a cognitive and intellectual kind. The crisis is both moral and intellectual.

Malfunctions and Dysfunctions in Childraising

Clearly, malfunctions and dysfunctions are not confined to education. Law, economy, religious life, the family, culture—any and all social arrangements are capable of not doing properly what the community expects them to do or of doing what the community does not expect, does not approve of or wish to promote. My concern are the interconnected malfunctions and dysfunctions of family, school and popular culture. I have presented the case of educational malfunctions and dysfunctions in a relatively discreet form. It will be convenient at this stage to do the same in the case of the family.

There is enormous evidence for the anxieties in question. The modern family is clearly failing. The view that it is in deep crisis is quite overwhelming. As Mitchell Pearlstein shows, the facts simply rebel against the thesis that all is well on the family front, that we are moving into pluralism or a new equilibrium. All such talk is cant. Pearlstein's guiding statistic is chilling and intractable. Almost a third of all children born in the USA are born illegitimate.[12] Far from presaging any kind of homeostatic readjustment, this witnesses a historically new dysfunctionality. There are millions of young people in the advanced societies of predominantly European culture for whom the one parent family is the norm either through outright illegitimacy or divorce or through the male parent having abandoned his responsibilities.

The growth of divorce has been staggering and unprecedented. Duncan and Hobson observe that in Great Britain today between one-third and two-fifths of all marriages fail.[13] And the phenomenon is almost all post Second World War. In 1911 there were less than 600 divorces in England.[14] On the actual etiology of this astonishing transformation, Duncan and Hobson also quote the emigre English historian at Princeton, Lawrence Stone:

> All the historian can say with confidence, is that the metamorphosis of a largely non-separating and non-divorcing society, such as England from the Middle Ages to the mid-nineteenth century, into a separating and divorcing one in the late twentieth, is perhaps the most profound and far-reaching social change to have occurred in the last five hundred years.[15]

The results of this have been predictably catastrophic. It is entirely proper to stress the unviable character, the dysfunctionality, of the one-parent family. As Morgan has noted, anthropology knows of no case of a successful culture where males have not been involved in family life.[16]

A dishonest campaign has been mounted by the opponents of the nuclear family and supporters of single parenting, to the effect that the apparently adverse results of the single parent family are really to be attributed to its poverty, not its social, cognitive and moral character. Morgan asserts to the contrary that the American and British evidence on the deplorable outcomes of the single-parent family is overwhelming, as well as comprehensive These are witnessed in data on health, mortality, school performance, intellectual development and employment. Adverse effects are also visible in behavioral and emotional problems-law-breaking, leaving home, drug-taking, early pregnancy and other measures.[17]

Nor, one can add, have the findings of Charles Murray, to the effect that American welfare has had a devastating impact on the American poor, especially the black poor, ever been remotely invalidated.[18] It is foolish and perverse to deny that the removal of one standard partner to the process of bringing up children dramatically alters the affective atmosphere of the home. And to attribute criminal behavior to poverty is as foolish and partial as laying the blame for inadequate schooling largely on the back of a parsimonious government. Morgan also stresses the huge fiscal burden of the single-parent family, one which applies to both sides of the split. Families without men need much more help than families with men, and men without families need much more than those who have them.[19]

Also compelling is Geoff Dench's thesis that the patriarchal family is largely a spontaneous theatrical device for making immoral and feckless males more amenable and civilized; while the political effects of divorce and separation and the pondered, legislatively backed influence of radical femininism, such as, for example, the increase in one-parent families and the encouragement given to then by fiscal arrangements, will increasingly criminalize many young men.[20] The Dench line is that men are stormy and morally unsettled creatures, who need family responsibilities to keep them in basic order.

The Deficiencies of Mass-Culture

The precise part played by mass culture in the moral and intellectual woes of the advanced societies of Western type is a curiously under-investigated subject. Some scholars are clearly well aware of its appalling impact. The British historian/journalist, Paul Johnson, for example, regularly fulminates against it, alleging, for instance, that pop music is the worst weapon ever aimed at the heart of youth.

The defenders of mass-culture, however, are to be found, not just among the masses to whom the "mass" in mass-culture refers, but more surprisingly among academics. As Harold Bloom observes: those who would destroy the Western literary canon, those who would rather read nihilists like Foucault than Shakespeare or Milton, are often to be found advocating the merits of mass culture, and even its status equality with high culture.[21]

For me this marks the effective end of a Marxist line on culture amongst today's aspiring radicals. Whatever else he was, Marx was a devotee of the classics. The only real Marxist presence today, in the afflatus of political correctness, is Engels, with his perverse hatred of the family.

There is not the space here for a sophisticated treatment of aesthetic hierarchies. Let me say simply that I believe that Mozart is superior to Lloyd Webber just as Dickens is superior to Harold Robbins. Though nothing definitive can be said to show the superiority of high culture, an immensely sophisticated and compelling structure of argument can be used to support its claims. Similarly, a large body of quite convincing argument is available for those who find mass-culture not to their taste.

When it comes to a critique of mass-culture one could as easily show its deficiencies by examining the output of television in general, or perhaps by analyzing trends in the cinema, as in a study of popular music. I choose the latter for purposes of economy. Popular music today is in an appalling state. Its lyrics are crude and vulgar and mostly do not rhyme correctly. Its melodies are feeble, thin, repetitive. The rhythm is always stodgy, sometimes deafening, but rarely characterized by the artful zest, the "swing" which Louis Armstrong used to attribute to successful jazz as its most salient feature. There must be more heterogeneity in popular music than strikes its casual observer. Manifestly there are standard and aesthetic hierarchies.

The overwhelming bulk of it is just bad. I share the aversion of the Oxford historian Professor Norman Stone, he being "allergic," so he tells me. The kind of music that follows one around shops, to the hairdresser's, down the hall at the university as one passes the students' bar, is almost all dreadful. Above all, it is going backwards. One could reel off the names of twenty or thirty popular composers of the 1930s better than anyone composing today. The beautiful melodies of Porter, Gershwin, Berlin, Arlen, Loesser, Mercer and many others, have no modern counterpart; nor do their lyrics, sparkling with wit and sophistication. I think any of these composers and lyricists would be astounded that an Andrew Lloyd Webber could be a multimillionaire as a result of his music, though in fairness I must add that in the case of Lloyd Webber there is nothing immoral or nihilist about his music.

Equally astounding, in America and Great Britain, is that this impoverishment has taken place against a backdrop of continuous expansion of upper secondary and higher education. The populations of these two countries are today certainly better qualified, or at any rate more certificated, than at any previous time. When we read Allan Bloom[22] or E.D. Hirsch,[23] we are struck by the failure of mass education as an agency of enculturation. Obviously there are millions in our society who like good theatre and music and such, but it is the majority who clearly do not who are the concern. We have been even less successful in transmitting the high culture of our civilization to the population at large than we have in equipping that population with basic reading and number skills. The effects of a phenomenon like modern pop music are uncertain. I am inclined, at first, to eschew any utilitarian or consequentialist arguments and attack it above all for its intrinsic awfulness. The moral content of this popular music is especially reprehensible. One just has to listen to the words, when indeed they can be distinguished from the general din. Crude, sometimes blatantly obscene, and never with the slightest moral or aesthetic sensitivity, the language of these songs appeals to the lowest in humans. It is frankly infantilising and against the adult world, as in the words of the song a few years ago, "We are the world; we are the children."

Can we live with this? The historical precedent is not good. Images of the fall of Rome or the doom-laden antics of the Weimar culture strike the mind's eye. Moreover, there is a *trahison des clercs* at work. The voices of corruption, some thirty years ago, were political ones, trying to get us—to put it at its simplest—to love Communism. They failed, never getting the project off the ground in the USA or Great Britain, and falling to Earth with a salutary bump even in France and Italy, where their prospects had once seemed bright. In parts of the East, and in many parts of Africa, sad to relate, they were for decades horribly successful.

Today the intellectuals, so-called, are often to be found furthering and encouraging the aesthetic as well as the moral corruption of the young. Robert Hughes notes that the Post-Modernists and Politically Correct spirits are not hostile to modern mass culture.[24] However surprisingly, the gurus of Post-Modernity are not opposed to pop music and the mass entertainments of modern capitalism. Indeed the insights of Post-Modernism have been directly focused onto the world of popular culture as a resource to be utilized without censure or even to be eulogized.

Intellectually this turn of events is quite staggering. The appallng Madonna is a good case in point. As Hughes points out, there is a Lacanian Madonna, a Baudriallardian Madonna, a Freudian Madonna and a Foucaultian Madonna. Hughes reports Melanie Morton as saying of Madonna that her melodies are such as to "prevent...ideological closure." Apparently, she undermines "capitalist constructions" and "rejects core bourgeois epistemas.[25]

It is a quaint picture, is it not? Post-Modernists, however, turn everything upside down. Hence Morton feels at liberty to depict Madonna as an opponent of the bourgeois order. We can just imagine her, first thing every morning, as she sits sipping her orange juice and deciding which capitalist and bourgeois epistemes she feels like undermining and rejecting today.

The implication is clear, however. The old-style Marxists, from the old maestro himself, were dedicated to high culture. The PC gurus of Post-Modernism are philistines pretending to be scholars, what the English-speaking opera and theatre-going middle classes, with historically inaccurate but justifiable contempt, used to call "peasants."

Thus is the very worst feature of capitalist society today, its mass culture, exonerated and excluded from the paranoiac indictment to which incomparably more ill-chosen targets are subjected. Perhaps there is method in the madness. If the education system had not infantilised the population so effectively, which is what thirty or more years of "progressive" methods in the schools of America and Great Britain have done, then the state of mass culture would not be so dire. These people and their immediate spiritual ancestors are the authors of the mess. It would not make much sense for them to criticism it.

What must not be forgotten is the economic space which this nonsense occupies. The time and resources which go into it are immense. There are millions of people worldwide who now depend on this grossly insensitive culture for their livelihood. There are many millions more who fill their heads with this and with almost nothing else.

Moreover, though the *a priori* case against all this is more important than the consequentialist, the latter does matter too. Though the precise effects of this so-called culture are hard to conceptualize and even harder to measure, it is difficult to predicate that the countless hours young peopleand even some not so young—devote to this do not have some very adverse consequences.

Pop Culture. Human Nature and Consumer Sovereignty

One difficulty, already mentioned, is that majoritarian pressures are not the same in the aesthetic world as in the world of basic morality. Crude majoritarian preferences, if they are allowed their way, will mostly give you traditional morals and basic literacy and numerary. In the long run they may even restore discipline to classroom and the home. But the masses seem to like pop music and the rest of popular culture. Indeed, many perfectly decent people seem blithely unaware of its moral turpitude. In matters aesthetic, human nature seems to drift easily towards low standards. Human beings readily take to rubbish in questions of art.

This being so, it is all the more important that their education be attended to, both in terms of basic competence and morals, and in terms of reaching out to the finer things of the mind. No one is saying this is easy. At least, however, this is what education should try to do. When we ask, "Why not?" it is hard to escape the conclusion that it is the elite and not the masses who have been at fault. The former imposed on the latter at school—just as they propagated similar ideas for home consumption—a morally and intellectually enfeebling pedagogy and curriculum. They made even less attempt to maintain high cultural standards than they did to secure basic intellectual competence, and any possibility that these would arise from the pressure of popular consumer sovereignty was effectively removed by the massive underquipping of the population at school, in terms of basic competence.

Clearly cultural standards do vary. There are historical changes. If I assert that today's musical tastes are especially reprehensible, I have been unashamedly looking back at a popular music of not so long ago which seems to me incomparably superior. I have not shown that modern culture is inferior, merely articulated some sense that an earlier popular music was better. Doubtless, as I have already intimated, there is no definitive geometry of the aesthetic, permitting incontrovertible demonstrations of the better and the worse. But there is a rich galaxy of measured and experienced argument available in support of high culture and none which gives plausible comfort to the contemporary aesthetic nihilism. In any case, I hope I have articulated a worry clearly shared by many conservative thinkers.

I have said that we have been even less successful in the transmission of high culture than we have in teaching basic competence in reading, writing and number. To this we could add our shocking failure to instill a sense of history in our populations and our even more surprising failure, in an age of science and technology, to transmit the rudiments of scientific understanding in an acceptable form. One can, in fact, reason one's way to the conclusion that these failures in basic literacy and other competencies are related to the aesthetic failure. Indeed, they virtually guarantee such failure.

After all, high culture too must have its own mechanics. There is less reason to be interested in eighteenth century music, for example, if you know nothing of the literature and the history of that period. Nor is lack of access to reading about these confined to illiterates proper. By definition there is likely to be a very substantial penumbra of inadequate performance even among many of those whose official classification would be "literate."

The teaching and appreciation of music suffer also from more specific shortcomings. There has been little sustained leadership from the best minds in music *vis-a-vis* the teaching of their subject in schools. Indeed, as in so many curricular cases, the initiative has been passed to the fatal dispensation of teacher education. There is no real attempt to teach proper reading of music in our schools as a routine part of the curriculum. An intellectually and morally inadequate life in many homes, and an equally dismal performance in many schools, tie in perfectly with the cultural disaster I claim to observe in contemporary popular music.

Glimpses of Cultural Hope

Although we humans are fallen and flawed, human nature has great potential, moral and intellectual. This is seen in the regular display of quiet virtue by countless human beings, as well as in the manifestation of Olympian goodness by small numbers of persons in every era. It is also seen in the magnificence of the best intellectual and artistic creations of our race. Human nature has also demonstrated its enormous potential in general economic terms. After all, the economic system we call capitalism is an immensely complex natural phenomenon, whose rules most people seem able to learn, however, provided they have the right kind of moral and attitudinal socialization.

What we need next is a tough combination of moral and cognitive as well as aesthetic formation for our young people, such as to permit our lagged cultural and cognitive life to catch up with the dramatic changes we have effected in the general economy. It will not be easy. The repair of moral ruin, even if it is only partial ruin, never is. There are some hopeful signs, some shoots of young flowers in the cultural desert. It is apparent that under certain circumstances millions of people are prepared to listen to good music, or rather listen while they watch its performance. It is also possible to transmit serious novels in televised form. What we need to understand better, in view especially perhaps of the extraordinary resources we have to work with, is why cultural and intellectual life in our societies is so mediocre. In the next section I will attempt to link somewhat more systematically the three questions I have treated separately so far: school, home and culture, and try to see what impact the activities of the state have on them.

School, Home, Culture and the State

It is not possible conclusively to demonstrate the interconnectedness of the three very large and fluctuating variables I have been concerned with: school, home and culture. No matter, in one sense. I incline on principle to that sociological persuasion which finds speculative social theory immensely more convincing than empirical sociological research, and I speak as one who works in both areas.

Two of these variables present no evidential difficulty. We have vast accumulated evidence about the sick condition of schooling and the family. It is the cultural variable which is elusive. Yet this variable is probably the key site of the social pathology which exercises us. Its addition acts to compound, beyondmeasure, the problems of understanding, since culture is relatively indeterminate, and the causal nexus in the resulting triad is in a sense inscrutable. If we want hard statistical data we must stick with the bald links between family and school. There are solid, reliable results here. For me, however, it is the cultural connection which is of real interest.

Once culture is brought to the reckoning that reckoning becomes, indeed, a blurred triangulation. It is impossible in these circumstances, to assign specific weights to the flow of malign influences. One knows that the poison of the culture is compounding the adverse mutual effects of family and school, but there is no way of expressing the results in any meaningful statistics.

This does not mean that the influences imputed are unreal. Why should it, since we know, already precisely and statistically, that two of the elements in the triad are in deep trouble? It is perfectly possible, on the contrary, to intuit the linked character of all three and to put forward a plausible account of the links. The conceptual framework is quite easily outlined. Malfunctions and dysfunctions in family, school and culture are fundamentally sustained and promoted by the state.

The state should not, in this context, be regarded as a fourth variable, giving us a quartet of interlocking effects. Instead it should be thought of as a nexus of publicly financed institutions and ideologies which has directly penetrated, destabilized and deregulated home and school and, rather more indirectly, contributed to the shocking banality and immorality of modern mass culture. It does this by the standard economic inefficiency which always characterizes public expenditures, compounded by the corrupt ideological currents which have appeared in recent decades in all the advanced societies of predominantly white European type. The brooding intellection which aims to weaken and fragment our society is born in the public sector and also nourished by the resources the state so helpfully provides.

The Dialectic of Mediocrity

There are enormous cognitive and moral shortfalls in our modern education systems and family structures. These influences interweave. Inadequate families imply lowered educability of children, which in turn means that the education system is impaired in its fundamental economic activity: human capital formation. I prefer, in general, to stress the argument from the other end, however the deadly contribution made by public sector education. Intellectually and morally inferior state education leads to cognitive, cultural and moral deficits in the population, to huge deficits in the distribution of private human capital, with weighty implications for family life, economic performance, civil responsibilities and so on. The interwoven shortfalls play off one another, in a dismal "dialectic of mediocrity."

Sustained by school and family failure and in turn sustaining them, lies the "kraken" of modern mass culture. It deadens the intellectual and moral lives both of family and school, reinforcing the empty, cynical and defected culture which we are familiar with from the works of Bloom[26] and Hirsch.[27]

Nor is the woe confined, as some might think, to lower strata. The adoption of antinomian attitudes and ideologies by the so-called intellectual classes is the middle class "educated" version of criminal behavior and rowdiness by the working classes. Both relate to the malfunctions and dysfunctions of educational preparation and family life. Being less prepared than they ought, the products of secondary education fall victim at university to Political Correctness and other pathologies. Lower down the scale the counterpart is the more ocular criminality of the working classes. And all of them are subject to the endless deintellectualizing influence of modern mass culture, with pop music perhaps its most devastating instance, though quiz-shows, sitcoms and soaps are scarcely more commendable.

It is the state which amplifies and embodies the woes of our civilization. We in the free societies have not escaped the destructive effects of statism. It is true that we have not endured the ultimate stasis, theparalysis and total subversion of moral life, in which uncorrected malfunctions and dysfunctions ultimately converge in uncontrollable state hypertrophy. Such was the case with Nazism and Communism, which we avoided and, indeed, finally overcame. We have nevertheless partially crippled our societies, made them less free, less secure and less prosperous than they should be, by allowing the State Leviathan too much part in our lives.

This argument is cogently spelled out by James A Dorn. He notes the adverse trends in the USA, not only of the breakup of families, but also of the amorality of public education, the eruption of criminal activity, the decline in civility, the lack of integrity in public and private life and the growth of litigation as the chief way to settle disputes.[28]

The state has produced legislation for which there has often been little popular demand, which has weakened the social fabric. There was no widespread demand that divorce be made the overwhelmingly easier thing it has become, for example. Nor were the attitudinal changes a result of popular demand. Rather, like other dubious changes, such as the relaxing of the law on homosexuality, they were the work of dedicated *bien-pensant* elites.

Can you eliminate shame and stigma from social life and still maintain the integrity of the family? Can you introduce the "ideology of infantile happiness," otherwise known as "progressive education," without paying a huge intellectual and moral penalty? In fact, both these sets of innovations have occurred. The state education system has generated intellectual changes which have both threatened and impaired its own performance and the functioning of the family too. Child-centered education and child-focused forms of child-rearing are among the central errors of our civilization, rivaling, indeed overlapping with, the reliance on ever-increasing doses of public expenditure as a social panacea. They lead to a shirking of responsibilities, as people who do not bring up their children properly expect schools to make up the deficit, and schools neither can nor will.

Patricia Morgan shows that the state treats unmarried or divorced or abandoned mothers better than poor married people.[29] At the very least it can be said that the state joins in the errors. Worse, it is indeed probably the principal locus of their genesis. The state has relaxed the laws on divorce, it fails to support married life as the norm; it softens the penalties incurred by women falling pregnant out of wedlock; it encourages soft determinism, it decriminalizes manifestly criminal action. I am, of course, speaking not of an abstraction but of the personnel, the ideological cadres of the state, who widely proclaim the determining influence of poverty on social ills and the helplessness of human beings in the face of their environments, just as they laud the curative powers of public finance.

Nor is it spiteful or otiose to note that many of the contentions which underlie modern welfare—views about marriage, sexual practices, race and culture, and perhaps especially rights—are cognate with those of Political Correctness.

The State and Antinomianism

When Schumpeter proposed that advanced societies tend to promote and reward antinomian thought, he did not elaborate on this important insight, formally or theoretically. Nor did he sufficiently observe that as well as antinomian thought, antisocial behavior is sometimes encouraged.[30]

He did not note the mechanisms whereby this thought and behavior are promoted. He did not relate antinomianism to questions of finance, private or public. Much later, when Paul Johnson produced his formidable history of our century, he echoed Schumpeter's insight and broadened it. His view is that modern mass education systems in the free societies are sources of disorder and disruption as much as of consensus and accord.[31] Johnson thus went beyond Schumpeter on the question of the mechanisms involved. He too failed, however, to say anything much about the provenance and financial sustenance of "radical" thinking. Given that one can assume that rich modern societies are bound to have elaborate education systems, how far is it significant how they are financed?

There has not been much study to date of the intimacy between malfunctions and antinomian disruptions on the one hand, and public finance on the other.[32] It is not appreciated how close the links are between moral and artistic nihilism and the temptations which seem to inhere in the spending of other people's money. I have often been informed by the very same people who fulminate against "middle class morality" (in my view just another name for civilization itself) that it does not matter if would-be teachers are not well informed on the traditional corpus of culture. They will know "other things." This turns out to mean the likes of pop music.

There is a case for identifying public finance as a source of many of our contemporary woes. The malady of the one-parent family, for example, is in good part a function of public finance. Money from the state allows people to do the single-parent family, just as with the British, our tax arrangements encourage unmarried cohabitation.

The question of the one-parent family goes beyond material support, however. The intellectual defense of these arrangements, too, tends to be mounted out of public funds. Publicly paid academics in social work and teacher education deny in lectures, in seminars and in print that the one-parent family is a problem. Those who dissent are subject to reprimand, as I have myself been on occasion. There is a strong convention against any criticism of the one-parent family in British teacher education, for example, as we have already noted. Indeed, this convention has exerted proven influence even on government reports.[33] Public finance permits forms of behavior which it then defends—it generates both the institutional and the ideological socialism which sustain this dysfunctional activity.

There are many other examples I could have used. The whole welfare state, the apparatus of intervention, and much of the administrative structure of equal opportunities on both sides of the Atlantic, and of Affirmative Action in the USA, are funded from public sources which also maintain their intellectual defense. Their justification comes mainly from their own salariat. This should signal a certain caution on the intellectual front. Does one ask a barber if one needs a haircut?

All the hobby-horses of the confused culture of guilt and envy which characterizes the advanced societies of European type—they are mercifully absent from Pacific Rim capitalism—have depended heavily on the state for their funds and on vested state interests for their ideological defense. In the USA and in Great Britain the cults of antiracism, antisexism, multiculturalism and all the others have been dependent on the state in this way. In the British case the vast expansion of soft social science since the1960s has also happened in this manner, just as now the huge afflatus of media studies, much of it to be taught by people in an advanced condition of Politically Correct, is also fed from public sources.

Once established, of course, such ills can enter the private realm. They can be taken up and are taken up in the private sector, and their legal enactments also have influence in private markets and private institutions. A pathology like progressive education, and *a fortiori* more advanced forms of the malady, like Political Correctness, will by their very nature be inclined to fan out, to colonize, to seek to spread their conventions and convictions. The provenance of such ideas, and their important institutional props, however, are to be found in public finance. We must repeat that along with these intellectually insubstantial doctrines there has developed a widespread cultural relativism (some might call it cynicism) to the effect that there are no genuine differences in aesthetic worth either between cultures or within them. To those who hold these ideas we cannot look for a cultural renaissance. They do not believe there is anything worth being reborn.

Some of the widespread malfunctions and dysfunctions are startling in their bizarre and wayward qualities. They are practiced in colleges where teachers are prepared as well as in general university life, and even have purchase on the life of schools themselves. Examples include taking minority cultures more seriously than majority native culture, or maintaining fanatical opposition to intellectual competition. When these malfunctions and dysfunctions become widespread, the ability of the curriculum to supply possibilities for proper investment or consumption decisions becomes radically reduced, with dire effects on family life.

These malfunctions and dysfunctions in education are exotic examples of that most exotic phenomenon of the free societies: their socialist education system. This education cannot help producing intellectual and moral confusion, since this is what its purpose is. Such education is characterized by quasi-institutional monopoly and secular deficits of seemingly intractable kind. These are analogue of the production deficits of larger scale socialism. Public money, suppression of competition, suppression of the rational division of labor and most of the other ills of socialism are the order of the day. It is only in such an environment that a corruption like Political Correctness (PC) could spring up. PC is the latest, unintended analogue of that Leninist bureaucratic poison which crippled Russia for seventy years.

Education has in good measure been undone by these developments, which together with equally undesirable changes in our arrangements for family life, deliver millions of helpless beings into the wilderness of modern mass culture. Unless we intervene directly, and painfully, into this vicious circle, this dialectic of moronisation, the whole structure will reproduce itself indefinitely.

The Mannheim Legacy

In the first half of our century the ground for these grim eventualities was carefully laid by Marx's disciple, Karl Mannheim, a man who still, astonishingly, is accorded a favorable image in some quarters.[34] He went so far as to advocate a class of moralistic experts to run part—an indefinitely large part—of all our lives. In one sense, his advocacy has been astonishingly successful, in teacher education, probation service and the ubiquitous phenomenon of "counseling."

The trouble is that the so-called experts have made a mess of it all. They have ruined many schools and families replacing good practice with bad. Where genuine elite counsel was required, for example in the arts curriculum, they offered either tawdry counsel in the form of defending a debased popular culture, or prevented the voices of genuine elite wisdom from getting a proper hearing.

In the end, however, and here we can assume once again a rather more hopeful note, the dream will be seen to be in tatters, since it is apparent that the Welfare State, which sustains and justifies that dream, cannot be prolonged indefinitely. The resources simply are not there to permit an indefinite public support for the present scale of the welfare system. Nor are taxable citizens willing to wait around while their wealth is stolen from them by a predatory state. The late Christopher Lasch identifies their unwillingness to face massive taxation as selfishness and lack of national responsibility.[35] Gerard Radnizky conceives it as an escape from a coercive theft-state into a new international spontaneous market order.[36]

The welfare state and socialist educational arrangements were tragic errors into which the rich Western societies stumbled largely by accident.[37] These arrangements are doomed, or at least they are if the wrongs they produce are ever to be righted. There are clear signs of public discontent over all this mismanagement, and a growing awareness that in these issues at least, we people of European culture and race, have something to learn from the East.[38]

ENDNOTES

[1] Digby Anderson (ed.) *This Will Hurt: The Restoration of Virtue and Civic Order*, National Review, New York, 1996.
[2] "Diligence Abandoned: the Dismissal of Traditional Virtues in the School" in Digby Anderson (ed.) *The Loss of Virtue* 1992.
[3] David Marsland *Welfare or Welfare State?* Macmillan, 1995.
[4] Charles Murray *Losing Ground: American Social Policy, 1950-1980*, Basic Books, 1984.
[5] Philippe Nemo *Le chaos Pédagogique* Albin Michel, 1993.
[6] I was working with him in Australia at the time, that country's education seeming to me to be a clear example of dysfunctionality.
[7] William Kilpatrick *Why Johnny Can't Tell Right from Wrong* Simon and Schuster, 1992.
[8] Dennis O'Keeffe *The Wayward Elite: A Critique of British Teacher Education*, Adam Smith Institute, 1990.
[9] Rita Kramer, (ed.) *School Follies: The Miseducation of America's Teachers*, The Free Press, 1991.
[10] Digby Anderson "Ridicule as a Means of Resisting Outlandish and Socially Damaging Ideas" in Digby Anderson (ed.) *This Will Hurt*, pp25-29.
[11] Robert Hughes, *Culture of Complaint: The Fraying of America*, Harvill, 1993, pp 111-129.
[12] Mitchell B. Pearlstein, "Fatherlessness in the United States," *The Family in Global Transition*, PWPA Books, St. Paul, MN 1997, pp.401-446.

[13] Alan Duncan and Dominic Hobson, *Saturn's Children: How the State Devours Liberty, Prosperity and Virtue*, Sinclair Stevenson, 1995, p317.

[14] Ibid. p317.

[15] Lawrence Stone, *The Road to Divorce, 1530-1967* OUP 1990, p. 442 (quoted in Duncan and Hobson op cit p317).

[16] Patricia Morgan, *Farewell to the Family: Public Policy and Family Breakdown in Britain and the USA*, IEA Health and Welfare Unit, 1995, Chapter Six, Conclusion.

[17] Ibid p. 116.

[18] Murray, op cit.

[19] Morgan op. cit. especially Chaps 1-2.

[20] Geoff Dench, *Transforming Men: Changing Patterns of Dependency and Dominance in Gender Relations*, Transaction Publishers, 1996, especially Chapter 8.

[21] Harold Bloom, *The Western Canon: The Books and School of the Ages*, Macmillan, 1994, Part 1 "An Elegy for the Canon."

[22] Allan Bloom, *The Closing of the American Mind*, Simon and Schuster, 1987.

[23] E.D. Hirsch, *Cultural Literacy*, Houghton and Mifflin, 1987.

[24] Hughes op. cit.

[25] Ibid.

[26] Allan Bloom, op. cit.

[27] Hirsch, op. cit.

[28] James A. Dorn, "The moral state of the union," *Orange County Register*, January 30, 1995.

[29] Morgan, op. cit. Chaps 1-3.

[30] J. A. Schumpeter, *Capitalism, Socialism and Democracy*, 1942.

[31] Paul Johnson, *A History of the Modern World: From 1917 to the 1980s*, Weidenfeld and Nicolson, 1983.

[32] David Frum has broken new ground. See his 'Dead Right: US Politics and Government, 1945-89," *New Republic*, 1994.

[33] For example, the Swann Report of the mid-1980s, which had been briefed to study the impact of the one-parent family but ducked out of this under pressure of objections. For a critical view of this outrageous document, see Dennis O'Keeffe, "Swann-Song of Prejudice," *Encounter*, December 1985.

[34] Karl Mannheim, *Ideology and Utopia*, multiple editions.

[35] Christopher Lasch, *The Revolt of the Elites*, W.W. Norton, 1995.

[36] Gerald Radnizky, "The Information Society versus the Churning Society" in Nils Karlson *Can the Present Problem of Mature Welfare States Such as Sweden by Solved?* City University Press, Sweden, 1995.

[37] It is not that Japanese or Singaporean schools are economically efficient. Nationalised production can never be so. It is simply that the relative absence of socialist ideology in Japanese schools makes them much less inefficient than we. In the advanced Western societies it is the combination in education of socialist institutions and socialist ideologies which generates the fatal malfunctions and dys-

functions. In advanced economies, most educational institutions are owned by the state and where they are private, are not capitalist. At the same time, many of the senior personnel of these systems are dedicated advocates of ideological socialism, sometimes even in very advanced and extreme forms like Political Correctness.

[38]We should imitate some of the school practices of the East without hesitation.

Chapter 5

FAMILIES AND EDUCATION: REFORM FROM ABOVE OR BELOW

Geoffrey Partington

Families and Children's Futures

A notable feature of recent debates about education and families is that there is usually little disagreement on basic facts. Radicals and conservatives generally agree there are strong links between family structures on the one hand and levels of educational achievement and modes of conduct among children on the other. There are disagreements about the relative influence of genetic endowment and environmental factors in explaining those strong links, but no one denies they exist. Family structures do not fix the futures of children, since there is no absolute determination of individual character either by heredity or environment, but they certainly exert a powerful influence on them.

There is also widespread agreement that, although family wealth is important in influencing children's futures, 'cultural capital'[1] is even more powerful. In respect to future intellectual achievement, for example, in many western countries coal miners have higher average earnings than school teachers, but teachers have more 'cultural capital' and their children have, on average, higher educational achievement than miners' children. This was also the case in the former Soviet Union. It is even agreed that several other attributes of families correlate more highly than wealth with the future law-abidingness and civility of their children.

There is little disagreement about the effects on children of broken families or lack of two parents. Research findings confirm the expectations of common sense that children from intact two-parent families have fewer emotional and behavioral problems, do better in school, have higher rates of achievement, and move more easily from dependence to autonomy. Radicals are among the first to demand that schools with a high proportion of children from broken homes need extra public funding, because of various disadvantages such children suffer. Similarly there is little disagreement that the presence rather than the absence of the mother in early childhood is highly advantageous to children's development.

Penelope Leach recently restated how and why a close relationship between a parent or quasi-parent and children is of great importance in cognitive as well as emotional development. Leach's emphasis was on parents' unique tendency to consider their children uniquely wonderful. She reminded us that "the spiraling strands of development that transform helpless newborns into sociable and socialized small people are plaited into their relationships with known, loved and loving adults." She observed that "those adults do not have to be parents or relations" but that "unfashionable and unpalatable though the fact may be, it is much easier if they are."

Leach conceded that the maternal care on which John Bowlby placed so much importance may be effectively replaced by "individualized, responsive, sociable care" provided by substitutes, but she insisted that this is virtually impossible to provide in residential nurseries and comparable institutions. The young child may respond well to one outsider, but not to a succession of strangers, however kind and industrious.[2] The most distinguished psychologist produced by the English nation explained the key educational role of the mother within families with his customary clarity. Sir Cyril Burt wrote:

> If...I were to single out the one feature in the home which showed the closest correlation to the child's school progress, it would be, not the economic or industrial status of the family, but the efficiency of the mother. We have already noted how closely this conditions the child's physical development during the first few years

of life. But in later years it has an immediate influence, no less profound, on the child's whole intellectual growth. At the same time, by affecting his comfort, cheerfulness, conscientiousness, and bodily fitness from day to day, it acts through subtle channels, indirect as well as direct. Wherever the child's mother is lacking in intelligence, in temperamental stability, or in general force of character, where she is indifferent to the mental welfare of her family, or herself overburdened by domestic worries or by frailties of heredity and health, there the child's whole mental and moral development suffers together.[3]

In general, the capacity of a mother to promote this development is reduced if she carries the whole burden herself, without the support of a husband.

Before the 1960s in Western societies, radicals and conservatives usually agreed it would be better for disadvantaged families to be in some key respects more like advantaged ones. The respectable poor were, by definition, more respected and self-respecting than the unrespectable. Few Victorian moralists were more condemnatory of the foolish and feckless than was Karl Marx, who regarded what he termed the *lumpenproletariat* as a major handicap to the emancipation of the genuine working class. The *Communist Manifesto of 1848* condemned capitalism for its supposed destruction of traditional family life, which, Marx and Engels hinted, might be reconstituted at a higher level after the proletarian revolution. 'Bourgeois' advocates of publicly provided education, such as Sir James Kay-Shuttleworth in England, Horace Mann in the United States and William Wilkins in New South Wales, were as concerned with moral instruction and the strengthening of family life as with reading, writing and arithmetic. Although some later radicals attacked these reformers for using schools as instruments of social control, the methods employed to foster law-abidingness among the young were not oppressive or draconian. In the words of Lawrence A. Cremin, Horace Mann's faith in the American common school combined 'elements of Jeffersonian republicanism, Christian moralism, and Emersonian idealism'.[4] To use Robert Bellah's expression: the American common school was based on 'civil religion', an undogmatic belief in traditional virtues combined with confidence that ongoing secular progress could be secured, for the masses as well as the classes.[5]

When about that same time socialists and secularists in Britain sought to exclude religious teaching from government-provided schools, they typically formed organizations such as the 1897 Moral Instruction League, which advocated ethical teaching little different from that advanced under religious auspices.[6] Women's suffrage movements were also committed to instilling moral values in the schools, with temperance and self-control among the cardinal virtues they extolled. Many Marxists, such as the Italian Antonio Gramsci who devoted considerable attention to education, placed great emphasis on hard work and self-discipline. Gramsci wrote:

> In education one is dealing with children in whom one has to inculcate certain habits of diligence, precision, poise (even physical poise), ability to concentrate upon specific subjects, which cannot be acquired without the mechanical repetition of disciplined and methodical acts...it is also true that it will always be an effort to learn physical self-discipline and self-control; the pupil has, in effect, to undergo a psycho-physical training. Many people have to be persuaded that studying too is a job, and a very tiring one, with its own particular apprenticeship—involving muscle and nerves as well as intellect. It is a process of adaptation, a habit acquired with effort, tedium and even suffering. If one wishes to produce scholars, one has to start at this point and apply pressure throughout the educational system in order to succeed in creating those thousands or hundreds or only dozens of scholars of the highest quality which are necessary to every great civilization.[7]

Gramsci understood that school education could best be built on the foundations of family education. His letters to his wife from a fascist prison are a moving testimony to his affection for her and their child, whom he had scarcely seen, and to the importance of the nuclear family.

The 'civil religion' of the common or government school developed during the late nineteenth century was rejected by the Roman Catholic Church but was by no means alien to its moral beliefs, unlike much secular teaching of the late twentieth century. The 'civil religion' was found satisfactory by most Protestants, including Fundamentalists, whose forerunners had established churches they considered to be in error. A century later 'Bible Christians' are the most prominent single group in several western countries in setting up new non-government schools because they have lost confidence in the moral teaching of government schools they once trusted.

Some radicals, of course, continued to acknowledge the value of the 'civil religion' and its moral principles. Oscar Lewis, the American radical political scientist, defined one key feature of 'the culture of poverty' as 'a strong present time orientation, with little ability to defer gratification and plan for the future'. Lewis recognized there are very real differences between poverty-stricken families which accept the 'culture of poverty' and those which strive to escape from it.[8] Unfortunately, the doctrines that have achieved political correctness in recent years reject earlier understandings. Instead they hold that every family culture or sub-culture is necessarily as valuable as any other, although with the Orwellian proviso that those of the disadvantaged or marginalized are more equal than others. In general, it is no longer an aim of western educational bureaucracies to encourage family structures characterized by high intellectual and moral standards and to persuade other families to be more like them. Instead of schools helping as much as they can to keep families intact, schools are forbidden to present two-parent families as normal and normative on the grounds that this stigmatizes the single parent or broken family. Stories and textbooks that portray young children in the home with their mothers are accused of sex stereotyping and denigration of working mothers. Differences in intellectual and aesthetic, as well as moral, understanding are taken to be merely arbitrary constructions of the powerful and wealthy to oppress various victims. The French radical sociologist Pierre Bourdieu wrote that culture is merely "a mechanism for the reproduction of social classes, that 'the school is required to perpetuate and transmit the capital of consecrated cultural signs', and that 'taste, in the wider sense of the word, is no more than competence in perceiving and deciphering clues which may, at the most elementary level, be totally extrinsic'. Instead of seeking the upliftment of families lagging behind, intellectually, culturally or morally, the school has now instead the task of praising and preserving their way of life."[9]

Under the new dispensation, no family may be urged to change its ways on the grounds that there is anything deficient in its culture. Such claims are now defined as 'blaming the victims', while all differences in educational outcomes are attributed to the malign effects of inequitable society. The English sociologist A.H. Halsey once claimed there is only "equality of opportunity if the proportion of people from different social, economic or ethnic categories at all levels and in all types of education are more or less the same as the proportion of these people in the population at large...If not, there has been injustice."[10] The French sociologist, Robert Boudon, wrote: "By inequality of educational opportunity (IEO), I mean the differences in level in educational attainment according to social background."[11] It is not only in terms of socioeconomic classification, but internal structure as well, that families must exhibit equal educational outcomes, if charges of inequity and injustice are to be avoided. Society is only fair if sober and hard-drinking families, sexually faithful and promiscuous ones, show similar patterns of achievement, according to John Rawls' 'principle of redress', on which he commented:

> This is the principle that undeserved inequalities call for redress, and since inequalities of birth and natural endowment are undeserved, these inequalities are somehow to be compensated for. Thus the principle holds that in order to treat all people equally, to provide genuine equality of opportunity, society must give more attention to those with fewer native assets and to those born into the less favorable positions...In pursuit of this principle greater resources must be spent on the education of the less rather than the more intelligent, at least over a certain time of life, say the earlier years of school.[12]

The family which gives its children every care and attention must suffer reverse discrimination in favor of the feckless family, if Rawls' principle of redress is to be satisfied. Such ill-considered abstractions made many types of fecklessness more attractive, so that the relative proportion of children born into 'less favored positions' increases rapidly. Rawls and his disciples rejected the wisdom of Aesop's fable of the ant and the grass-hopper. The grasshoppers moved to center-stage of social concern.

This new political correctness facilitated successful challenges to established family values, including those of the 'civil religion', but change did not take place overnight. There has been a two-stage process at work, one that is constantly extended into new fields. In the first stage, all values are denied any possible status as moral absolutes on the grounds that all ideas, practices and structures are relative and open to revision. Once traditional moral certainties have been ousted, there is a vacuum into which new absolutes of political correctness are thrust. Daniel Patrick Moynihan explained how in the United States 'Defining Deviancy Down' has taken place.[13]

In such redefinitions, relationships and conduct regarded until recently as deviant are accepted as normal and unexceptional. Homosexuality, lesbianism, illegitimacy and cannabis addiction fall into this category, although tobacco smoking has moved in the opposite direction. In addition, Charles Krauthammer noted that, although deviancy is defined down so as to normalize some previously acceptable activities, it is also defined up to include the previously acceptable.[14] Homosexual intercourse has been redefined as normal, but disapproval of homosexual intercourse redefined as homophobia. Street violence and grievous bodily harm related to robbery have been explained as inevitable and understandable responses to the inequalities of capitalist society, but mild physical chastisement by parents of their own children redefined as child abuse. Courtship overtures by males to females have been redefined by some feminists as attempted rape: Andrea Dworkin described romance as 'rape embellished by meaningful looks'. Armed with such redefinitions Catharine MacKinnon could claim that about 47 percent of women are victims of rape or attempted rape. These are stage-two operations in the destruction of families, or even in their prevention.

Although the politically correct assert the equal value of all ways of life, they also assert that some families are so disadvantaged by their way as to require massive compensatory support from governments. They also advance policies that increase the numbers of those they deem disadvantaged. Charles Murray has noted that gaps between different geographical areas and social groups in Britain have increased significantly in recent years, largely because of differential rates of single parenthood and illegitimacy. Between 1987 and 1992 the percentage of births outside marriage rose in England from 23.3 percent to 31.2 percent, yet as recently as 1974 even the twenty districts with the highest proportion of unskilled workers averaged only 11 percent. The collapse of the traditional English family structure has now spread beyond the most depressed inner-city areas and affects high percentages of the unskilled, both white and black but not brown, because of stronger family structures among groups of South Asian origin. Many two-parent working class families now seek desperately to escape from housing estates and schools dominated by single-parent families. A few radicals, such as Professor Halsey, now recognize the dangers to equality as well as to general prospects in life posed by family disintegration. In consequence he has been the object of considerable abuse from the unreconstructed politically correct, especially from radical feminists.

Unlike Professor Halsey, most Western radical intellectuals continue to regard evidence that a mode of life has very negative consequences for the participants as grounds for demanding increased public expenditure to make that mode more tolerable, instead of trying to reduce its incidence. The politically correct now reject as mere prejudice support in schools or anywhere else for marriage as against informal sexual unions, or for intact as against single-parent and broken families. Far from presenting the two-parent family as normative, schools in many western countries attack the 'traditional' family as patriarchal and oppressive, the transmitter of sexual domination of women by men and subjection of children by parents.

In Australia, as in many similar countries, there has been a big change in how families are studied in the secondary as well as well as the primary school. In particular, non-families are redefined as families. Sociology courses, when first introduced in secondary schools during the 1970s, taught that biological links and potential if not actual raising of children were crucial to the definition of families, but a revolution has taken place since then. Recently, I gave a group of graduate student-teachers of social studies a passage on families from Kevin Piper's 1976 *Evaluation in the Social Sciences for Secondary Schools*. Piper was Senior Research Officer in the Australian Council for Educational Research when this was published and in good standing in progressive circles. He introduced the unit in what was then standard fashion:

> Anthropologists and sociologists have identified a number of 'family' types....It should be noted that the term 'family' as used here refers to a group of people who are related to each other by blood or by marriage, and who are living together in the same dwelling or collection of dwellings.

This definition included extended kindred groups who do not live together in the same dwelling or collection of dwellings, but in 1976 Piper did not conceive of 'families' that were not related by blood or marriage. Several graduate students were distressed by the passage, because previous lecturers had followed the Australian organizers of 'The Year of the Family' in counting as families non-kindred groups excluded from the category of family since time immemorial by ordinary folk and until the last ten years by even the most radical sociologists and anthropologists.

School materials which deal with families exhibit very rapid changes of emphasis, since political correctness itself is highly unstable. As recently as the mid-1980s leading radical feminists still demanded that women and men be shown roughly equally in family contexts, especially with small children. The political aim then was to challenge any residual notions that, especially during the babyhood of her children, a mother's place is in the home. By the early-1990s men were disappearing once more from school readers, since, the former aim achieved, the new objective was to ensure that fathers or other males are perceived as marginal to children and families.

Unsurprisingly, over the last twenty years, in countries which have experienced these changes, many parents have lost confidence in the schools their children attend. This number is by no means confined to parents with strong religious beliefs, or indeed any positive religious beliefs at all. My own research in South Australia found that many children from government schools to non-government schools with a religious dimension did so despite, rather than because of, their general attitude to the Christian churches.[15] They saw the non-government schools as generally likely to be less trendy and more oriented to traditional values than were their neighborhood government school. Some parents fleeing government schools were opposed specifically to their attitudes to families and human relations. Such parents were rarely opposed to sex education as such, but feared that schools were legitimizing activities, notably gay sex, which are at the very least dangerous and imprudent, certainly much more so than cigarette smoking, against which students are frequently warned. Parents have found some non-government schools little better in these respects than the government schools they deserted, but they continue, sensibly, to shop around.

There are thus very good reasons for concern about the treatment of families in many school systems in the western world. Unfortunately, it is much easier to expose educational policies as highly detrimental to the interests of families and social fabrics than to find solutions. Two main strategies should, however, be pursued. One is to reform government school systems, so that their moral integument is closer to the 'civil religion' of common or government schools a century ago. The other is to expand parental choice, so that as many children as possible are in non-government schools. The two policies are not in conflict with each other, but they usually appeal to different groups among those dissatisfied with the current educational malaise and the steps needed to achieve the one are quite distinct from those required for the other.

'High-Doctrine' or 'Low-Doctrine' Schools?

I have fully conceded that in many countries at particular times the provision of state education has brought considerable benefits. I concede, for example, that in the late nineteenth century the American common school with its 'civil religion' achieved, among other things, considerable success in assimilating and integrating into the United States millions of migrants from alien cultures, while at the same time showing respect for most of the traditional family structures of these diverse migrants. So did Australian government schools as recently as the 1950s and 1960s. However, I do not believe that this policy is likely to succeed in the 1990s, certainly not as the main strategy of educational reform. The main reasons are that the 'majority culture' is now so fragmented that it can no longer assimilate and integrate effectively and that the dominant ideology of the schools no longer values traditional family structures. In conditions of increased cultural diversity it becomes ever more difficult for schools to command consensual support, unless they abandon all distinctiveness and every 'high doctrine'—to borrow an expression from Canadian academic Mark Holmes.[16] Even conscientious teachers not of a radical disposition opt for the lowest common factor, or 'low doctrine', in any expression of values, because they fear there is no consensus in support of anything of a more positive character, even within relatively monoethnic communities. As a result of massive population movements and major changes in systems of belief, general all-purpose schools possess very few symbols and narratives which link fundamental moral values with widely shared traditions and practices. Yet, the 'low doctrine' solution of avoiding any activity or moral advocacy not shared by every group in diverse communities means that schools cannot transmit effectively any coherent set of positive values, including those once distinctive of the 'civic religion'. And it is vital that children have symbols and narratives to underpin fundamental moral values.

'Multiculturalism' is often the form assumed by such 'low-doctrine' schools. 'Multicultural' can be contrasted with 'monocultural' as containing an expanded range of substantive values and practices, to which students might gain access through public cultural manifestations, as well as through an extended cultural curriculum. What has taken place far more often, however, has been a major dilution of the literature and history of the majority culture, without much increase in significant knowledge of other cultural traditions, certainly not in sufficient depth to sustain beliefs and values. In primary schools there may be some pleasant celebrations of diversity in ethnic foods, costume and dances, but even these fade in most secondary schools. In Canada, a pioneer of attenuated multiculturalism, outside Quebec, attempts to avoid offense to families whose ancestors were not around or held to have been 'marginalized' when mainstream traditions were formed including dropping the celebration of Christmas and drastically reducing accounts of how the main national institutions developed from British models. In consequence feelings of rootedness are weakened, generally to the detriment of family and national loyalties.

The claim is often made that national unity would be promoted if governments ignored diverse family sentiments and forced all children to attend the same school system Australia is one case that suggests the contrary. In Australia during the 1870s the most persistent single divisive political issue was the refusal of governments to fund Roman Catholic schools. The belief behind these policies was that lack of funding would force Roman Catholic families into government schools and that, as a result, sectarianism would be overcome and greater national unity achieved. Just the opposite resulted: greater sectarianism and reduced national unity. In less than half a century since Roman Catholics have been able to choose their own schools without severe financial penalties, that sectarianism has almost completely disappeared.

Parental Choice

I hold then that governments should permit the operation on equal terms of a variety of 'high doctrine' schools, as well of course, as 'low-doctrine' government schools for those families that want them. I would prefer that parents send their children to schools of their choice which I dislike, rather than that they be compelled to attend schools which meet with my approval. Critics of my position may draw attention to features of various sorts of 'high doctrine' which they particularly dislike, whether at the ultra-permissive or the fundamentalist end of the spectrum. Given a choice as a parent, I would not send my children to a school based on religious fundamentalism, Christian, Islamic, Aboriginal 'Dream-time', or any other, nor to one based on political correctness. Yet, in the West it is political correctness, not some variety of fundamentalism, which threatens parental choice. Furthermore, the dangers fundamentalist schools pose may be less dire than those who would deny them existence maintain. Peshkin, one of the sharpest critics of Protestant Fundamentalist schools in the United States, acknowledged that their students

> achieve above-average scores on national tests, they receive good in-
> struction in English; and they are taught by hardworking, dedicated
> teachers. Christian schools create a safe environment in physical and
> moral terms; they emphasize character training; they promote a sense
> of community; and according to my data, their students are noted for
> their low alienation and also for personal qualities that make them
> attractive to local employers.[17]

Peshkin is repelled by the cultural narrowness and indoctrinative inten-
sity of many such schools as I am, but he rightly praised 'the principled
protection of aberrant institutions', which 'is not commonly found elsewhere in the world' (that is, outside the liberal democracies), but has
become 'bred in the bones of our society' and 'integral to the particular
form we give pluralism'.[18]

An Islamic education based strictly on the Sunna is feared by many
people in Western societies who are radical in outlook. Educational
demands typically made by Muslims may seem very likely to leave Islamic children ignorant of much of the cultural life of Western societies, but those of us who argue for the rights of Christian parents must
be prepared to extend them to families of other faiths on comparable
terms. Direct initiation by government schools of Muslim boys and
girls into life in a pluralist liberal-democracy is usually difficult to achieve,
however well it is carried out. In separate Islamic schools in Western
societies, Western culture would still exert great influence on Muslim
youth, especially perhaps on girls. There might well be sharp and continuing inter-generational conflicts among Islamic families, but these
are preferable to the creation or strengthening of a unified hostility
towards the host society among Muslims by excluding them from financial support comparable to that of Christian schools. A much wider
degree of parental choice in education might help to deepen attachment to Western societies among many Muslims. Provided that success
success, there would probably be considerable parental resistance in

Islamic schools, as there is now in Christian schools, against extreme cultural compartmentalization and anti-intellectual tendencies.

Just as many radicals object to any public subsidies for religious schools, many conservatives deplore the idea that schools much more flamboyantly radical than current government schools might be in receipt of taxpayers' money. Some conservatives join the politically correct in arguing against vouchers and similar systems on the grounds that many parents are ignorant about educational questions and should be guided by experts, although they disagree, of course, as to just who the experts are. Some opponents of parental choice point out that in TV and cinema viewing, or in patronizing 'junk foods', parental choice is often mistaken. No doubt it is and no doubt many parents will make mistakes in their choice of schools. It is very doubtful, however, whether many will choose worse schools than many of them get on a no-choice basis. Some bizarre schools are chosen now by those who can afford choice, but by-and-large parents who can exercise a choice to go outside government school systems make sensible choices. There are bad and foolish parents and circumstances of cruelty or neglect which justify removal of children from parental custody, but such powers should be exercised with care and discretion. Parents who are considered fit persons to have charge of their children should be the key decision-makers about their education. Even if some parents choose schools which are worse in various ways than government schools have been in general, this may be a necessary price to pay for the ability of other parents to choose something a lot better. At the very worst the 'respectable poor' will be better able to get their children into more tranquil classrooms in which special indulgence is not constantly given to the alienated and bloody-minded and extra resources provided to those who abuse all the resources already available to them. It is time to give incentives to sense and virtue, not to folly and vice. It is also time to attack the elitism of the radical intelligentsia. In other aspects of life, including the sale of food and drink, house construction and motor manufacture, there is both public regulation of standards and individual choice between a variety of providers. So it should be in education. Again, I am willing, within broad limits, to leave it to parental choice.

My only restrictions would be that schools, publicly funded or not, should not be permitted to advocate violation of the criminal law and that in all funded schools secular instruction should be fully open to inspection and examination.

The politically correct often allege that choice in education leads to greater social inequalities than does the imposition of uniformity, but gaps in average family income between government schools in prime residential areas and those afflicted with socioeconomic problems are often as great as, or even greater than, those between government and non-government schools. Some opponents of parental choice claim that all background factors allowed for, government schools are just as good as non-government ones, although rather more concede that non-government schools are generally better but contend that this is unfair. Some express fears that parents might 'shop around for schools as they might for grocery stores, changing their choice every few months and that this is unfair since education and the school deserve some commitment'. Yet very few parents for whom choice is currently available make such frequent changes; even if they did so it is hard to see that they should be prevented from doing so. Other opponents of vouchers use the opposite argument: that most parents are so apathetic about their children's education that they would not take advantage of choice.[19]

The politically correct often dismiss increased parental choice in education as a 'right-wing' position, but it has been supported by many radicals. William Godwin, in his time perhaps the leading British atheist and anarchist, but now known as the husband of the pioneer feminist Mary Wollstonecraft and father-in-law of the poet Shelley, argued in his 1798 *Political Justice* that state intervention "could not fail to strengthen the hands of government and to perpetuate its institutions," which he considered ripe for destruction, not candidates for perpetuation. John Stuart Mill wrote:

> If the government would make up its mind to require for every child a good education, it might save itself the trouble of providing one. It might leave to parents to obtain the education where and how they pleased, and content itself with helping to pay the school fees of the

poorer classes of children, and defraying the entire school expenses of those who have no one else to pay for them A general state education is a mere contrivance for molding people to be exactly like one another: and as the mold in which it casts them is that which pleases the predominant power in the government, whether this be a monarch, a priesthood, an aristocracy, or the majority of the existing generation, in proportion as it is efficient and successful, it establishes a despotism over the mind.[20]

Opposition to compulsory schooling in the Western world during the last thirty years has come from both right and left of the political spectrum with radicals such as John Holt, Paul Goodman, and Ivan Illich advancing policies similar to those of conservative home-schoolers, although offering very different reasons in favor of freedom from state control. Paul Goodman followed William Godwin in branding compulsory schooling as "compulsory miseducation."[21] John Holt claimed that most schools are counter-educational and teach children 'to think badly, to give up a natural and powerful way of thinking in favor of a method that does not work well for them'.[22]

Research carried out in the United States by Coleman and his associates suggests that extension of parental choice is likely to raise rather than lower educational standards, most of all in the case of minority groups.[23] In a later study Coleman and Hoffer also found that students attending schools based on closely-knit communities with a common set of religious beliefs and moral values were, on average, higher achievers and less likely to be dropouts or in trouble with the law, than other students whose families were similar in terms of income or occupation. This went for single-parent families and other families in trouble, as well as for 'normal' families. The main exemplars of this benefit were Catholic parochial schools, Jewish schools, and Evangelical or 'Born-Again' schools. Coleman and Hoffer found that some non-religious independent schools could not call upon more 'moral capital' than could some government schools. Some rural and small-town government schools were richer in moral capital, although not intellectual capital, than many prestigious independent schools. Even in the case of independent schools loosely attached to churches and catering mainly to families sharing some important social values, the parents rarely knew each other and seldom constituted a community, except in the most formal sense.[24] None of these ongoing problems is, however, likely to be solved by increased governmental intervention into education.

In general, parents give more careful thought to the education of their own children than do even enlightened schools, educational authorities or governments about the education of children of others. Through questionnaires and interviews I ascertained why 329 families in South Australia had transferred their children in an unforced way (i.e., not because of change of residence or employment, or because the children had come to the end of primary school) to other schools.

Among parents leaving government schools, reasons for their decisions were, in descending order of importance:

- Concern about standards of work in school;
- Concern about quality and commitment of teachers;
- Concern about student behavior in school;
- Concern about job prospects of child;
- Concern about moral standards of school;

Concern about religious atmosphere of school came sixth.

The top five reasons for parents transferring children from non-government schools to government schools were:

- Concern about job prospects of child;
- Concern about quality and commitment of teachers;
- Concern about standards of work in school;
- Concern about student behavior in school;
- Concern about moral standards of school;

Concern about class size and school facilities came sixth.

What is characteristic about parents changing their children's schools is not necessarily so of those making initial choices of schools for their children. My modest inquiry, however, like the massive research by Coleman and his colleagues, suggests that there will be moral as well as intellectual benefits from extended parental choice.[25]

Reform from Above

I do not wish to disparage all the efforts made during the 1980s and 1990s in countries such as the United States and Britain to improve the intellectual and moral standards of government schools. Despite many detailed criticisms which can be offered, movements towards a national curriculum in Britain and higher levels of student competency in the United States stopped some of the rot which had been spreading so rampantly. Yet much more seems achievable by the extension of choice from below than by governmental reform from above.

'Low-doctrine' schools which seek to be all things to all people generally lack effective sanctions as well as shared positive values. They easily become anomic schools with high rates of truancy and student disobedience, reflected in high rates of teacher stress and strain. These matters are not readily cured by central committees, whether appointed by 'right-wing' or 'left-wing' governments. In South Australia, for example, the Liberal Party, the main conservative alternative to the Australian Labor Party, was elected as the state government with an overwhelming majority of votes at the end of 1993. South Australian government schools combine high per capita expenditure with low levels of staff and student morale. In May 1995, the new government issued a 54-page closely-typed draft of a new manual of discipline for government schools, entitled *Procedures for Suspension, Exclusion and Expulsion of Students from Attendance at School.* A brief glance at the first page suggests that the other 49 will be of little value, since it starts with the proposition: "Educational disadvantage is socially constructed." Offending individuals are given advance exoneration by conferment of victim status. This document urges schools to ensure that "students who are identified as educationally disadvantaged" are not "significantly over-represented in suspension rates" or in any other form of punishment, were such a reactionary term now useable. Proportionally, some groups are, of course, very much 'over-represented' in comparison to others. Children from one-parent families are significantly 'over represented' with children in intact two-parent families, children of current or former criminals compared with those of the law-abiding, Aborigines compared with non-Aborigines, boys compared with girls, and so on.

Even the politically correct do not suggest that the 'educationally disadvantaged' are 'over-represented' because they are being, have been, or will be 'picked on' unfairly by hostile teachers seeking scapegoats. In the case of boys, who are suspended at about ten times the rate of girls, there will, of course, be no heart-searching to reduce their lower-representation', unless they have an additional characteristic, such as being non-native English speakers. Yet there is little need for special consideration for non-native English speakers, all of whom are deemed 'educationally disadvantaged', because many ethnic groups with strong family structures have a much lower than average rate of school suspension.

Under the Liberal reform the unfortunate teacher, and then the principal, will have to spend even more time than hitherto in considering not so much the seriousness of individual offenses as the affinity of the offender and recent relevant statistics. Teacher organizations will be able to complain more stridently that their members have little time or energy for actual teaching. Furthermore, the document is written in a legalistic format which will encourage litigious parents, especially individuals with experience in the courts and groups with ready access to publicly-funded lawyers, to challenge schools whenever their children are suspended or even detained after school. Non-government schools, too, have their difficult students and parents, but because parents have freely chosen a school whose disciplinary code, as well as other aspects of its provision, correspond fairly closely with their own values they are less likely to be uncooperative. The all-purpose government school, seeking to be all things to all people, is in a position of weakness which even benign and resolute governments, if such can be found, find it hard to strengthen. The educational policies of the last Liberal government in New South Wales were in some respects worse than those of its left-wing predecessor (and now successor). As Lucy Sullivan noted,[26] its *Girls Growing Up* performs "the extraordinary feat of presenting an exposition of sexual relationships, pregnancy and motherhood without discussing marriage," except on one occasion when girls are warned that they may be too young and immature to marry, although they are assured they are old and mature enough to have a baby and look after it themselves. Sullivan noted that the booklet "fosters the view that the sex of the partner is irrelevant, and that having multiple sex partners is a normal state of affairs."

Many Australian parents, and for that matter non-parents, find strange the recent policies of educational bureaucracies and the academic doctrines that support them, but, unlike the situation in parts of the United States of America, such parents are generally unorganized and no match for the special interest groups who dominate educational decision-making in the public arena. To gain election it is thought wise, even for center and right-wing parties, not to challenge special interest groups more than is necessary, since these may then provide even more money and propagandist energy for the other side. Teacher unions, even more than public service unions, are outstanding political campaigners. I do not suggest that the moral and intellectual defects of current public schooling cannot be affected at all for the good by governmental action. It certainly can. Yet any such changes are very difficult to achieve and it is at the grassroots level of increased parental choice, rather than centrally through implementing improved public policies, that the main hope for substantial change resides.

Nothing of great importance is easy to achieve, but the schools of Western societies are likely to become much more effective contributors to the moral health of their communities if key features of the former 'civil religion' can be restored to government schools and if extended educational choice can be offered to parents. Both are important, but of the two the second way is likely to prove the more successful. 'Empowerment' of the poor, women and many other groups classified as oppressed or victimized is a constant radical rallying cry. Let that cry be taken seriously. The most effective way in which families, especially poor and the single-parent families, can gain greater educational power is, whenever possible, to possess extended school choices.

ENDNOTES

[1] This was a favorite phrase of Pierre Bourdieu's. See reference 9.

[2] Leach, P. (1994). *Children first: what we must do now and are not doing for our children today.* London: Michael Joseph, p. 7.

[3] Burt, Sir C. (1961). *The Backward Child.* 5th edition. London: University of London Press, p. 133. For the posthumous character assassination of Burt in the cause of political correctness see: Fletcher, R. (1991). *Science, Ideology, and the Media: The Cyril Burt Scandal.* London: Transaction Publishers; Joynson, R.B. (1989). The Burt Affair. London: Routledge; Snyderman, M. and Rothman, S. (1988). *The IQ controversy, the media and public policy.* New Brunswick, NJ., USA: Transaction Publishers.

[4] Cremin, Lawrence A. (1964). *The Transformation of the School. Progressivism in American Education 1876-1957.* New York: Vintage Books, p. 9.

[5] Bellah, R.N. (1975). *The Broken Contract: American Civil Religion in a Time of Trial.* New York: Seabury Press.

[6] Hilliard, F.H. (1961). "The Moral Instruction League, 1897-1919" in *The Durham Research Review,* 111 (12).

[7] Gramsci, A. (1971). *Selections from the Prison Notebooks* (ed. and trans. Q. Hoare and G.N. Smith). London: Lawrence & Wishart, pp. 37,42.

[8] Lewis, 0. (1961). *The Children of Sanchez.* New York: Ransom House, p. xxvi.

[9] Bourdieu, P. (with Passeron, J.) (1970). *Cultural Reproduction* (trans. R. Nice). London: Sage Publications, p. 19; Bourdieu, P. (197 1). "The thinkable and the unthinkable" in Times Educational Supplement, 15 Oct, p. 1255; Bourdieu, P. (1971). "Intellectual field and creative projece in M.F.D." Young (ed). *Knowledge and Control,* London: Collier-Macmillan, p. 178.

[10] Halsey, A. H. (1972). *The Halsey Report.* London: HMSO, p.345.

[11] Boudon, R. (1974). *Educational Opportunity and Social Inequality.* New York: Wiley, p. xi.

[12] Rawls, J. (1972). *A Theory of Justice.* Oxford: The Clarendon Press, pp. 100-1.

[13] Moynihan, D.P. (1993) "Defining democracy down" in *The American Scholar,* Winter, pp. 17-30.

[14] Krauthammer, C. (1993). "Defining deviancy up" in *The New Republic,* 22 November.

[15] Partington, Geoffrey. (1989). "Parental Changes of School in South Australia" in *Australian Educational Researcher,* 16 (4), pp. 27-44; Partington, Geoffrey. (1990). "Changing Patterns of School Enrolment in Australia" in *Australian Educational Researcher,* 17 (3), pp. 65-84.

[16] Holmes, Mark (1992) *Educational Policy for the Pluralist Democracy: The Common School, Choice and Diversity.* London: Falmer Press.

[17]Peshkin, A. (1989). "Fundamentalist Christian Schools: Should They Be Regulated?" in *Educational Policy* 3 (1), pp. 48-9.

[18]Peshkin, 1989, p. 52.

[19]On vouchers consult Peacock, A. T. (1983). "Education voucher schemes—strong or weak" in *Economic Affairs,* 3 (2); Seldon, A. (1986). *The Riddle of the Voucher. An inquiry into the obstacles to introducing choice and competition in state schools.* London: The Institute of Economic Affairs; West, E.G. (1982). "Economic vouchers: evolution or revolution" in *Economic Affairs,* 3 (1).

[20]Mill, J.S. (1910). "Essay on Liberty" in *Utilitarianism, Liberty and Representative Government.* London: Dent and Dutton (Everyman edition), p. 161.

[21]Goodman, P. (1964). *Compulsory Miseducation and the Community of Scholars,* 1964, New York: Vintage Books.

[22]Holt, John. (1968). *How Children Learn.* London: Pitman.

[23]For an excellent summary see Coleman, J.S. (1981). "Private schools, public schools, and the public interest" in *The Public Interest.*

[24]Coleman James S. and Hoffer, T. (1989). *Do Students Learn More in Private Schools Than In Public Schools?* James Madison Institute for Public Policy Studies.

[25]Partington, 1989.

[26]Sullivan, Lucy. (1994). "Choosing Blind" in *Education Monitor,* Autumn, pp.2-3.

Chapter 6

RESTORING AMERICA'S CIVIL SOCIETY THROUGH COMMUNITY-BASED INITIATIVES TO STRENGTHEN THE FAMILY

Robert L. Woodson

Although trends toward family disintegration and rising rates of out-of-wedlock births are now present in virtually every sector of American society, these phenomena have taken their greatest toll in low-income communities that lack the economic stability which would, at least temporarily, buffer their destabilizing effects. A reversal of these trends in low-income areas—and a reestablishment of the primacy of community and familial bonds in these neighborhoods—will provide a model of revitalization which can be applied at every economic level.

This paper, therefore, will focus on the causes of family dissolutions in low-income neighborhoods. Second, it will show the relationship between the disintegration of family and a shocking rise in the negative social indices in the United States. Last, it will describe models of successful community-based initiatives that have worked to reestablish family bonds and to prepare youths to develop the qualities, values, and skills necessary for them to responsibly fulfill their roles as parents in the future.

Injured by the Helping Hand

A major factor in the quality of life of low-income people has been the impact of government policies and programs purportedly instituted to meet the needs of their neighborhoods. While such programs have supplied financial support and services, they have done so in a way that has also brought injury to the individuals they served. Many of the regulations of these programs and restrictions on their recipients that have weakened family and community bonds, discouraged family formation, and undermined the values that promote strong families—a work ethic, the value of savings and delayed gratification, and the value of self-determination.

Public housing residents, for example, have been charged rents equal to 30 percent of the household income. This discouraged formation of families that would have two wage owners, since the rent formula could drive payments even above market rates for comparable properties. An alternative that many women in public housing took to avoid such "marriage penalties" and the risk of losing their benefits, was to omit male adults in their households from their leases. In communities strained with high unemployment rates and few job opportunities, the authority of the male was already precarious. When absence from the rental agreement reduced men to illegitimate occupants, their authority was further diminished, and, rather than functioning as stabilizing figures in their communities, they became "invisible" men.

A number of initiatives have been launched at both the national and state levels to reform such counterproductive policies and practices. In New Jersey, for example, Representative Wayne Bryant, a black Democrat, is an ardent proponent of welfare reform who was moved to action by the rising social instability of the low-income neighborhoods in his district. He recalled that these were once neighborhoods which may not have had material wealth but, nonetheless, enjoyed a wealth of values and tradition. He recalled that in earlier times, all the adults of the community fulfilled a parental role to all the children. If a group of boys were to get out of hand, for example breaking bottles at a curbside, one of the men who lived on the street would be certain to stop them and to order them to clean up their mess. There was a sense of order and stability, of right and wrong. The neighborhoods have now changed. The vast majority of its men are now either absent or invisible.

To put the neighborhoods in his district on the path to economic and social recovery, Rep. Bryant developed a comprehensive Family Development Act. The act included several bills which eliminated regulatory disincentives for family formation and offered low-income families pathways to self-sufficiency. One of its bills addressed the surge in out of wedlock births and specified that, with ample warning, women on welfare should not be given increased benefits from the government for children born after they were on the welfare rolls. Previously, the continual increase in benefits had certainly not discouraged a rising rate of out-of-wedlock births nor had it alleviated the plight of a growing population of children who may never know their fathers. Although Bryant's proposal did no more than introduce welfare recipients to the financial considerations those working families must deal with in planning their families, his Family Development Act—like similar legislative proposals that have been made at national and state levels—met with vehement opposition from lobbyists who had an interest in maintaining the status quo of the welfare system.

The Impact of Family Dissolution on Social Stability

Those who oppose reform to policies and a bureaucratic system that have weakened the family are very vocal and well-versed in the tactics of the political arena, yet there is a fast-growing recognition on all sides that the deterioration of our low-income communities has reached crisis proportions and that something must be done. Rampant family dissolution has been paralleled by a steady rise of negative social indicators, and concern has risen across political and ideological boundaries.

Since 1960, illegitimate births have increased by more than 400 percent. By 1990, 28 percent of all births in the United States were out of wedlock. Among blacks, the illegitimacy rate was 65.2 percent in 1990. The divorce rate in America has increased by 200 percent while the marriage rate has declined by almost one-third to an all-time low.[1]

At the same time, juvenile crime has risen sharply. Reports from the

Federal Bureau of Investigation indicate that the rate of arrests for juvenile violent crime has more than tripled over the past three decades along with an upsurge of single-parent households. Moreover, a study published in 1988 in the Journal of Research on Crime and Delinquencies revealed that the rates of violent crime and burglary in a community were closely correlated with the proportion of single-parent households in the community—not to poverty or racial composition—when adjusted for family structure. Recent research has shown that 60 percent of repeat rapists and 75 percent of adolescent murderers do not have two parents in their households. Studies have also shown that children from single-parent homes tend to fall behind in terms of academic performance; they are three times more likely to fail a grade, they are more often tardy or absent, and they are more likely to be subject to disciplinary action. Statistics show that they are also twice as likely to drop out of school and are more likely to use drugs and/or have psychological disorders than are children from two-parent homes. Tragically, they are also more likely to commit suicide, which is now the third leading cause of death among teenagers.

Addressing Problems at Their Root

Even if, throughout the nation, policies and legislation were to be put in place to promote family cohesion and parental responsibility, the problem would not be solved. By nature, government initiated solutions can deal only with the external elements, the consequences, of a problem. When the root of a problem is spiritual, it is beyond the realm of the professionals employed by the government. Enforcing garnishing salaries for child support payments does nothing to establish the life-giving bonds of parent and child.

The root cause of the rampant family dissolution in our nation is spiritual, and while its solution lies outside the realm of government activities, proven solutions do exist in faith-based, value-driven efforts of individuals and organizations within the afflicted communities. The solution to an epidemic of family disintegration is not to enforce changed behavior but to awaken a sense of parental responsibility, fidelity, and a sense of commitment in the hearts of men and women.

In essence, the solution is to produce an internal transformation in the values that guide an individual's life choices. Government agencies do not have the capacity to address the problem at this level, but hundreds of community-based grassroots leaders throughout the nation have proven that they do.

Residing in the communities in which they work, they have a first-hand knowledge of its problems and have won the trust and respect of those they serve. Many have "achieved against the odds" and have been personally victorious over the difficulties they are guiding others to overcome, and their daily lives provide a tangible example of the principles and values they promote.

The key to the remarkable impact that many grassroots initiatives have had is that they are faith-based and driven by a clear set of values and principles. Their strategies of revitalization are founded on a notion of reciprocity, and follow the model presented in the parable of the prodigal son. In this parable, when a man's son wasted his portion of his inheritance in a life of debauchery, the father could not meet the young man in his debauched state, offering support and sustenance. Instead, he had to first wait until the son "came to himself" and returned home before he could be embraced. In the same way, community leaders first call the individuals they work with to themselves, undergoing an internal transformation of values and vision that results in a sustained change in behavior and in the direction of their lives.

In areas ranging from family preservation, to ending parents' alcohol and drug addictions, to establishing effective methods of placing foster children, hundreds of dedicated community activists have claimed a beachhead against America's social dissolution and have engendered lasting internal transformations of the people they have served.

Guiding Teen Parents to Fulfill Their Responsibilities

One arena in which effective efforts have been made to halt a cycle of family dissolutions is to work with teen fathers and mothers, encouraging family formation and equipping them with the skills and guiding principles they will need to fulfil their responsibilities as parents. Several of the hundreds of such community-based programs that have been launched throughout the nation are discussed below.

Teen Fathers: The National Institute for Responsible Fatherhood and Family Development—Cleveland, Ohio

In the Hough neighborhood of Cleveland, a grassroots outreach program for teen fathers was launched singlehandedly by one of its residents in 1982. Since its inception, this effort, called the National Institute for Responsible Fatherhood and Family Development (NIRFFD) has offered guidance and support to more than 2,000 teen fathers, many of whom had been high school dropouts or involved with drugs. As a result of the program, 97 percent of the young men began providing financial support for their children, 71 percent did not have any more children outside of marriage, and, although only 12 percent had full-time work when they entered the program, 62 percent were employed full time and 12 percent had part-time jobs after joining it; hundreds of the young fathers married the mothers of their children; and hundreds more went through court procedures to legally establish their paternity of their children.

The program's founder, Charles Ballard, understood from firsthand experience the confusion that teen fathers face. Having fathered a child when he was seventeen, Ballard could neither comprehend nor cope with his parental responsibilities and took refuge by enlisting in the service. When circumstances later led to criminal charges against him and to his incarceration, Ballard underwent a conversion experience. After his release from the service, he took on the responsibility of raising his young son, and went on to complete his education to equip himself to serve other young fathers.

Like many grassroots leaders who have been able to reach young people who were intimidated by—or resentful of—professionally-designed programs, Ballard possessed an empathy and personal concern that allowed him to break through their barriers.

If asked what his program teaches his young men, Ballard will reply that his success is not a matter of lecturing but of tapping the latent sense of responsibility and love within their own hearts. Often, simply initiating contact with their offspring will result in creating a desire to take care of them. As Ballard recently stated, "Instilling the love of a father for his children is the most powerful 'job' program."

Much of the young men's openness and trust of Ballard is a result of the authentic sense of respect he has for them. One young man who recently married the mother of his children and is currently working toward his college degree recalls his first encounter with Ballard:

> "I remember it like it was yesterday. He looked me straight in the eyes and called me 'sir'. He showed me respect that I had never known. I know now that MY goal is to become a lawyer. And I will be the best lawyer, because I have a family, and because I have respect."

Because of Ballard's personal investment, the young fathers in his program willingly accept his "tough love approach," including the requirement that all participants be either employed or involved in a program of education or training. A number of them have chosen to stay on with the program as mentors and several have established satellite centers to reach teen fathers in other inner-city areas. Program activities have also been expanded to serve older single fathers and single mothers with male children. Services now include assistance in locating employment and educational opportunities and housing, as well as guidance in health, nutrition, medical care, and parenting skills.

Teen Mothers: The Beth Shalom House of Peace: Lancaster, Pennsylvania

The majority of programs for teenaged mothers have been facilities that have cared for them during their pregnancies or maternity homes to help them in the birthing process. Few facilities or programs exist to assist the young women after their children are born and to prepare them to take on their new responsibilities as parents. The Beth Shalom House of Peace in Pennsylvania (a state in which in just one year 29,200 teenaged girls became pregnant) is one facility that was created to offer support and guidance to young women who find themselves alone and untrained, with a child to support.

A safe, secure living environment is crucial for the mother and child's health and the development of a strong parent/child relationship. Beth Shalom was designed to provide a loving, spiritually nourishing family atmosphere as well as stepping stones to independence. The residents of the program have apartment-style living quarters but come together regularly for group meetings and for large family-style dinners with the directors, a married couple in residence who are available to the young mothers virtually 24 hours a day. In addition, to help them to deal with the stresses of their new role, Beth Shalom offers practical guidance and counseling. The young mothers learn the value that simple acts such as holding and talking to their babies have for their wholesome development, and they receive instruction in matters of safe and healthy child care. In addition their training includes working out a household budget and on-the-job training such as shopping trips in which the shopper who makes the wisest decisions receives a prize. In contrast to many programs of short-term care, most residents of Beth Shalom stay in the home for two years, providing a calm trustable for both the new parent and her child during its initial formative years.

Requirements of the home promote a stable, wholesome lifestyle and ensure that the young women will be prepared to take advantage of future job opportunities. All residents are urged to attend a Sunday service at the church of their choice. Girls of high school age must go back to school or earn their GED. Those who have graduated from high school must be enrolled in a program of training so that they will be prepared to support their children. A goal of the program is to achieve self-sufficiency and to step up from welfare dependency. Many of the program's participants were, themselves, children of teenaged mothers who were on welfare. Beth Shalom was created to break that cycle, and to offer new vision and opportunities for young women—and for the next generation.

Parents of Watts–Los Angeles, California

When the founder of the Los Angeles-based initiative Parents of Watts, "Sweet Alice" was asked how her group got its name she replied simply, "Because that's what we are."

In fact, the grassroots project, with a host of programs operated through eleven facilities, does perform the role of "Parents" of the community, offering loving support, guidance, information, and training. Sweet Alice and her staff are on call virtually 24-hours a day to meet the needs of a broad range of residents of the Watts district, from men who were formerly incarcerated who are seeking to find jobs and begin productive lives in society, to at-risk youths who have dropped out of school, to pregnant teenagers who need essential information and guidance regarding the care of their babies.

Many of the functions of Parents of Watts have both an immediate and long-range impact on stabilizing family structures within the community. One of the group's houses which has been effective in preventing teen pregnancies employs a strategy that does not dwell on the sexual behavior of the girls it serves, but, instead, focuses on giving them a vision for their lives which will, in turn, affect their behavioral choices. The facility serves girls who have dropped out of school or who are in danger of dropping out of school, stressing the possibilities of the future rather than the failures of the past and is known as the "College Prep" project. The effort has had extraordinary success and has currently placed 123 young women in colleges throughout the country.

As "Sweet Alice" remarked recently upon returning from one student's college graduation, "Once they have new vision and values for their lives, the pregnancy prevention part is taken care of."

College Prep activities include motivational trips to boost the self-concept and goals of the girls and an educational program in which teachers from schools in the area come to the home to tutor the residents in targeted subjects.

Additional programs conducted by the Parents of Watts include a home for pregnant mothers, a crisis center, and a youth retreat home for youths aged seven through twleve which teaches life skills and social skills and gives spiritual guidance and inspiration.

Fulfilling Parental Roles Through Safehouses

Efforts have also been made to offer support, guidance, and security to at-risk youths, who come from households that are unstable, dangerous, and often abusive. Through experiencing the personal commitment of adults who are authentically concerned about their welfare, these youths are able to begin a process of healing. In this oasis of spiritually nourishing support, they can develop the value and vision for their lives that will allow them to grow into responsible, loving adults who will be equipped to fulfill the role of parents themselves.

In low-income neighborhoods, from Texas to Washington, DC, to Florida, an unheralded miracle is underway as thousands of children are given a second chance to live lives of success, health, and fulfillment.

Hundreds of committed men and women have selflessly responded to the critical needs of the children they witness daily in their communities and have opened the doors of their humble homes and public housing units as safe-havens from the turmoil of the streets.

Many of these safe-havens began serving just a handful of youngsters but became virtual magnets, attracting hundreds of young people. These oases of safety and support offer a place to study, watch television, share simple meals, and, most important, speak with a trusted confidante about pain and fear that have been held behind floodgates of personas of tough independence.

"I Am That I Am"–Dallas, Texas

In the poverty-ridden community of South Dallas, Texas, one woman, Delores Beall, was moved by the plight of children in her neighborhood who were afraid to go home in the evening where they were often physically and/or sexually abused, yet were terrified to stay in the streets in the violence of a world of drug and alcohol abuse. She began driving around to apartment complexes each evening after she came home from her job, picking up from 30 to 40 youths each night for an impromptu after-school program she set up in her small four-room rented house. The program grew quickly, as more and more children got word of the "center," and has, since 1985, developed into a volunteer-staffed training center that operates from 4:30 p.m. to 8:30 p.m. offering tutoring in math, reading, and computer skills, as well as a well-balanced meal (for some children, the only meal of the day). To date, Beall's program has served more than 4,000 children.

It would be a euphemism to label the children Beall works with as "at-risk." Most already bear massive scars from wounds of a daily battle for survival. Beall describes the South Dallas community she serves as an area in which "Twenty-one thousand seven hundred seventy six men and women are unemployed causing 9,136 families to receive some type of public assistance. Sixty-five percent of these households have children under 18 years of age. There are more than 120 alcohol and beer stores in the area and at least 26 crack/cocaine houses that keep many adults in the neighborhood preoccupied. Consequently, many children are abused and neglected. Children as young as seven years of age are selling their bodies to survive."

After a number of Beall's students were raped or beaten by family members when their mothers were sentenced to jail on drug charges, Beall realized that her program had to be expanded to meet residential needs as well. She launched an aggressive and passionate fundraising campaign which enabled her to purchase a 185-acre tract of land with fields, timberlands and a small lake that will be the site of a residential home for severely abused or neglected children as well as a summer camp with classes in carpentry, horticulture and wildlife. Further news-letter pleas from Beall rounded up donations of a variety of resources including dishes, mattresses, furniture, farm equipment and building supplies for cabins that will be constructed on the land.

As director of this "Back to Nature" camp, Beall recruited a former gang member that she had counseled in the late 1960s who now has established a 15 year track record of service to foster children, retarded individuals, ungovernable juveniles, and runaways.

The camp will, in Beall's words, "take abused and neglected youths out of their alcohol and drug-abusive homes where they have been sub-jected to their parents' mood swings, and have reacted with anger, hurt, hostility, and retaliation," and, through a process of healing, the camp "will produce sane citizens that have learned anger management, problem solving, and impulse control." Beall's program receives no government funds which would come with guidelines that limit treatment to 30 days. As she explains, "It takes from one to two years for some of these children to readjust their lives."

Impassioned to seize any and every resource to nourish her children, Beall has even directed ads in her newsletter to local corporations, asking them to allow her students to take field trips to their firms during the Christmas holidays. She explains: "One successful way to teach a poor child to work and not to use drugs is to take him out of his public housing project, away from the drive-by shootings, and show him the real world where work can bring stability and success."

Statistics from just one year of service are evidence of the success of Beall's project. In 1992 alone, 825 children under the age of 18 were served. Four hundred eighty-eight children were persuaded to stay in school. Of these, 234 were accepted into A and B Honor Rolls, one was inducted into the National Honor Society, and seven attended local colleges. None became pregnant. In addition, the children joined in a number of community service activities, cleaning the yards of 25 elderly residents and delivering 200 hot turkey dinners to senior citizens during the Thanksgiving holiday.

In frank and moving terms, Beall describes the children she serves:

> Many folks do not understand the cause of these kids' problems and have written off this generation as 'hard to reach,' 'self-serving,' 'violent,' and 'aloof.' If they could only talk to one of our children, they would quickly see that this younger generation consists of forgotten children. They are rejected in their own community, unwanted at home, and neglected in the school system. They are also fighting to overcome generations of poverty, substance abuse, and welfare. Something has to be done to change these circumstances. These kids are our future.

Northeast Performing Arts–Washington, D.C.
There is a cruel irony to the names of certain neighborhoods in

Northeast DC—names like "Parkside" or "Paradise." Children in these areas have struggled to survive against oppressive odds and in the face of continual violence:

> A small boy carrying his mother's groceries encounters a triad of teen-agers trading sex for drugs in the hallway.

> Children run from the lot that they use as a play area as police and members of a drug posse open fire.

> The mother of three small children bends to an offer to rent her unit to drug dealers in exchange for extra funds for her household. Her toddlers watch as four men are dragged from their living room, doused with gasoline, and set on fire outside their window. Residents who race to the rescue are turned back with threats of the same fate.

Yet, despite the trauma and destitution of this environment, no less than 35 young people have risen up to pursue college degrees. Many of these students work side-by-side with younger children in the community, mentoring, counseling, and sharing their vision. Others, shutting out the desolation that surrounds the building in which they are rehearsing, perform their leaps and dance movements with dreams of one day earning the applause of audiences in the finest entertainment arenas. The aspirations of these young people have been salvaged and revived through the undaunted commitment of one woman, Rita Jackson.

Rita recognized that a key to the liberation of the neighborhood's children rests in their education. Yet, she had experience enough to recognize that the possibility of their education was interwoven with a host of other goals that must also be achieved: providing a safe and secure haven from the surrounding violence, meeting basic needs of food and clothing, reestablishing confidence in their ability and potential, and providing an outlet for their frustrations and a base of healing for those who have endured physical, sexual, and psychological abuse in their homes.

Ms. Jackson looks back on the first days of her outreach when she offered her two-bedroom public housing unit as a safehouse for eight youths, all of whom have now completed their college education. The first child Rita took in was an eleven-year-old named Isaac whose brother had been killed on the street. She describes the early days of her efforts:

> The kids would just sleep on the floor, and you can imagine how crowded that little place was. I would be stepping on arms and legs, but I would just announce, "Move out of my way, I'm coming through." In the morning, they would fold up their blankets and clothes and would get ready for their day—school and other activities.
>
> We had very little. We would dole out tokens so they could get to and from school. We would budget to get tennis shoes for one child one month, and save to buy what someone else needed the next month. I would plan and save to make sure we could celebrate Christmas, and at least we never went hungry.
>
> Sometimes our suppers would be peanut butter, sometimes beans. But I'd say, just as my mother used to tell me, "No one outside will know what we are eating unless we tell them." If we had chicken, it was one piece a person, and I'd ask them to fill up on potatoes. I had a limited income but I was not going to put them on the street."

Rita's effort grew from providing shelter, solace, and spiritual support to offering a number of diverse programs. Today, more than 800 young people claim her as their "adopted mom." Rita gave by "offering what she knew best." She began by giving dance lessons to ten young people in the community. As word spread through the neighborhood, more and more youths began to show up at her door. And when the troupe performed in other neighborhoods, youths who lived there would come to Rita after the show and ask if they could become involved.

Not only did her program grow in terms of the number of youths it served but, as she recognized more needs, Rita responded and offered an ever-expanding range of activities. Rita muses, "I never had a grand plan to establish all these projects. But wherever I saw a need, I tried to help."

"Save Our Seed," for example, is a mentoring program in which young people take responsibility to tutor others. "College All Aboard" was launched to help young people prepare, both academically and financially, to go to college. This included assistance in completing college applications, help in gathering information about possible scholarship opportunities, and guidance in choosing a college. As of 1993, this program has enabled more than 80 young men and women to attend college.

In a recent conversation, one of Rita's young proteges recalled the impact on the young people of the housing development when one of Rita's kids, Isaac, went off to college. "It made a big impact when Isaac went to college. He was just one of us. He was our age, and he was an average kid, hanging around with the rest of us. He was not a super student. When he went to college, it sent a powerful message to us all– Yeah, we can do that too!"

Rita recognized that even those who had received scholarships and grants still needed money for books, materials, and living expenses. With jobs scarce, Rita worked to provide entrepreneurial opportunities for her young people and created Young Entrepreneurs Succeeding (YES) which offers guidance in conducting market studies, product development, and financial management for youth-owned businesses. With the support of YES, one college-bound teen launched a balloon company that netted $3,000 in the course of a summer. In addition, to enhance the youths' skills in writing and graphic design and to give them a sense of greater involvement in the community, Rita helped her students to create a neighborhood newsletter called the *Northeast Page*.

Yet, amid this flurry of activities, Rita's "kids" have explained that some of the most valued contributions she has made in their lives have been informal and intangible. Alonzo Patterson, whose future was rescued through Rita's care and concern, explains, "Many of the kids who come to Rita's house have never had the experience of eating at a fully set table. They have never had a family conversation where their ideas and feelings can be voiced.

"Simply sitting together in the living room, watching a television program and sharing their comments, brings a sense of cohesion and belonging into the splintered lives of many of the kids in the housing project. For many young people who have been abused by their relatives or who first witnessed drug abuse in the example of the adults in their own homes, Rita's compassion and acceptance have provided an outlet for the flood of emotions—pain and anger, surrender and revenge—that they carry in their hearts.

For some youths who were nearly overpowered by the difficulties they faced, Rita's guidance has meant, literally, the difference between life and death. One young man who made it through college set out for New York City to launch his career but found his dreams dashed. Despondent, he was on the verge of suicide when he called Rita. "I was in tears," he recalls. "I told her I was a failure." He still carries Rita's reply in his heart, "Son, if you don't accomplish another thing, your life has already been a success. Look at what you've done so far."

The youth pulled himself together and returned to his neighborhood where he now works as a substitute teacher and the director of a local community center, with hopes of going on to law school.

In a world fraught with challenges—and often with defeat—Rita has a clear message for her kids. Failure is not in her vocabulary:

> I tell my kids, 'If you don't succeed at something, that is 'preparation' for something else. It's not failure. Whatever trials you go through are of value. You are being prepared for something larger.'

Mel Blount Home for Boys–Claysville, Pennsylvania

Mel Blount, of All-American football fame, learned the values of tenacity and self-discipline long before his sports career began, stacking tobacco in the predawn darkness by the light of a kerosene lamp, helping his dad with the chores of his Georgia dirt farm. He often went barefoot and the family home had neither indoor plumbing nor electricity.

Although his father died before he had a chance to witness his son's stellar football career, his example and motivating guidance were a constant presence that encouraged Mel to give his best. In addition to images of his father leading a family prayer circle and working long and hard hours to boost his family from poverty, Mel was motivated by a story in which his father's confidence and righteousness had overcome the hatred of angered whites in a hostile South. When a group of vigilantes arrived on their properties in search of a fugitive, Mel's father, despite his wife's pleas to stay in the house, strode confidently through the midst of the intruders who, one by one, dropped their guns. Mr. Blount's calm declaration, "My family obeys the law. You'll find no criminals in this house," was sufficient to make the posse retreat from his property.

As a football star, Mel had many young fans who, out of admiration for him, would often confide in him. He heard from two boys who had dropped out of school, others who were left alone at home, and some who came from abusive households. Their faces and stories stayed with Mel throughout his football career and immediately after his last year in pro-football he moved to fulfill a dream he had nurtured for these youths—establishing a farm where they could stay and learn the values that his father had taught him. In 1983, Mel and his brother opened a licensed youth home just 200 feet from his mother's back door. Mel put thousands of dollars of his own money into the project and raised thousands more with the help of his former teammates and business contacts.

Residents of Blount's farm willingly adhered to the schedule he had learned in his childhood: rising at dawn to clean the stables; attending classes at the local public school or studying at home school; completing additional chores; studying in the evening and going to bed early. The boys washed and ironed their own clothes and washed the dishes and cleaned the kitchen after every meal. The program is based on the premise that young people want and need structure in their lives. It is built on a solid framework where expectations and responsibilities are clear and where respect for self and others is paramount. From sunup to sundown, the daily discipline of farm chores and class work teaches the boys responsibility, pride, and respect for the order and beauty of creation.

An accomplished horseman, Blount works with the boys to teach them to ride and to care for animals.

Of the more than 100 youths who graduated from Blount's program, 85 percent remained in school, found employment and stayed free of drugs and alcohol.

Healing Families That Were Torn By Drugs

One of the most tragic factors of the dissolution of family and societal bonds that we witness today is the trap of drug and alcohol addiction. A cycle of despair has emerged in which family degeneration and conflict has resulted in substance abuse and substance abuse has caused even greater devastation of the family.

The high recidivism rates and low success rates of conventional therapy-oriented treatment centers seem to indicate that there is little prospect of turning this situation around. However, throughout the nation, faith-based programs for drug and alcohol addiction offer clear signs of hope, with success rates that range as high as 60 percent.

Victory Fellowship–San Antonio, Texas

A paradigm of such effective substance abuse programs is San Antonio-based Victory Fellowship which, since its inception twenty years ago, has freed more than 13,000 drug addicts and alcoholics from their addictions. Not only does Victory Fellowship have a program for every member of a family—husband, wife and children—its core staff, itself, is a family. The organization's founder, Pastor Freddie Garcia and his son-in-law, Juan Rivera, focus on the needs of the men while wife Ninfa and daughter Josie serve the needs of the women and children. In addition, Freddie and Juan offer premarital instruction to prepare men and women for their family responsibilities, as well as marriage counseling to help couples meet the challenges of their roles as husbands, wives, and parents.

Both of the parallel programs for men and women focus on applying Biblical Christian principles to the challenges of daily life. And both begin with a first phase of rehabilitation which includes daily prayer, scripture reading, and, later, practical application of service to the community in hospitals, convalescent homes, and outreach on the city's streets.

As women learn to embrace their responsibilities as mothers, wives, sisters, and responsible community members, they also learn practical skills through a program coordinated by Josie which includes personal hygiene, housekeeping, cooking, child care, bookkeeping and financial and organizational management. The women also serve in a prison fellowship ministry through visits or letters and help care for infants and toddlers in the nursery.

Even the children learn the value of service through Victory Fellowship's version of the Boy Scouts (with ranks such as the Arrows and the Royal Rangers) as well as a version of the Girl Scouts (including ranks of the Daisies, Stars, and Missionettes). Toddlers learn a respect for tradition and recognize the Bible as a book that is to be carefully handled.

Emphasis is placed on creating the security and warmth of a family environment. Meals are prepared and served family style, and facilities are coordinated by house parents (married couples) who are available for guidance and support virtually 24 hours a day. Some residents function as older brothers and sisters, empathizing with the challenges that others are striving to overcome and encouraging them in the process of rebuilding their lives.

Victory Fellowship's holistic program has not only reclaimed thousands of lives that had been lost to drug and alcohol addiction, but has also inspired the self confidence and moral direction needed for men and women to fulfill their responsibilities to their spouses and children.

Restoring Intact Households vs. Institutionalization

In many cases, where a disability has disrupted the structure of a household and has limited the capacities of a family member, professional guidance has been to follow the easiest course and simply to institutionalize the afflicted individual. However, personal outreaches from concerned members of the community have, in many cases, made institutionalization unnecessary and made it possible for the disabled individual to continue to live with his family where he can enjoy the personal relationships that are essential for his physical, mental, and emotional health, and where he can also fulfill his supporting and loving role as a family member.

One to One–Beaver County, Pennsylvania

The One to One project was founded in Beaver County, PA, to link those who have suffered disabilities to volunteer "advocates" from the community who can offer support and assistance in practical procedures. Since its inception nearly ten years ago, One to One has made a positive difference in the lives of more than 100 individuals who would otherwise be destined to lives of isolation within institutions. The association performs a simple function of identifying people with disabilities and linking them to others in a pool of volunteers who are best equipped to meet their needs.

One partnership that was brought together through this organization was between Daryl, who was interned at the State Navy hospital and a basketball coach, Rick, whose training and personality could reach Daryl and bring him to the point where he could return to his home.

Another beneficiary of One to One's program was Jack, a former pilot who worked as a courier for NATO for 20 years but underwent back surgery that left him paralyzed. Jack was linked to Jim, a pilot with USAir with whom he felt an immediate relationship. When the two met, Jack was in living in a nursing home. Jim inspired him with new vision and a belief in the importance of his roles as spouse and father in his family and then helped Jack to go through the procedures and paperwork involved in applying for a mortgage loan. On Thanksgiving Day, 1995, Jack and his family, reunited, moved into their first home. "If it had not been for Jim," One to One's founder A.J. Hildebrand remarked recently, "Jack's family would be a single-parent household, and he would still be in that nursing home."

Creating Families Through Adoption

Throughout the nation, an adoption and foster care system has solidified into a virtual multimillion dollar industry whose procedures and regulations do not always promote the interests of the children it was created to serve. It is often more profitable financially for an agency to place a child in a continual stream of foster homes (keeping the child on their rolls) than it would be to place the child in a stable adoptive home. For this reason, it is common for boys and girls to spend their entire childhood lives in the domain of the foster care system, to be released only when they "age out" at eighteen. At present, there are 500,000 children in the system.

Many households that would be willing to provide stable, loving homes for these children are daunted by the snarl of red tape, rules, regulations, and adoption fees and procedures.

The Extended Family and Informal Adoption

Grassroots efforts have met the needs of many children who otherwise may have been destined to live within the foster care system. In the black community, in particular, extended family and kinship networks have provided both homes and daycare services for working parents. Nearly half of all black working mothers who need child care depend on relatives for such services. In fact, studies have shown that black families informally adopt ten times more children than are placed through formal adoption services.

Community-based Adoption Placement

Although conventional professional adoption services have often explained their low records of placement by citing a dearth of black parents who are willing to adopt, one 1981 survey revealed that nationwide, as many as two-thirds of the black households polled said that they would be interested in taking in a foster child, and one-third registered an interest in legal adoption.

Community-based initiatives to identify adoptive homes for children have made their services more accessible to families and have been far more effective. In Detroit, one such initiative, Homes for Black Children, is an example of a successful, independent, community-based adoption agency that, with relative ease, found homes for purportedly "hard-to-place" foster-care children. In its first year of operation, this agency placed 137 children while the combined efforts of 13 traditional adoption agencies in the area placed only 96 children. The director of the agency, Sydney Duncan, helped to facilitate the adoptions by such commonsense steps as locating her office in the neighborhood where prospective parents lived and by keeping office hours in the evening to avail her services to working parents.

Throughout the nation, there are a number of such successful community-based initiatives to ensure that the greatest number of children possible can abide in stable homes, and they, also, have been more successful than many conventional adoption agencies. Many of these groups have used the extended family approach to prevent the unnecessary placement of black children in foster care. Their starting premise is that an adoptable child can be placed within the black community. In some cases, the agency, through its supportive services has become a part of the extended family network by initiating regular contact with the parents and children of families that are dealing with multiple problems. Homes for Black Children, for example, operates a Family Preservation Program whose sole purpose is to keep a family intact and functioning as a unit.

A number of community leaders from low-income neighborhoods have proposed that churches might also be used to identify prospective adoption families and link them to children who need homes. The church's personal knowledge of its congregants and its moral standards and principles are important characteristics that should qualify them for the role of screening agents of prospective adoptive homes.

Conclusion

Although nationwide the trend of family dissolution has, perhaps, had its most disastrous consequences in low-income communities, it is within many of these same neighborhoods that successful initiatives have been launched to alleviate the negative effects of family disintegration and to offer the support and guidance necessary to preserve and reestablish the family unit.

These grassroots initiatives have been effective where professional programs designed and implemented from the outside have had little effect—and have sometimes even exacerbated the problem. Grassroots leaders have addressed the problem at its root, on the level of morals and values, and as on-site examples of the principles and values that are needed to sustain a strong and healthy family, they have the capacity to engender substantial and sustainable positive change in the lives of the people they serve.

ENDNOTES

[1] William J. Bennett, *The Index of Leading Cultural Indicators* (New York: Simon & Schuster, 1994).

Chapter 7

PROGRAMS OF TRADITIONAL AGENCIES FOR FAMILIES

David M. Genders

Hard times have befallen child welfare services in the United States. Increasingly larger numbers of children enter care. At the same time, services needed for children and their families are under pressure to reduce costs and scale back the scope of services available. Traditional residential treatment programs are looking at treatment philosophies, lengths of care and goals of their programs.

Many feel that programs providing services are unable to appropriately address key issues facing families and children needing care and protection. Political and financial pressures are putting children at risk of further neglect and abuse. Opinions have been voiced that we should return to "orphanages" as the best solution for a financially strapped, over-burdened system.

In the late eighteenth century and early nineteenth century, orphanages became places where children were sent to provided surrogate care. Orphanages attempted to care for children in a group setting staffed primarily with female adults who provided basic care and nurturing. Parents frequently turned their children over to orphanages because of personal health issues, lack of income or lack of a second parent. Children from a family with one parent were referred to as "half orphans." Family members maintained limited contact and the general expectation was that a child would be raised in the orphanage.

Over the years, residential treatment programs have grown to become a major source of care and treatment. Over 450,000 children in the United States are currently served through a variety of large and small group care programs in the foster care system. Unfortunately, many agencies still maintain a mission of primary treatment for the residents in their care giving lip service to family participation.

To emphasize a system that downplays family services and makes individual care primary, is disturbing. While recognizing a need to provide protective care, children must still be served in an environment which promotes healthy development, physically, educationally and spiritually, with every effort to involve family and extended family members as a function of the treatment process.

In the United States, family life is rapidly changing. Over the past 34 years, the ranks of children living in mother-only families has swelled to 24 percent. Combined with children living in two-parent families projected to experience divorce, the total of children living some portion of their life in a single-parent home rises to more than 50 percent.

Every state in the United States has experienced an increase in families where a single mother is the primary care provider. The 1990 census figures identified 4.5 million children living in neighborhoods where more than 50 percent of families were headed by a single female.

Census Bureau data confirms the increase of female-headed families and quantifies difficulty that accompany being a single parent. The poverty rate is 36 percent for single-parent families compared to 7 percent percent for married-couple families. Quality of family life is drastically affected by the absence of a stable two-parent family and the role modeling of fathers.

It is with this brief backdrop on family trends and developing conditions that we consider program efforts which can work to protect and recover the lives of children affected by abuse, neglect, inadequate nurturing and developmental growth opportunities while maintaining an emphasis on family participation and integrity.

Care and protection for children is often sought outside of the home and sometimes the community of a child. Children are placed in residential treatment group homes or foster care programs away from their families with primary focus given to the care and treatment of the individual. Once placed, family involvement may be limited or mandated by another entity such as the courts or welfare system. Participation by parents may be to satisfy a legal mandate rather than repairing family integrity. Family members frequently do not see their child in placement for periods of time depending on the structure of the program and the policies of a given agency. It is typical for a residential program to designate a period of time following placement as an "adjustment" time and restrict interactions with parents, siblings and/or significant individuals in their lives.

While the history of residential care services has long been one of focusing on the care and treatment of individuals, there is a need to re-tool our focus and our efforts. Residential treatment programs must use the strength of their history and position in community service and their resources (however meager they might be) to reach out to families and to grapple with the multiplicity of problems and issues which face many families today.

Organizing for Change

Assuming for a moment that well-established residential treatment programs operate with a sense of understanding of the greater picture of social welfare and human development, agencies must assume a major role in integrating, not segregating families. Expanding the scope and services of traditional residential care programs requires vision and resources. The potential is enormous and can draw upon the strength of the base program.

To accomplish such a goal requires organizational change and a commitment to viewing program objectives in a totally new light. Individual treatment must change to family treatment. Agency programs must extend their scope of activities to encompass the constellation of individuals who make up the family/extended family matrix and a child's "natural" environment. Opportunities for intervention and treatment services must exist outside of the boundaries of traditional residential treatment programs. Everyone, from administration to childcare worker/counselor and educator, must develop an image of a child as a part of a whole, not a singular individual. Treatment objectives must incorporate the totality of a child's family, regardless if the family may be a single parent, aunt or uncle, brother, sister or grandparent.

The behavior and needs of a child in care are rooted in the relationship, or lack of relationship, experienced as a member of a family constellation. A natural tendency has been to view a child as the charge of an agency since they are the individual in direct care. Changing one's mind-set becomes difficult, yet imperative to effectively integrating a resident into the fabric of family life. The role of therapy is best served from a view of the whole. Saying, "I work with the Johnson family" is a very different perspective than, "I work with Bobby Johnson." Saying, "I have eight families on my caseload," is very different than "I have eight *children* on my caseload." Working with children in a holistic manner emphasizes the place of the child in the family structure, communicates inclusion and drives a vision of reunification as a product of therapeutic intervention. While the goal is to preserve the integrity of the family structure, the actual outcome may, in some cases, be other than an ideal "family relationship." Nevertheless, the process serves to preserve the importance of a child's identity as a family member and establishes a tie to their family heritage and culture. Family religious orientation and moral values are made a part of a child's heritage.

Family-centered Group Practice

A comprehensive description of Family-centered group care practice can be taken from work done by the Albert E. Trieschman Center, Needham, Massachusetts, USA., in connection with their Carolina's project carried out in the southern states of North and South Carolina, USA. Taken from a paper prepared by the Albert E. Trieschman Center, and attributed to Frank Ainsworth, and Richard W. Small, Ph.D., "Family-centered group care practice is characterized by institutional structures, services, supports and professional practices designed to preserve and, whenever possible, to strengthen connections between child(ren) in placement and their birth parents and family members. Whether the function of group care is to provide short-term shelter, long-term care of residential treatment, education or training, a primary goal is always to work towards the child's optimum involvement in family life, even in situations where total reunification is not possible."

According to Ainsworth, Small and Nelson:

"The key assumption integral to family-centered group care practice is that child and family are irrevocably linked and that the best long term interest of the child can only be guaranteed by ensuring that birth parent(s) and family members continue to be respected and have a Place in their child(ren)'s daily life." The Carolina's Project is a wide scale effort to change the view of agencies toward families who have children placed in their programs.

A wide geographic spread of rural and urban treatment programs are reflected in the Carolina's project Staff of the Albert E Trieschman Center in Needham Massachusetts are working with the participating treatment centers to enhance their focus on families. Goals were developed to establish benchmarks for involving parents in the activities of agencies.

The following goals outline the extent of participation sought by the project and demonstrate the considerations necessary to truly develop a family-centered program.

- 75 percent of the agencies will have revised their mission statement to include a greater emphasis on family involvement.
- 50 percent of the agencies will offer at least one additional service that directly involves working with families to prevent placement or to *assure* earlier reunification (e.g., home-based, kinship care, wrap around, etc.).
- 50 percent of the agencies will actively involve parents in staff in-service training.
- 50 percent of the agencies will include parents or former parents of clients on their board of directors.

- 50 percent of the agencies will have child and youth care workers who will communicate directly with parents on a weekly or biweekly basis.
- 90 percent of the agencies will actively involve parents in the screening and admissions process.
- 90 percent of the agencies will actively involve parents treatment conferences.
- 50 percent of the agencies will actively involve parents in the orientation of new parents.
- 75 percent of the agencies will implement systems for regular consumer feedback from parents.
- 75 percent of the agencies will modify their programs to make the agency more accessible to parents and extended family members including grandparents, aunts and uncles.
- 50 percent of the agencies will incorporate strategies for involving extended family members in sharing the care of the child/youth in care (kinship care).
- 50 percent of the agencies will offer education and peer support groups for parents.
- 90 percent of the agencies will offer in-service training on cultural diversity.
- 75 percent of the agencies will have set aside a welcoming family room.
- 75 percent of the agencies will increase family involvement in on-site activities by 50 percent.
- 75 percent of the agencies will have produced an updated parent's manual.
- 90 percent of the agencies will have clearly articulated grievance procedures that are shared with parents prior to the admission of their child.
- 90 percent of the residential programs will provide in-home support and services to families of children or youth in their programs.

Committing to family-centered programming requires the involvement of every segment of agency operation. Personal transportation, provisions for taxi and bus fares, gasoline monies and support for sibling childcare can all contribute to empowering parents to be involved with their child(ren).

Treatment Focus of Children in Care

Treatment issues in a family based therapeutic environment place high emphasis on interactions, the cause-effect relationships which make up daily family life. While individual therapeutic work remains a component, it became less of a medium for treatment of the individual, rather more of a component of a broader spectrum of family dynamics. Family involvement is more frequent, and arranged to ensure successful family interplay as opposed to more rigid, formally scheduled meetings. Ideally, programs organized to actualize daily interactions of family and child, hold the greatest potential for increasing family unity.

Establishing Family Ties

Ideally, a child is referred to a program because efforts for preventative care, kinship care and "family" based care, such as treatment based foster families, have been attempted and/or evaluated with respect to a child's treatment needs.

When placed in a residential program, as should be in any placement, the first goal of staff must be to "map" family relationships. Staff must develop an understanding of the potential for family involvement and commitment. Interest and attachment must be clarified and evaluated for maximizing treatment participation. In cases where natural parents—one or both—are unable or unwilling to take an active role in treatment and reunification efforts, support must be sought from relatives in the family constellation. Pacific Lodge Youth Services in Woodland Hills, California, USA, works with boys ages 13 to 18 years who have been placed by county departments of probation and children's services. At admission, approximately 10 percent of the boys have significant contact with their families. This is to say, a relationship in which the family maintains influence and control of the boy's behavior and the boy demonstrates participation with the family. Treatment efforts to identify family, relatives and friends result in a significant increase in family involvement and responsibility for the management of boys' lives. At discharge more than 60 percent of the boys return to family/extended family living and participation in neighborhood schooling and recreational activities.

Personalizing Care with Family Involvement

Involving families members in the activities of a residential program offers opportunities for a multitude of learning/sharing experiences for the family. A residential program must look for, and open itself to the participation of family members. Staff must not be annoyed or threatened by the presence of families but encouraged by family efforts to interact with their child(ren) positively.

With boldness, and creativity, we must look to find ways to integrate family life and agency life for the enhancement of children's treatment and preservation of family relations. Meal planning and preparation, snack times, reading before bedtime, typical housekeeping chores, individual play, educational activities and religious devotion are areas ripe for family integration and participation in residential living.

Personalized activities such as fixing a child's hair, participating in the purchasing of clothing or doing personal chores together offer realistic, life-based opportunities to establish emotional bonds and develop more effective communication patterns among family members. Enhancing communications serves to improve conveying thoughts and emotions and increases respect and appreciation for the rights of individuals to express themselves. Trust becomes a product of respect and participation of the family members.

Residential programs hold an unparalleled opportunity to offer support systems that ensure family contact.

Bringing Order to Family Relationships

Utilizing the structure of residential life, families experience order created by agency staff and programming. Direct and indirect modeling are employed to establish a base of relationship building not possible with a periodic office visit where often key issues are discussed without other members of the family.

Incorporating families means including participation of siblings, grandparents, and possibly other extended family members and/or unrelated individuals who participate significantly in a given child's family life and culture.

Residential Treatment as an Educational Environment for Family Development

Maintaining an open, inviting environment creates trust and places families at ease. Families participate, not attend. They become engaged in the child's life, not threatened by their care by others. Each venue for interaction as a family is an educational experience in living in a cooperative environment. If structured with care, skills are taught which build a base of personal care skills, interactive play skills, communication skills and problem solving skills. Families enhance respect for one another's feelings and opinions, their differences and their anxieties. They also learn to enjoy the accomplishments of one another and to experience empathy.

Residential programs can represent an important resource to families who experience pressures that affect their clarity of thinking and behavior. Families can be faced with a medical trauma or catastrophe, loss of emotional control or burdens that compromise their ability to manage life's issues in a rational manner.

Community Life of Residential Programs

Residential programs operate in an organized, planned and generally regimented fashion. Time is provided for personal care, nutrition, treatment, educational therapy and play activities. Many activities and events can be classified as "community activities." By this I refer to those activities shared as a larger group or on an agency-wide basis. Such activities can be group play, watching television, eating meals, studying, quiet time games, chores, school, religious observations, and such. These events offer a fertile time to model, teach and interact.

Integrating families into the "community" events of the agency can take the form of invitations to picnics, group dinners, open structured play, or simply joining during quiet-time or TV times, to participate with the child as a family activity. Such opportunities offer time when families experience the structure, discipline and interactive skills implemented by staff, childcare/counselor, and caseworkers. These times are opportunities for parent(s) and child(ren) to be involved with one another in a non-judgmental environment. At the same time, staff have the opportunity to observe "real life" relationships and utilize their observations within the more formal "family individualized" therapy sessions. Community-style interactions can provide a less threatening and more natural therapeutic environment than traditional office meeting-style therapy sessions. The more natural and respectful interactions between child(ren) and parent(s)/guardian(s) can be developed in the group environment and improves the ability to effect a natural carryover of behavior patterns to home environments and family life.

Family Services Beyond Residential Care

Residential programs hold the strength and opportunity to provide specialized services to children and families beyond the walls of the institution. When the view of services is family-based, prevention oriented and driven by a belief that the best interests of children are supported by programs that work to enhance family ties, an array of services hold potential as outreaches of agency programming.

Family Preservation Networks

A Family Preservation Network is a cluster of services organized and managed by a lead agency. The lead agency manages cases through evaluation and referral to programs within the network. Generally, the programs are community based and reflect the population ethnicity and cultural values.

Typical services provided through a preservation network are individual and group counseling for issues such as drug and alcohol abuse, family therapy, parenting skills, job skills and financial. Medical service issues also often are a part of prevention services. Family Preservation Networks also provide in-home services, childcare, job counseling as well as counseling, behavior management and assistance with legal and social system issues that might impact the ability of a family to function.

Family Preservation Networks utilize services which are community based, offering greater opportunity for ethnically and culturally sensitive responses that can enhance acceptance and utilization of assistance by families. The managing agency monitors the treatment process, services and family participation. The primary charge of prevention services is to offer families the resources that can support resolution of issues that tear at the fabric of family unity. Family Preservation Services are organized to avoid costly, family segregating services that threaten the integrity of families and protect the moral structure of the family unit.

Programs designed to deliver services in the manner of assigning needed treatment components, must ensure that they do not overwhelm families by having them referred to multiple resources for treatment. An example would be a family assigned in-home services to strengthen homemaking and parenting skills and also having the family participating in possibly a drug and alcohol outpatient counseling program and other outpatient offerings.

Respite Care

Use of respite care is an important service that offers professional support to the family or single parent through temporary care of a family member combined with counseling or guidance to assist with the issue. Using the facilities and programs of established agencies is a perfect opportunity to effect short-term care with intervention therapy.

If left unsupported, an event or trauma in one's personal life may result in neglect, disrespect or abuse of a child or family member. Temporary losses of emotion often lead to more permanent issues of family disenfranchisement. Removal of a child from parental care can frequently be avoided with proper, non-threatening interventions targeted to give temporary relief to an otherwise potentially threatening situation.

A variety of services can support remediation of issues which could be employment related, medically related, result of a tragic event or a psychological episode. Relieving the pressure and responsibility of childcare gives time and space for emotional recovery.

Often a single adult family experiencing a tragic event, lacks the necessary resources to manage multiple needs and events without reaching an emotional crisis. Respite care offers a time out opportunity to give time to bring order into one's life.

Respite can prevent emotional trauma and disintegration of family support and integrity.

In-home Services

In-home services are services dedicated to helping families build skills necessary to more effectively parent children and to develop homemaking skills. Often abuse and neglect come as by-products of adults being inadequately prepared or trained to act in the capacity of a parent to a child. They may also lack basic skills necessary to manage such tasks as house cleaning, buying groceries, preparing meals and developing a daily routine. Residential treatment programs are ideally suited to participate in the identification and initiation of direct services that can serve to keep family and child united.

Providing for Youngsters Without Family Ties

Peers as "Family"

Often in residential care, children are truly abandoned or without willing family participation despite the best of efforts by many individuals and treatment programs. For these youngsters, the role of residential programs must be goal oriented for future achievement and success. Peers provide an immediate and daily resource for development of positive relationships which are success oriented and esteem building. Peer relations in a residential setting have many of the same characteristics of family relations and require like interaction patterns, communication skills, sharing and mutual respect for the personal and psychological milieu.

Resident programs can develop peer cultures that act as extended family and offer youngsters a reality base through which to test the efficiency of their actions and appropriateness of their behavior. Peers offer recognition for accomplishments and encouragement to reach for tangible goals. Peers become a form of "extended family" when children become independent and begin establishing their life as a citizen in the community, working, continuing their education and participating in age-appropriate personal activities.

Emancipation Support

Emancipation programs are an important part of programs for young adults preparing to leave group care programs. In states such as California, adolescents must be prepared for independent living at age eighteen. Government supported treatment terminates and adolescents without benefit of preparation can find themselves with bags in hand and no plans or resources to support their independence.

Emancipation programming is a critical service for adolescent children growing up without the support and guidance of family or relatives. Residential programs have a responsibility to ensure proper education, training and orientation to community life. Without adequate preparation, treatment efforts and valuable public and private resources are lost. Youth without preparation for independence revert to former patterns of behavior and survival.

With preparation, young adults can transition between residential care and independent living. Preparation must emphasize education, job training, money management and development of supportive contacts in the community.

Each life-skill component needs specific training and emphasis for success. Each adolescent must be supported and encouraged to complete requirements for graduation from high school (12th year) with the award of a diploma marking the completion of studies. Advanced or technical education pursuits should be encouraged and financially supported.

Many life-skill training areas offer opportunities to link adolescents with adults in the community who represent "pseudo-family" relationships. "Special friend" relationships offer a connection with the community and a valuable resource for a child entering community life. Volunteer community instructors can teach real-life survival skills such as job interviewing, dressing properly for interviews and how to complete a job application. Other skills are money management, transportation utilization and an understanding of potential community resource utilization. Pre-emancipation consists of supervised training opportunities such as part-time work in the community, saving money and searching for living arrangements which are supervised by staff as a specific placement objective.

The actual transition to independent community life must be supported and assisted by staff and peers. The search for living accommodations, collection of furnishings and actual move, should be supported. Continued financial support for education assist in reaching long-range goals a reality.

Pacific Lodge Youth Services' Response to Emancipating Youth

Pacific Lodge Youth Services (PLYS) provides comprehensive support to each boy who emancipates, to live independent of family participation. Before discharge, each boy has secured full-time employment and has developed a relationship with a volunteer "special friend" in the community. The "special friend" acts as a pseudo-parent figure and provides a contact in the community. Special friends include boys in family outings and activities and keep contact to participate in their integration to community activities.

PLYS staff maintain frequent contact to provide counseling and support. PLYS provides educational support up to an amount of $500 for each semester a boy successfully enrolls and completes college level academic studies or specific technical training.

Financial participation by PLYS includes payment of first month rent or deposit for housing. Furnishing of an apartment is supported through the acquisition of donated furniture, appliances and cookware. Each child is provided with appropriate linens and personal care items' to begin their "new life." In addition, an endowment fund is established to provide low interest loans for housing support in the event a boy makes a move to another community and needs temporary assistance. Successful "graduation" from the PLYS program is not limited by time or age for boys to receive support for personal issues and educational pursuits. In the past year, a former resident of 25 years completed an Associate of Arts degree in nursing with the financial assistance of Pacific Lodge Youth Services.

Community Based Programs

After Care Support

The best of care by any program, particularly long or short-term residential care, requires support, encouragement, tracking and reaching out to ensure that children leaving a group care program are provided assistance and guidance. This is a critical, yet difficult, area of service. Aftercare is generally an unfunded service component of care. Along with increasing regulations for confidentiality and funding, reaching out to past residents is challenging. Strong networks of communications and clear opportunities for continued personal support must be provided to enhance extended contacts and interactions with youth served in residential group care programs.

Community Based Programs

Responsible Teen Sexuality, and Prenatal Care Outreach Program

St. Anne's Maturity Home in Los Angeles, California, USA developed a comprehensive program to serve as an extension of their residential program. Through several regional offices, services were provided to support responsible teen sexual behavior and prenatal care.

The responsible teen sexuality program centered around a curriculum of sex education and self-esteem building activities designed to reduce teen pregnancy. Annually, more than 15,000 students of high school age participated in multiple session courses. Teens explored interpersonal relationships, peer pressure and media exploitation of sexually oriented, seductive advertising. Presentations included a comprehensive education on the reproductive process and facts about sexual intercourse, sexually transmitted diseases and emotional impacts of sexual relationships.

Counselors presenting the courses also worked with pregnant teens to keep them attached and under the care of their family or supportive individuals in the community. Counselors insured that teens received guidance in birth options and proper prenatal care.

The intent of the programs was prevention and support for family involvement. Presentations on teen sexuality included planned opportunities for parents to participate in the program for family involvement in children's lives and a recognition of the value of the services being provided in and for their community.

FESNAC (Franklin Elementary School Neighborhood Advocacy Council)

In a treatment to prevention continuum of services, FESNAC is the combined effort of two large historically situated treatment centers in the greater community of Pasadena, California, USA, to recognize an opportunity to work within the community to improve family life and general living conditions. Two agencies combined their concerns and expertise in an effort to help families in a community take charge of improving conditions at the community elementary school and in their surrounding community. Viewing a child as the center of an ever expanding circle of support encompassing family, community, school and government, the project was designed to strengthen community with the elementary school as a primary component of community activity for families.

Franklin Elementary is a walk-to-school. With support of a grant,

Five Acres Boys' and Girls' Aid Society, Altadena, California, USA and Hillsides Home for Children, Pasadena, California, USA., embarked upon a join effort to improve family participation in the improvement of their community school and neighborhood surroundings. With the involvement of the school principal and approval of the school district, questionnaires were completed by parents, members of the PTA, teachers and children to determine what were perceived to be critical needs and concerns. The responses ranked in order of concern, from concern for the deteriorating condition of the school and surrounding community, safety and security to a need for a place where children and families alike could go for help and assistance with a broad range of personal and family needs.

A steering committee of parents was elected and a plan set for meeting monthly. Five Acres provided space for meeting and refreshments. Two staff, under the direction of Five Acres and Hillsides Home for Children are assigned to the project. Some financial support is provided directly from the project budget for activities. At this writing, a project to physically improve bathrooms at the school has been completed. Directors of both agencies' staff and parents worked side by side to improve conditions for children attending the school. The focus is to empower families to organize and develop activities that enhance the physical conditions of the community and to organize opportunities based at the school to offer direct services. Suggestions for services have been counseling, childrearing classes and English proficiency classes.

To date, there is still a great reliance on the organizing agencies. As the program progresses, empowerment will rest in the hand of the Advocacy Committee and families in the community. This is an interesting and vital activity by established residential programs to strengthen families and structure their participation in the improvement of the community and the resources made available for families.

Conclusion

Residential treatment programs hold the potential to significantly enhance family integrity and the protecting unnecessary separations of children from their parents and/or extended family ties. Through program evaluation and restructuring, families can be brought into the milieu of residential programs and made a part of the treatment and healing process necessary to resolve family issues and improve the quality of family relationships. Not all children will enjoy an opportunity to return to life with their families for one reason or another, but the potential is there to significantly enhance their tie to family heritage and a recognition of their place in a family structure. Children will have an increased opportunity to understand their heritage.

Residential treatment programs must recognize the importance of a child's family and community and ensure delivery of services that emphasize and respect the value of strengthening and supporting those ties. Programs must continue to be designed and implemented that meet family and child needs in the comfort of their natural environment. With innovative programming, we can continue to use the historical and technical strengths of well-developed programs to reach outside the wall of traditional inpatient treatment approaches to deliver services.

The cultural, moral and ethical embodiment of an individual is established through a process of integration with family, relatives, friends and the community. Taking services to the community to solve problems once approached by removal of individuals for "treatment," offers hope maintaining attachment and sensitivity of one's heritage and cultural identity. Residential programs have developed a sophistication over the years as programs focused on the treatment, care and protection of children. Breaking traditions in treatment emphasis is not easy, but crucial if we are to truly consider Families as key to the long-term success of children's treatment.

REFERENCES

Ainsworth F. (1991). "A No 'Blame'Approach To Work With the Families of Children and Adolescents In Residential Care." *Child and Youth Care Forum*, 12,5,301-311

Burford G. and Casson C. (1989). "Including Families In Residential Work. Educational and Agency Tasks." *British Journal of Social Work*, 19,1,17-37.

Fanshel D. and Shinn E. B. (1978). *Children In Foster Care: A Longitudinal Investigation.* New York: Columbia Universily Press.

Fanshel D., Finch S. J. and Grundy J. F. (1990). *Foster Children In Life Course Perspective.* New York: Columbia University Press.

Festinger T. (1983) *No One Ever Asked Us...Postscript to Foster Care.* Washington, DC: Child Welfare League of America.

Garland D.S.R. (1982) Residential care workers as primary agents of family intervention. Child Welfare and Youth Care Quarterly, 16,1,21-34.

J. Stevenson-Hinde (Eds.). *The place of attachment in human behavior.* New York: Basic Books.

Jacob Kepecs and Albert E. Deemer, Some Efforts to Meet a Critical Period in Child Placing, Child Welfare 21, (1942), p.2.

Jenson J.M. and Whittaker J.K. (1987). Parental Involvement in Children's Residential Treatment. From Preplacement to Aftercare. Children and Youth Services Review, 9,2,81-100.

Keith-Lucas A. (1987). "What Else Can Residential Care Do? And Do Well?". *Residential Treatment for Children and Youth,* pp. 4,25-37.

Kelsall J. and McCullough B. (1989). *Family Work in Residential Child Care: Partnership in Practice.* Cheadle, Cheshire: Boys' and Girls' Welfare Society.

Maier H. W. (in press). "Family Welfare Paves the Way for Child Welfare". In J.F. Giligun, I.M. Schwartz, G.D. Melton and Z. Eisikovitz (eds.). *Rethinking Child Welfare.* Lincoln, NE: University of Nebraska Press.

Maluccio A.N., Warsh R. and Pine B.A. (1993). *Together again. Family Reunification in Foster Care.* Washington, DC: Child Welfare League of America

Marshall B. Jones, Decline of the American Orphanage, 1941-1980, Social Service Review 67 (1993): 459-480.

Proch K. and Howard J.A. (1986). "Parental Visiting of Childrenin Foster Care". *Social Work,* 31,2,178-181.

Small R. Ainsworth F. and Hansen P. (1994). *7he Carolina's Project-Working Paper no. l.* Needham, MA: Albert E. Trieschman Center.

U.S. Bureau of the Census, 1994. "Marital Status and Living Arrangements": (1993), *Current Population Reports,* Series p.20-478.

Chapter 8

SIGNS OF HOPE IN TROUBLED TIMES: US PROGRAMS THAT WORK FOR CHILDREN AND FAMILIES

David S. Liederman and Mary Liepold

For children to thrive, families must be able to meet their needs: adequate food and shelter, emotional nurturance, education, health care, and protection from harm along with opportunities to explore and develop toward independence. For families to thrive, communities must be able to meet their needs: safe neighborhoods, adequate and affordable housing, accessible health care, living wage jobs for all who are able to work, income supports for those who cannot work, and services ranging from playgrounds and public transportation to police and fire protection.

The things children and families need come from a variety of sources: from the parents' own efforts: from relatives, friends, and neighbors, usually as part of reciprocal relationships from nonprofit community institutions, including religious and civic organizations; and from municipal, state, and federal governments. Although different families draw their primary resources from different ends of the spectrum, no modern family functions purely on its own resources, and few or none depend purely on public largesse. Wealthy families draw on the public infrastructure in numerous ways, and poor families often supplement public assistance by participating in the informal economy of goods and services.

The last years of the twentieth century are a time of dramatic changes in the field of services for children and families. The federal government has canceled its 61-year-old guarantee of income assistance, along with entitlements to food stamps and basic services for immigrants who are in this country legally and pay taxes. The "devolution revolution," a social experiment on an unprecedented scale, has shifted responsibility for meeting the needs of the neediest families to the states, which may, in turn, shift them to their constituent counties. New federal cuts of $23 billion in food stamps over six years and $54 billion in services and benefits overall for the same period, signifying either the fact or the perception of a declining public willingness to fund social programs, will further erode the safety net for poor families.

Even before devolution received official federal sanction in the summer of 1996, states had been experimenting with ways to reduce the number of families on public assistance and drive down other health and welfare expenditures. The forces that are converging to reshape the nation's social service delivery systems include managed care—a risk-sharing, cost-shifting mechanism that was pioneered in health care and is now being applied to mental health and child welfare services—and privatization, with the resulting competition among nonprofit and for-profit providers for clients and resources. Each of these developments has great potential for harm—and perhaps for good.

Challenges and Opportunities

Public and private agencies are experimenting with service integration, linking social services, health care, and education across the boundaries of programs and departments to address whole children and whole families. Departments of federal and state government, hospitals, religious congregations and denominations, universities, corporations, and foundations are partnering with private agencies and other community institutions to produce results that none of them could have achieved alone. Some of these collaborations are developed at the local level; others are put together in response to initiatives from federal government agencies or national foundations. So far, this process has produced mostly scattered pilot programs, but its potential for replication is enormous. State child welfare agencies are reconfiguring in a variety of ways. In some fifteen states, most social service programs are already county administered, but each has a unique pattern of apportioning responsibility. More new patterns will emerge over the next decade. While some states decentralize, driving responsibility for most day to day operations down to the county or district level, others are recentralizing, consolidating services for children and families that had been scattered among four or five departments of state government to create new agencies focused on children and families.

In Tennessee, five years of planning have led to a consolidation of programs that serve children and families in the new Department of Children's Services. This state has evolved three distinct variations on managed care for its Departments of Health, Mental Health, and Children's Services. The architects of the latter (children's services) expect to avoid mistakes that were made in shaping the first two experiments. Illinois' governor enacted a similar consolidation by executive order in 1996 but was forced by the legislature to accept a modified consolidation plan that merged three cabinet agencies with parts of three others to create a new Department of Human Services.

Private agencies, meanwhile, are re-examining their missions and reshaping their array of services. Since most private child welfare agencies are dependent on state contracts, few can afford to ignore state-level changes. Their future depends on how they adapt to the new way of doing business.

Some are merging to form strong multi-service agencies that will be positioned to compete for contracts under managed care and in other newly privatized service areas. Some maintain their identity but enter into regional alliances, provider networks, and continuity of care contracts. Some, undoubtedly, will resist change and attempt to operate as they always have. And some will be forced to close their doors.

More with Less?

Managed care is based on the promise of doing more with less:

improving the quality and availability of care while cutting costs. Many people question the wisdom of applying managed care principles to child welfare, but there is one overarching principle that definitely transfers: the emphasis on prevention and early intervention. In both health care and social services, providing the right kind of help right away can often eliminate the need for intensive and expensive intervention later on.

In health care, although planners divide the population into varying risk pools, they begin with the assumption that everyone will need services sooner or later. That premise is not yet widely accepted with regard to family services. Still, experts and casual observers agree that many of the supports traditionally available to families, like extended kinship networks, are diminished or absent for contemporary families of all classes and ethnic groups. Some of the most progressive, most promising new directions in child welfare do begin with the premise that every family needs support at some time or other. For this reason, they focus less on child welfare in the traditional sense than on child and family well-being.

They catalyze change by bringing good ingredients together across conventional boundaries: supportive relationships and concrete help; highly skilled professionals and trained volunteers; public and private sector ideas and resources. Civic organizations like Kiwanis and Rotary International have launched national immunization and child health initiatives. Local housing authorities, national foundations, city governments, health care and social service providers, and residents of public housing have worked together in the federally funded Family Unification Program to keep children out of foster care. Child advocates in every community are advancing the notion that healthy families are everybody's business.

The extent of buy-in varies from place to place, but communities that invest in young children and their families are betting on lower levels of family breakdown, dependency, and crime in the long run. Although none has sustained that investment long enough to see dramatic reversals in several systems at once, there are encouraging signs.

Community-Owned Prevention: Keeping Families Whole

In 1996, Pinellas County, Florida, celebrated its "50th year of putting children first." Pinellas was the first county in the United States to create a special taxing authority for children. Since 1946, a constant percentage of property tax revenues has gone directly to the county's Juvenile Welfare Board. The assessment, which averages $42.03 a year for each homeowner, funds a wide range of prevention and early intervention activities.

One of the Board's projects to mark the half-century was a survey of community attitudes conducted by an independent research firm. Among other questions, citizens were asked how they would distribute a dollar among different levels of services for families. On average, community members chose to allocate 50 cents to prevention, 27.5 cents to early intervention, and 22 cents to treatment. Pinellas citizens understand the importance of prevention. And of the nearly $21 million in local money the county spent for child and family programs in the '95-'96 fiscal year, 48.25 percent went to what the board calls primary prevention, including subsidized childcare, the Healthy Families Pinellas home visiting program, neighborhood family centers, school-based clinics, and substance abuse prevention.

Although every jurisdiction must provide many kinds of services simultaneously, and some services at every stage of the life cycle can be characterized as preventive, most people understand that it is easier to build a child than to repair an adult. The most effective and economical prevention programs focus on infants and young children—and their parents. Early, preventive family support is to child welfare what immunization is to health care.

As of fall 1995, according to J. Knitzer and S. Page in *Map and Track*, 37 states had developed at least one state-funded initiative intended to prevent problems for young children and their families: home visiting, family support and parent education, or pre-kindergarten programs like enhanced Head Start. Eight of these states—Colorado, Georgia, Minnesota, North Carolina, Ohio, Oregon, Vermont, and West Virginia—had what the two experts considered comprehensive family support strategies in place, often involving public/private partnerships.

Since parents are the constant influence in most children's lives, many of these promising programs provide services in the home to build parents' competence. Three extended families of home visiting programs,

Healthy Start, Parents as Teachers, and the Home Instruction Program for Preschool Youngsters (HIPPY), differ in their purpose and their timing. They are alike in that they all send trained para-professionals into family homes to show moms and dads how they can meet their children's needs. The visitors model interaction that promotes bonding (or in the case of HIPPY, school readiness) along with parenting skills and positive discipline techniques.

Home Visiting: The Healthy Start Model

Home visiting programs are sweeping the country, many of them inspired by the widely acknowledged success of Hawaii's Healthy Start. The Hawaii program began with two private agencies in the 1970s and was adopted statewide in 1985. Healthy Families America, a program of the Chicago-based National Committee for the Prevention of Child Abuse (NCPCA), promotes adoption of the Hawaiian model nationwide. Healthy Families programs now operate in 100 communities in 20 states, and NCPCA coordinates a national network of home visiting trainers. In these programs, visits start at birth or even during pregnancy.

Like the widespread home visiting programs in Europe, Healthy Start originated as a public health effort. Soon, however, its remarkable success in reducing child abuse and neglect caused it to be maintained and replicated for that purpose as well. Hawaii settled one of the most basic questions any prevention program must answer—whether to provide services to all families or only those at risk—by adopting a compromise. Healthy Start begins in the maternity ward, where information provided by new mothers is used to identify candidates. If a mother shows any of the risk factors on a highly inclusive list of 15 factors (including lack of family supports, immaturity, poverty, school failure or dropping out, history of abuse or neglect, alcohol or drug use, and others), she is matched with a salaried visitor from her own community who makes the first visit before she and her baby go home.

The visitor comes to the home every week for the first year, nurturing both mother and baby, modeling infant care skills and positive parenting behavior, and linking the family with community services such as income support, well-baby care, and parenting classes, as appropriate. Visits continue with decreasing frequency until the child is five. Visitors are alert for any sign of danger, but in Hawaii the friendly support has been so effective that no incidents of child abuse or neglect were reported for 99 percent of the families involved during the first four years the program was in operation.

Other state and local programs have developed variations on this model, either independently or under the aegis of NCPCA. Some begin the visits before a child is born, like Bright Beginnings, the home visiting program in Albany County, New York. Women who are pregnant or have an infant under three months are referred to the program if it appears that they could benefit. They may receive services for up to five years, until the child enters Head Start or kindergarten. Bright Beginnings is a project of the Albany County Health Department, with family support workers provided by a private child welfare agency, a college, and a health center.

In Palm Beach County, Florida, any new mother who bears a child at St. Mary's Medical Center or Good Samaritan Medical Center—not just those considered at risk—may receive a visit within days after she arrives home from a team composed of a nurse, a social worker, and a bilingual parent-aide. Visits are voluntary; mothers may choose not to receive a visit after having the program explained to them by hospital staff. The program will gradually be extended countywide as part of an initiative that also includes universal prenatal care and a 24-hour "warmline" for parenting emergencies. The Children's Services Council of Palm Beach, one of the program's sponsors, is a special taxing district modeled on that of Pinellas County, Florida.

Home Visiting: The PAT Model

Parents as Teachers, or PAT, began in 1981 as a pilot project to promote school readiness in four Missouri school districts. In 1984 it was extended statewide by legislative mandate. It is now being replicated, on some scale, in 44 states and the District of Columbia, as well as in five foreign countries.

In Hawaii's home visiting model and many of its mainland offshoots, although every mother and child unit receives one visit, families are selected for home visiting only if they appear to be at risk for family dysfunction. Parents as Teachers was designed to be available to every family with children from birth to five. It combines home visiting less intensive than in Healthy Start (four visits each school year and more if special needs are noted) with three additional components: parent group meetings, regular monitoring of children's health and developmental status, and referrals to other agencies as indicated. The home curriculum is based on the work of two preeminent experts in early childhood development, Burton White and T. Berry Brazelton.

Home visits stop when a child turns three, but other activities continue. Parents may re-enroll with the birth of another child. In Missouri, where PAT originated, program administrators work hard at outreach to be sure they attract a mix of middle-income and low-income parents. Still, communities with a concentration of poor families and recent immigrants tend to have larger programs.

Significantly, when PAT was evaluated in 1991, the group meetings proved less popular than the home visiting component. Attendance at group meetings had fallen off significantly since the pilot projects. Even when the programs scheduled meetings at various times throughout the day, provided transportation, and offered donated door prizes as incentives, parents—especially poor parents—had a hard time attending meetings away from home.

The evaluation revealed another limitation, which may now have been corrected in at least some locations. Although the children overall scored significantly better than a national sample on norms of achievement, children of parents for whom English was not a first language consistently showed the smallest gains.

Home Visiting: The HIPPY Model

The focus is on three, four, and five year-olds in the Home Instruction Program for Preschool Youngsters (HIPPY), which was pioneered in rural Arkansas by the National Council of Jewish Women in 1984. It is modeled on a program developed in Israel to help new immigrant families adapt. The goal is to prepare children for school and prepare parents to play an active role in their education. Home visits occur every other week for two or three years. Group meetings are held in the alternate weeks. The HIPPY national office at Columbia University Teachers College in New York City offers training and disseminates information nationwide. Today there are 107 programs in 29 states involving some 15,000 families.

A 1990 study by the U.S. General Accounting Office, "Home Visiting: A Promising Early Intervention Strategy for At-Risk Families," reviewed evaluations of 72 home visiting programs and confirmed numerous benefits, including fewer low birth weight babies, fewer reports of child abuse and neglect, higher rates of child immunizations, and more age-appropriate development in children. The programs have spread widely since then, but they are still not available to all the parents who could benefit from them.

Family Support Centers

Family support or family resource centers offer a wide range of preventive, family-building services, which may include home visiting, but their agenda is larger than any one program or service. Though they tend to be located in neighborhoods with a high incidence of environmental risk factors, they provide the kind of services that can benefit every family.

The passage of the 1993 federal Family Preservation and Support Services Act was an early indication of the growing national interest in these services. The act provided funding and a time line for states to develop individual plans. Remarkably, funding for the Act not only survived the budget cuts of 1996, but was reathorized and funded for five more years.

The 1994 "Goals 2000: Educate America Act" authorized $10 million for family resource centers in 28 states. Although their inspiration comes from education, not from child welfare, these centers will clearly promote child and family well-being. Most family resource centers offer parenting classes as well as informal opportunities for parents to share concerns, borrow books and toys, take or teach classes in areas from crafts to computers, and obtain job training, child care, developmental screenings, medical care, and other essential services. The centers funded by Goals 2000 are using either the Parents as Teachers model or the HIPPY model for parent education.

The centers that Goals 2000 funded in its second year, which began October 1, 1996, were scattered, largely in the nature of pilot programs. Several states have developed statewide family resource and support programs, but many of these are also still in the pilot stage. Even in Minnesota, where the effort has been growing steadily since 1974, only 40 percent of the state's children under four were participating in 1993-1994, the last year for which statistics are available.

Family *preservation* services are often court ordered or agreed to by a family whose only other alternative is losing a child to foster care. Participation in family *support* services is voluntary. People have to want to come, and they have to like what they find. Since community ownership is vital, successful programs usually begin with a survey of community needs and community resources. A program may start by filling one obvious gap—perhaps school-age child day care—then expand to meet other identified needs. Programs that work are culturally responsive, involve parents in planning and administration, and devote considerable energy to outreach.

Although each family support program finds its own balance between formal and informal programming, hours are usually flexible and accommodating, and dropping in is encouraged. A program in full swing looks like a cross between a 19th-century settlement house and a modern community center. It differs from the former in being staffed by highly skilled professionals, as well as volunteers, and linked to a range of community services that didn't exist in the 19th century. In any century, however, personal relationships among staff members, clients, and other community helpers are the key to success. Professionals see participants as a resource and value them for their ability to help themselves and each other.

Connecticut, Iowa, Kentucky, Maryland, Minnesota, Missouri,

Oklahoma, New Mexico, Washington State, and Wisconsin all have ambitious and expanding statewide networks of family resource centers. Maryland's nonprofit Friends of the Family serves 5,000 families each year through a network of 22 family support centers in 17 of the state's 24 jurisdictions—and it is still growing. Friends is a public/private partnership initiated by the state's Department of Human Resources in 1985. Funding comes from four state agencies—Human Resources, Education, Mental Health and Hygiene, and the Office of Children, Youth, and Families—plus foundation, corporation, and individual contributions. Local centers are sponsored and run by county agencies, youth service bureaus, churches, a community college, a housing authority, a school district, and a coalition of community groups. They are linked into a network and mediated by the central Friends office, which takes care of fundraising, advocacy, training, technical assistance, monitoring, and more.

North Carolina's Smart Start is a comprehensive state and local planning initiative to develop and coordinate programs for families and young children. It began with an effort to improve the quality of home- and center-based child day care. After two years (1993-1995), the number of child care centers earning the state's top AA rating had jumped from 328 to 478. The effort also includes a network of 16 family resource centers and a child health component, in which immunizations and health screenings are provided in clinics and mobile health vans. Parent involvement is a major component. The North Carolina Partnership for Children, a public-private corporation, orchestrates the statewide effort. Between 1993 and 1995 the private sector contributed $14.5 million in cash and in-kind services.

Many private child welfare agencies operate family support centers as part of their array of services. The Jane Addams Hull House Association in Chicago, Illinois, is a direct descendant of Jane Addam's original Hull House, founded in 1889. Today, the agency has six community centers, 35 satellite locations, and 700 employees. Kingsley House in New Orleans, which celebrated its 100th birthday in 1996, is a modern-day settlement house with similarly deep roots in its community.

Co-Location of Services

Because they provide such a wide range of services, including preventive or primary health care, education, and counseling, family support centers illustrate the growing trend to co-location of services. Across the country, systems that often serve the same families but have traditionally operated on parallel tracks are sharing not only information but also quarters.

In Franklin County, Ohio, the police department staffs a desk in the child protective services office. In the Department of Housing and Urban Development's HOPE VI program, recently funded at $550 million, housing authorities in 38 cities will collaborate with community agencies to provide health care and social services to residents of public housing and the nearby neighborhoods. The program is expected to create both entry-level and career ladder jobs for residents onsite. In Boston and San Diego, hospitals house integrated support services that combine domestic violence intervention and child welfare services and advocacy. Elsewhere, day care center clients can register to vote, collect food stamps, and schedule child health and development screenings when they come to drop off their children.

One of the most attractive manifestations of co-location is the community school. Although critics have predicted that turning schools into community service agencies will compromise academic achievement, the evidence suggests that making families and communities healthier also makes children better students.

Around the country, schools are opening before first light and closing after dark. They're open weekends and through the summer with services and activities for the whole family. The Children's Aid Society of New York now operates six schools in New York City neighborhoods where parents can learn parenting, gain job skills, and involve themselves in their children's education as volunteers and paid parent aides. Young children participate in rich and varied after school programs; older children work in them as aides or small group leaders.

Baltimore's Woodbourne Center, one of the oldest child care facilities in the U.S., is also embracing this new idea in family empowerment. The collaboration involves the agency, the Baltimore city schools, the city's Department of Social Services, and its Health Department.

Families and Schools Together

Since 1993, Family Service America has been promoting national replication of Families and Schools Together (FAST), a research-based, experiential model for strengthening families and helping children succeed in school. The program begins with an eight-week series of small group sessions that bring several families together with a team of community helpers. Participation is sustained by monthly meetings over a two-year follow-up period. Evaluation results have shown significant gains for participating families. Since its beginnings in Madison, Wisconsin, in 1988, FAST has spread to 250 sites in 25 states and Canada and won widespread national recognition.

Mentoring

The California Mentor Council, a body representing business, the entertainment industry, community-based mentor programs, and public entities, was created in 1996 by executive order. Its charge is to develop and implement a strategic plan for recruiting and training 250,000 mentors for at-risk children and youths by the year 2000.

The scale of this objective underlines the fact that mentoring, like home visiting, is a sweetheart of a program. It has had a visible impact over many years and is easily understood by the public. In long-established programs like the national Big Brothers/Big Sisters and their hundreds of smaller local offshoots, children benefit from one-on-one relationships with caring, committed adults. The most familiar mentoring programs match a young person with an older role model; others match parents, both young and not-so-young, with role models of their own. The warm, informal, one-on-one nature of the relationship is the same in either case.

Although a social worker can play a mentoring role, mentees benefit from knowing that someone is choosing to spend free time with them on a volunteer basis. Public/Private Ventures did a series of evaluations of Big Sisters/Big Brothers matches between 1992 and 1995. In a controlled study of 959 youngsters 10 to 16, half of whom were matched and half were not, the mentored youngsters were found less likely to start using drugs and alcohol and less likely to hit someone when they were frustrated. They had better school attendance and performance and better attitudes toward completing homework, and they got along better with parents and peers than the children who remained on waiting lists.

Around the country, agencies and other community institutions have developed their own variations on the theme of mentoring. Some programs focus on reinforcing ethnic, cultural, and religious identity, like Jewish Big Brothers in Los Angeles and Sisters Taking Care in Chicago, which links at-risk African American girls with successful older counterparts. Some focus on sports and the outdoors; some on academic success or adult literacy. Some link children who have been in trouble with the law with police officers or even judges who volunteer their time. Some pair children in residential care with community members who take them to church, to special events, or to spend a weekend in their home.

A number of agencies offer whole-family foster care, in which mothers and children are taken into the home of another family together. Ideally, a mentoring relationship is formed between the two mothers in the course of daily interactions, and the relationship continues even after the mentored family moves out and begins to fend for itself.

Unfortunately, most mentoring programs have long lists of would-be mentees and far shorter lists of would-be mentors. Adults in the middle of their lives generally have all they can do to juggle jobs and family responsibilities, so mentors are drawn mainly from the smaller ranks of recent college graduates and recent retirees. As a result, the candidates with the most potential to succeed in relationships are selected for the opportunity and the less charming candidates, those most in need of a caring relationship, are never matched.

Parent-to-Parent Support

Programs like Parents Anonymous, founded in California by Jolly K. 26 years ago, strengthen families through parent-to-parent support and education. Parent volunteers team up with professionals to conduct small group support meetings and provide classes and referrals. The growth of the Parents Anonymous movement, which now reaches 109,000 people in 39 states, is testimony to its effectiveness. In Illinois alone, the Children's Home and Aid Society sponsors 47 local groups, many of them organized and facilitated by formerly abusive parents. Some groups are composed of fathers, teen parents, or grandparents raising grandchildren, all helping each other to become better parents.

Does Prevention Work?

The greatest challenge for all these preventive services, particularly in an age of budget cutting, is to demonstrate effectiveness. The National Commission on Child Abuse and Neglect (NCCAN) explains in the preface to each of its annual reports how difficult it is to obtain an accurate count of child abuse and neglect reports, given the diversity in standards, procedures, and even the meaning of terms from one state to another. In spite of all these difficulties, it is clearly easier to count the Child Protective Services (CPS) reports that are filed than to count the ones that aren't. How does one document successful prevention?

Some results can be quantified, over time. After a 27-year longitudinal study, the Ypsilanti, Michigan, High Scope/Perry Preschool Project was able to determine that the graduates of its enriched preschool program had achieved more than control group members in terms of income, education, family stability, and other measures. Early gains had been maintained into adulthood. But most individual services or programs can address only a few of the many factors that influence a family's success or failure. That's why wraparound services like family support and full-service schools have a good chance of success. But a child who walks from a caring home to a supportive school through a drug-infested, violent neighborhood is still at risk. Clearly, communitywide efforts supported by positive state and national policies have the best chance of success.

Children and families grow best in wholesome, hospitable environments. Even in the most inhospitable environments, many families raise their children more or less successfully, but the fact is seldom noted. Programs like Big Sisters rate a human interest story in the inside pages of most newspapers now and then while the tragedies make page one. The fact that funding continues to be available for mentoring, home visiting, and other preventive services is a tribute to the faith and hope of governments and private donors alike, and to the willingness of communities to recognize a need and address it.

The Search Institute, based in Minneapolis, is promoting what it calls "developmental assets" and the "asset-building" process. (Like other youth development programs around the country, this one views young people themselves as assets, not as problems to be solved.) The institute's Healthy Communities, Healthy Youth Initiative encourages jurisdictions to identify the resources that strengthen children—primarily positive relationships and positive opportunities—and to launch all-out, communitywide efforts to build on them. The Institute is planning a statewide program for Colorado's communities, under a contract funded by the Colorado Trust.

Early Intervention: Picking Up the Pieces

Inevitably, in spite of the best-coordinated, most personalized, and most proactive prevention strategies, there will be some incidents of child abuse or neglect. The decisions that immediately follow a report of child maltreatment, often made by young, relatively inexperienced, and over-stressed workers, are crucial for the child, the family, and the community. Child protective services (CPS) is blamed when a child dies after being left at home or returned home. CPS is also blamed when families are investigated or children are removed without due cause. In either case, errors in judgment have been made, but the responsibility goes far beyond this overburdened, under-funded system.

The National Incidence Study of Child Abuse and Neglect, released in September of 1996 by the U.S. Department of Human Services, showed the tragic results of national neglect. Nationwide, between 1986 and 1996, the number of cases reported to CPS doubled, the number of serious abuse-related injuries to children quadrupled, and the number of investigations stayed the same. Something is terribly wrong with this picture.

Several major national and state efforts are now underway to reshape child protective services. Like most of the projects already cited, they involve national organizations, state governments, foundations, corporations, and caring individuals.

Child Protective Services Reform

The Edna McConnell Clark Foundation, after focusing its considerable resources on family preservation for most of a decade, has recently turned its attention to improving child protective services—the gateway to the child welfare system.

In many public agencies, this gateway, where the first report of child abuse or neglect is received and critical decisions are made, is guarded by workers whose explicit or implicit instructions are to screen out as many reports as possible. The message families in trouble receive from the system is "Go away and come back when you're worse."

Thanks to the Clark Foundation, the Child Welfare League of America, the Freddie Mac Foundation and a handful of progressive states, governments are modeling a radically different approach to CPS intervention. In some jurisdictions today, every CPS report is seen as an opportunity to help a family. The emphasis is on determining what needs to be done to protect the child and strengthen the family, not on proving or disproving the specific allegation.

Competent intake assessment is the key to separating the minority of cases that call for fast, authoritative intervention–the immediate removal of a child–from the majority that call for supportive services. An important part of each assessment is an inventory of the family's internal strengths and external supports, as well as its needs. To make this process as reliable and as uniform as possible, under the Clark Foundation Initiative "Community Partnerships for Protecting Children," a CWLA team has developed new national assessment tools.

Community partnerships are central in this new approach to CPS. Both in making the intake decision and in following through on it, child welfare agencies need to work closely with a range of other systems. In communities that pull together to strengthen families, people who work in the public and private child welfare agencies, the police and the courts, the medical community, income assistance and housing agencies, the schools and child care centers, the religious community, businesses and civic organizations, and other entities that deal with families are getting to know each other and setting out to develop a common language.

In these communities, a family that does not present an immediate danger to a child can be quickly connected with services to alleviate the stress that led to the report and to build on the strengths identified in the assessment. Maybe the child needs an Individual Education Plan and another school placement, glasses, a hearing aid, medical care, or medication. The parents may need a place to live, food stamps, drug and alcohol abuse treatment, child day care or respite care, family counseling, mediation, or parenting education. All of these and more can be provided for far less than the cost of removing the child to out-of-home care. In Florida, a neighbor, a teacher, or an extended family member may enter into a Community Support Agreement with the agency and the family. This individual will monitor the status of the child, offer help when it's needed, and report trouble if it arises.

Domestic Violence Intervention

In many cases, a parent who comes to the attention of CPS needs, among other services, a domestic violence restraining order. As areas of social service endeavor, child abuse and domestic violence have separate histories and separate personnel. One is well established, the other still struggling to achieve respectability. Yet the families they serve are frequently the same. Studies document overlap in at least half of all cases [Hangen 1994].

Agencies and programs that understand this connection provide admirable examples of cross-system collaboration. Massachusetts has developed the nation's first Department of Social Services Domestic Violence Protocol. It establishes guidelines for child abuse and neglect investigation, safety assessment and planning, interviews with children, case documentation, and services for children, parents, and offenders. The department has hired domestic violence specialists to help child welfare staff assess and respond to situations where women are in danger. Multi-disciplinary teams coordinate services for parents with services for children.

California, Michigan, Minnesota, and Florida have also developed coordination plans. Some programs link specialists in child abuse and domestic violence with hospitals, homeless shelters, and visiting centers as well as with each other. The National Violence Against Women Act, signed by President Clinton as part of the 1995 crime bill, has funded a range of small-scale programs around the country, as well as a National Domestic Violence Hotline.

Much remains to be done to improve services in both areas and the linkages between them. The long-running O.J. Simpson murder case served to raise public awareness on domestic violence issues, but also revealed the wide range of opinions on the topic and the extent of the denial that still surrounds it.

Family Preservation

The 1994 Family Preservation and Family Support Act conferred legitimacy, along with federal funding, on a child welfare services modality that was being gradually embraced by the field and generally misunderstood by the public. (The terms in the act's title, incidentally, are oddly reversed, since family support, the prevention of dysfunction, ought to precede—and hopefully prevent—remedial family preservation.)

The backlash against the philosophy and practice of family preservation that is being felt today is probably in proportion to the immoderate enthusiasm that accompanied the selling of the Seattle-based Homebuilders model over a decade ago. It promised to save money, to do more with less. Almost inevitably, then, it began to be prescribed as a panacea and to be used in cases where it was a poor choice. At the same time, the original, intensive family preservation model, which required almost round-the-clock involvement with a family by a single social worker or a social worker-case aide team over several weeks, was being watered down. Some overwhelmed public agencies began to say they were doing family preservation when in fact they were doing little more than routine casework for many families. Inevitably, tragedy struck in the form of child deaths.

Family preservation is not a panacea. Neither is it a sellout. It can be effective for many families if two principles are kept firmly in mind. First, keeping children safe is our first responsibility. Second, whenever it is possible to keep children safely at home, they should remain there.

Whenever the order of these two propositions is switched, especially in a cash-strapped system, there is bound to be trouble.

In recent years, some public child welfare systems that have been put on the defensive by highly publicized child deaths have backed away from whatever version of family preservation they had been using and sharply increased the rate at which children are separated from families. In most cases, once the media spotlight fades, these systems drift back to doing business as before. They do so for several reasons. There still are not enough foster parents for children who need care or enough social workers to arrange and monitor family foster care placements. Out-of-home care is effective for many children but it is expensive, and dollars, like other resources, are still in short supply. Finally, if they listen to children, they know that in all but the most extreme cases children prefer to remain at home, and they suffer intensely from separation. As the saying goes, "You can take the child out of the family, but you can't take the family out of the child."

At the same time, some jurisdictions continue to learn from their mistakes and improve the quality of their family support and family preservation services. Because of outstanding advocacy during 1996 by the child welfare community, entitlements for family support, family preservation, child protection, adoption, and foster care survived the budget buzz-saw. The challenge for the system is to use national and community partnerships to continue to improve these services.

New Roles for Residential Care

At some agencies, residential care now plays a major role in family preservation. Traditionally, child welfare services have been viewed as a continuum, with the interventions closest to home at one end and residential care at the farthest extreme. Today, the ends are meeting. Multiservice agencies deploy residential care at various points in the continuum, and residential agencies are reaching into homes and neighborhoods.

Although they may be housed in the buildings where children once grew into young adults, most of today's residential programs are built around stays of 18 months or less. In the world of child welfare, residential care is a service to support families, prevent long-term separation, and promote reunification. Agencies may, for example, use the controlled environment of the group residence to train parents in effective ways of interacting with their children, or offer a respite to a family near the breaking point.

Many residential agencies with a narrow geographic base, often founded decades ago for the express purpose of helping children in an environment away from the dangers of the city, have opened branches in inner city neighborhoods so they can help families prepare a home to which the child can return. As often as not, this involves meeting concrete needs, not just changing attitudes and behaviors. In 1995, Ruth Dykeman Children's Center, of Seattle, Washington, had 13 workers employed full time in home-based services.

Because Bellefaire Jewish Children's Bureau in Cleveland, Ohio, draws children from all over the country, the agency literally goes the distance to involve families. Bellefaire buys airline tickets so families can come in for therapy, and sometimes sends staff members on home visits so they can interact with the whole family. The agency reserves two efficiency units in its employee residence for visiting parents, and is currently seeking funding for a program that would accommodate families for residential treatment every Friday, Saturday and Sunday.

Family Reunification: Putting It Back Together

"Blood is thicker than therapy," in the words of longtime agency executive Don Brewer. Whether the setting of choice is residential care or family foster care, child welfare professionals who are responsible for a child removed from a family almost always view their custody as temporary. Since most of the children who leave out-of-home care in any given year return home—including 86 percent of the teens and young adults who have been prepared for independent living—it makes sense to plan for family reunification.

Through a program called Homeward Bound, 378 of the 452 children who entered out-of-home care with the Florida Children's Home Society between 1992 and 1996 were safely reunited with their families or extended families—an 82 percent success rate over the four years. The program has also dramatically reduced the length of time children remain in foster care, from about three years to about 10 months.

The hallmark of the program is teamwork among a small group of professionals and para-professionals assigned to each case. This team always includes a caseworker, a highly trained foster parent or parents, and a therapeutic homemaker—a home visitor trained to teach and model basic parenting and household management skills, such as positive discipline, cooking, cleaning and budgeting. It may also include a professional counselor. All the members of the team work closely with the biological parents. A close working relationship between foster parents and biological parents cuts down on loyalty issues for the children and fosters reunification. Parents usually visit the foster home within 24 hours after the child is removed from their home. Program directors believe it is important to capture parents' initial motivation and work with it toward reunification.

As the record shows, the majority of families the program has served were able to make the changes necessary to create a stable home for their children. When parents could not change, the agency moved to terminate parental rights and place the child with extended family members or in an adoptive home before precious months and years had elapsed.

St. Christopher's—Jennie Clarkson, based in Westchester, New York, has received high marks for its family reunification program from the toughest judges of all: biological parents. The agency began an experimental program three years ago that shifted the focus from children to families and incorporated parent feedback at every level. Each parent is assigned a personal advocate within the agency, usually a fellow parent who has overcome his/her own problems. Caseworkers are on call 24 hours a day, seven days a week. Drug rehabilitation services are provided immediately upon request; there are no waiting lists. Parent representatives sit on the agency's personnel committee and have a say in hiring and firing. The program has not only shortened foster care stays but also drastically cut recidivism. According to St. Christopher's sources, about 33 percent of children nationwide who are returned to their parents wind up in foster care again. At St. Christopher's, the number is less than 3 percent.

Aftercare

As budget cuts and managed care have combined to shorten the average length of stay in residential care, forward-looking agencies have made a virtue of necessity by crafting their treatment plans in successive phases. Instead of treating a child for a year or longer and then returning him to the same troubled environment he left, they may plan for six months of residential treatment that actively involves parents, siblings, and extended family members, followed by six months of intensive aftercare and three months of attenuated aftercare, or follow-up. The success of reunification will depend not only on the quality of the treatment and of the relationships that have been forged during the first phase, but also on the network of formal and informal community helpers that will take over some of the agency's responsibilities for the child and family.

Long-Range Monitoring and Services

If the transition is skillfully managed, and the stresses, dangers, and temptations of the familiar environment are not too overwhelming, many children and families will eventually be able to make it on their own. No amount of budget-cutting fervor, however, should be allowed to obscure the fact that some families will need services and case monitoring over the long range if outcomes for their children are going to be satisfactory. These include many families involved with alcohol and other drugs and HIV/AIDS. Richard Barth describes a Los Angeles program that formalizes informal family supports. In practice, the program puts a backup family in place, providing comfortable, familiar surroundings and dependable care for the children when parents relapse [Besharov 1994].

Perhaps managed care will be able to accommodate this necessity somewhat gracefully, since monitoring of chronic conditions is already familiar to the medical community. Perhaps not.

Adoption

Of all the U.S. children who left out-of-home care in 1980, only about 8 percent were adopted [Curtis, Boyd, Liepold & Petit 1995]. Still, adoption is the permanency plan the public most easily recognizes as a "happy ending," and one the Congress seems perennially eager to support.

Recent legislation to award adoption tax credits, although welcome, seem less critical to child advocates than the maintenance and expansion of funds for subsidized adoption. Most of the children who are adopted within the public child welfare system—about 40 percent of all U.S. adoptions in 1989—met their state's definition of "special needs." [Curtis, Boyd, et al. 1995] They were school-age children, sibling groups, members of minority groups, and children with physical or emotional disabilities. Many of these adoptions were made possible by federal subsidies. A 1993 study by Westat Corporation estimated that the families who adopted 40,700 children with IV-E subsidies between 1983 and 1987 alone are saving the federal government $1.6 billion in long-range costs.

Many of the families who adopt children from public agencies started out as foster parents. Most earn low or moderate incomes. Even if they do not qualify for subsidies, they benefit from ongoing agency support. Adoption is the beginning of a story, not the end; it is a lifetime process, not an event. Respite care, adoptive parent support groups, and periodic, reassuring calls or visits are among the services top-flight agencies commonly provide. Adoption arrangements that fall near the wide end of the continuing spectrum of openness—particularly likely in public agency adoptions, where children are often of school age and have strong family attachments—require extra professional help for all parties.

Adoption works, even for children with severe special needs. State agencies reported a disruption rate of only 3 percent in CWLA's 1995 survey [Curtis, Boyd, et al. 1995]. A study released in 1995 by the Minnesota-based Search Institute found that adopted children ranked as well as their peers or better on most measures of adjustment.

Preparation for Independent Living

Some children grow up "in the system," never able to return home permanently or find adoptive parents. States generally assume responsibility for children in foster care only until they reach the age of 18. But few young people can provide for all of their own needs at this early age. Independent living programs prepare children for emancipation by teaching personal care skills, job skills, and relationship skills. Some residential agencies begin offering this preparation in the early teen years. Some provide supervised experience with budgeting, time management, and household management as a transition to independence. Ideally, older youngsters have a chance to practice being on their own by living in a supervised apartment or other transitional arrangement while they begin work or receive job training.

Children in stable families learn these things from their parents, and children in stable foster care arrangements may learn from their foster parents. Children in residential care and those who move from one care setting to another may have few opportunities to learn them.

Sakonnet House, a program of Family Service in Providence, Rhode Island, has won national recognition for its independent living and youth development program focused on girls 11 to 15 who cannot live at home. Other Family Service programs are available to the young women after they leave Sakonnet House.

In most cases, independent living services are the system's last chance to help. Young people who make the transition successfully are on their way to becoming productive members of society. Those who fail are likely to wind up homeless and jobless, dependent on public assistance for the long term. Federal legislation passed in 1988 gave states the option of extending independent living services to all youths in foster care. In 1990, states were given the option of providing these services up to age 21. Federal independent living awards to the states are currently capped at $70 million a year. States vary considerably in the degree to which they avail themselves of this assistance.

Conclusion: Looking Ahead

Over the next decade, we will probably see more of what we are seeing now: a diminishing role for government in meeting the needs of families. This trend could easily lead to increasing poverty, family dissolution, and violence.

On the plus side, at least in some states, efforts to coordinate comprehensive services for young children and families may grow and take firm root. As managed care extends itself from the health care context into mental health and social services, we may also see improved coordination and utilization of services. The managed care emphasis on prevention, continuity and coordination of care, and meticulous record-keeping could result in greater accountability. At the same time, its focus on the bottom line could deny services to children and families who need them. We will definitely see blending of a variety of governmental funding streams and cost shifting between systems of care. We may also see an even greater commitment to the well-being of children on the part of the business community. Some socially conscious corporations are doing well by doing good. Others may follow their example.

Expanding the Social Sector

The programs described above could make a measurable difference—but only if families can count on basic supports like adequate income, food, shelter, and health care, and only if their size and scope can be multiplied many times over. Futurist Jeremy Rifkin suggests one way to do the multiplying. As governments and markets, the two sectors that have traditionally anchored the economy, continue to shrink, a third sector could expand to provide jobs and family support. It's what Rifkin calls the social sector—currently 9 percent of total employment in the U.S. [Rifkin 1996]. Jobs in the social sector place a premium on the things computers can't do—specifically, nurture, comfort, stimulate, educate, engage, challenge, link, and empower human beings through human interactions. The social sector already exists, in America's rich, diverse nonprofit community, but in this futurist vision its role would be greatly expanded.

In the social sector people are people, not units of production and consumption. They perform jobs that build and strengthen communities, quality-of-life jobs in family service, counseling, health care, education and research, child care and youth development, the arts, religion, and advocacy. Rifkin sees this sector as peopled by two kinds of workers in addition to the professionals who work there now. There would be the fully employed, whose impulse to volunteer spare time would be reinforced by tax credits of the type they already receive for donating goods to non-profits, and the otherwise unemployed, who would receive a "social wage" in return for their service. Expanding the current supply of home visiting programs, family resource centers, mentors, and full-service schools could engage many people in both categories. "More often than not," says Rifkin, "the combination of small professional staffs and large numbers of volunteers offers the ideal combination of expertise and empathy needed to assist others."

Creating the Children's Investment Trust

Paying the social wage to put displaced workers into the service sector would be easy if the nation took a cue from Pinellas County. Some national organizations are encouraging the creation of a Children's Investment Trust, or CIT. Working Americans would fund the trust by contributing $10 a year for every $10,000 they earned. Someone who earned $50,000 a year would pay $50, and someone who earned $100,000 would pay $100. All told, this would provide at least $7 billion a year for meeting children's needs. The money would be spent at the state and local level for prevention programs like those described above.

Whichever path our nation and our communities choose, children have the most to lose and the most to gain. As Richard Louv put it in *Childhood's Future* (1991), "When the safety net unravels, the smallest bodies fall through the fastest." And as Pearl Buck observed decades ago, "If a society succeeds for its children, it succeeds for everyone. But if it fails the children, it fails us all."

REFERENCES

Allen, Mary Lee, Brown, Patricia, and Finlay, Belva. (1992). *Helping Children by Strengthening Families.* Washington, DC: Children's Defense Fund.

Barth, Richard P. (1995). Long-Term In-Home Services. In Douglas Besharov, editor, *When Drug Addicts Have Children.* Washington, DC: Child Welfare League of America.

Curtis, Patrick, Boyd, Jennifer, Liepold, Mary, & Petit, Michael. (1995). *Child Abuse and Neglect, A Look at the States: The CWLA Stat Book.* Washington, DC: Child Welfare League of America.

Garland, Diana. (1993). "The array of family-centered residential services". Chapter 4 of *Church Agencies: Caring for Children and Families in Crisis.* Washington, DC: Child Welfare League of America.

Hangen, Eric. (1994). *Interagency Nonviolence Team Pilot Project Program Data Evaluation.* Boston: Massachusetts Department of Social Services.

Juvenile Welfare Board Research and Development Center. (1995, January). *Pinellas Profile: An Index Measuring Change in Pinellas County,* Vol. 11. St. Petersburg, FL: Author.

Knitzer, J., & Page, S. (1996). *Map and Track. State Initiatives for Young Children and Families.* New York: National Center for Children in Poverty, Columbia University School of Public Health.

Rifkin, Jeremy. *The End of Work. The Decline of the Global Labor Force and the Dawn of the Post-Market Era.* (1996). New York: G. P. Putnam's Sons.

Roehlkepartain, E. C., and Benson, P C. (1996). "Healthy Communities, Healthy Youth: A National Initiative of Search Institute to Unite Communities for Children and Adolescents." Minneapolis, MN: Search Institute.

Tierney, J. P. & Grossman, J. B, with N.L. Research. (1995, November). *Making a Difference: An Impact Study of Big Brothers/Big Sisters.* Philadelphia: Public/Private Ventures.

U.S. General Accounting Office (GAO). (1990). *Home Visiting. A Promising Early Intervention Strategy for At-Risk Families.* Washington, DC: Author.

Chapter 9

WHAT CAN BE DONE TO RECLAIM THE FAMILY

Ralph Segalman

Can We Change the Family?

Much can be done to reinforce the intact family in the Western world.

Possible Actions at National and Regional Levels

Recently, a group of leaders interested in family reclamation listed proposals for government action in behalf of the family.[1] Rep. Steve Largant indicated that the central government needs to know that no one loves children more than their parents, despite the current bureaucratic and political ethos which claims that the best interests of children are served by a "village" which for them is represented by a huge indivisible central government. This ethos is faulted in that it deals with the parents as less than fundamental to the rearing of children. Largent believes that the central government needs first of all to return the power of decision-making for children to the parents and the elected local school boards,. (He relates that once there were 130,000 school boards in the US, and now there are less than 15,000. This, he indicates, is an example of the huge power shift from local to federal agencies which accompanies federal financing.) James Dobson recommends the revival of the marriage culture and believes that the culture of divorce and illegitimacy is associated with centralization actions. His recommendation is that the central government should end what he calls "the confiscatory tax structure which undermines the financial stability of families." He proposes that taxes not be set at making a level playing field for all players, instead it should be tilted in the favor of families. He believes that government should reform welfare to end the current incentives for conceiving children outside of marriage. In addition, he believes that government shall define marriage as between a man and woman and to lend support to the state of such marriage. David Blankenhorn recommends the elimination of the anti-marriage bias in the Earned Income Tax Credit code, and suggests that tax exemptions for children in families be doubled, in order to make taxes on intact families less onerous. He also recommends that adoption be made easier and take place directly after the birth of adoptable children. Kay James cautions big government to cease intrusions into family life and to adopt the medical caution that "above all, do no harm." Until now James reports that government actions, intended or not, have been onerous on the family. John Engler, D. James Kennedy, John Ashcroft, William Galston, Paul Weyrich, and Dan Quail join in the support in many of these recommendations. We would add to these recommendations the following:

Consideration for increased tax deductions for intact families where children under age 25 are attending school at family expense in high school and college and are in good standing. For families where one parent does not work out of the home additional exemptions should be granted as an additional incentive for parent-rearing of children. This is a very important change if families are to be formed and thrive. This change should be part of a government policy at all levels to promote families with children and to tax those who do not marry and do not support children. This is a logical policy to adopt if the democrative society expects to progress and survive, and if the society is to reward those who rear its citizens and workers of the future.

If the society is to seek to improve the milieu for marriage and the family, one particular change is probably more important than any other. This is a change everywhere which would make divorces not only difficult to secure but socially stigmatized. If divorces are hard to get, and are stigmatized, the vision of marriage in the culture will be more highly valued and young and old would make strong efforts to marry more selectively and to work harder to prepare themselves for marriage and in their marriages, to work harder to make their marriages a success. Also, if the communities and churches dealt with courtships as if divorces were calamitous and very difficult to secure, it is most likely that these churches and communities would have a plethora of enduring marriages.

Consideration of special tax deductions for retired volunteers working within the scope of a religious or philanthropic local organization in a pro-family activity such as tutoring of inner-city children, big brother/sister programs and similar activities (see local below).

Grants to local and state programs which violate the principle of subsidiarity are counterproductive for families. The principle of subsidiarity requires that no law shall be enacted if the subsidiary institution is otherwise able to carry out its functions. Thus the government at any level may not interfere with a family and its membership if the persons in the family can carry out their own responsibility with their own leadership and resources. Thus no one unit shall be aided or interfered with by another institution if it can responsibly carry out its needs on its own. No state may do for any community that which it can do for itself. The federal government should not do anything which states can carry out on their own. Even in emergencies no state can continue to involve itself in local governance on anything but a temporary basis. Similarly no community may continue to involve itself in any family on anything but on a temporary, emergency basis until it becomes able to again be self sufficient.

Recently Patrick F. Fagan and Walter F. Horn have made some suggestions on "How Congress Can Protect the Rights of Parents to Raise their Children."[2] Fagan and Horn indicate that there have been repeated threats to parent's rights from the legislative, executive branches and judicial branches of government at all levels—federal, state, and local—and from the humane professions (psychiatry, psychology, social work, child care, etc.). Thus they provide the substitutive rationale for a

Parental Rights and Responsibilities Act to codify the fundamental right of parents already articulated by the U.S. Supreme Court. It would give parents the standing in law to protect their rights in relation to their children, in the following way: to direct and provide for their children's education, to make health and mental health decisions (with necessary legal exceptions), to discipline their children (within the limits of child abuse laws) and to direct and provide for the religious and moral formation of their children.

Possible Actions at the State Level

No-Fault Divorce

A number of Family Policy Councils have been organized in at least 28 states, promoting various pro-family issues. The Michigan Family Forum, for example, is pressing for reform of the No-Fault state divorce law.[3] The thrust of this legislation is to make divorce less accessible to couples with children, to encourage the resolution of marital problems and to provide a mechanism to help couples build family life.

Bringing Back the Fathers

Because of the large number of divorces in many states, and the large number of single-parent families dependent on welfare (state and national) many of the state legislatures, usually with federal bureaucratic encouragement passed laws which sought to force fathers not in the home to support their children. These laws usually do not provide for the fathers' rights of visitation. In many instances, mothers would express anger at their ex-husbands for late payments of support or for their ex-husbands' associations with younger women, for their pre-divorce actions, and for their continued conflicts, etc. Often the mother sought to get even with them by denying them visitations or by seeking to influence the children against them. As a result, many of the fathers seek to even the score in the conflict by late payments, by omitting payments, etc.. The result, in most instances was in an increase of the social distance between the father and his children, even to the point that they no longer had any contact. Many local family councils are now concerned with this problem and are considering a revision of state law to promote and protect the rights of fathers and their children to see each other as long as the fathers are contributors.

Fathers in the Inner City

Currently the models of successful men for children in the inner cities (and especially in public housing projects) are usually anti-social in effect. The men observed by the children are usually the boyfriends of their mothers, drug distributors, and pimps. These men usually boast about their manliness, aggressiveness, and about their seduction achievements and their illegal activities. In order to replace these anti-social models it is necessary to make available to children models of men who are successfully employed, who carry out their paternal duties to their families and who have potential pro-social leadership possibilities for these neighborhoods. Thus legislatures should consider the possibility of selecting intact families for public housing on marginal incomes and for rent vouchers at low rates as long as such families provided good role models. Such fathers and mothers could then become examples for neighborhood in-service leadership training etc. Legislative changes in line with these policies should be pressed, to determine whether this helps bring back the fathers in the inner city.

Foster-Care and Adoption of Children

Currently, the situation of many children in foster homes is dismal and dangerous. This issue requires detailed analysis.

The contemporary ineffective and frequently destructive program involving ten billion dollars in the foster home industry requires redesign. The foster home system was originally established on an assumption that foster parents could be found who would volunteer to provide the same care to other peoples' children as if they were their own, if they were paid the bare costs of caring for the children. This arrangement had a built-in restriction in that the child they accepted in care could never become their own child under adoption, and that the child could be removed at any time when the child's true parent was ready to again accept him home. The dilemma built into the system was that any couple interested enough in a child to provide him the kind of loving care that they would give their own would also want him to stay on and be theirs. But the moment that kind of bonding and personal commitment developed between foster-parent and child, the child care workers would probably want to move him for fear that he might never want to leave. Not to move him under such circumstances was usually a precursor of trouble for the child welfare worker in the future. If, on the other hand, the foster parent did not reach out to the child to convince him that they really cared for him, he would become difficult to control and in all probability would be reported to the worker as a "problem child." In time we find that most foster children are reported as "homeworn" by so many placements as to become "un-placeable." Many of these children had been moved from place to place, usually caring for no one and having no one who cares for them. The problem of child rearing occurs not only in foster homes but in day care settings, residential institutions and even in affluent homes. If the care is so good that the child finally becomes bonded to the parent-surrogate then the natural mother becomes concerned that the child is too attached to a stranger and not attached enough to her. The problem of having to raise a child through a surrogate is so difficult as to make it clear that neither a village nor a hired surrogate can be expected to effectively raise a child. The only satisfactory alternative to parental raising is probably that of a close relative or committed friend who is so closely tied to the parents as to be able to act in their stead, and in turn to convey to the child that they sincerely care for him and his parents. Another alternative is that of the person who aspires to become a parent of the child and who feels that there are strong enough possibilities for the surrogate to invest himself in a commitment to the child, and vice versa.

Thus instead of seeking out foster parents who do not want to became adoptive parents, the society should seek out potential fosterparents who are eligible to become adoptive parents and who are ready to make a commitment to children.

Similarly, in the case of pregnant young women who are unready or unable to make a realistic commitment to the child the potential mother should be strongly encouraged during pregnancy to place the child for adoption. Better the chances of a successful adoption placement and a successful rearing for the child rather than the high probability of the social pathology of life as a welfare raised, shopworn, multiplaced child.[3]

Already there are hundreds of voluntary agencies sponsored by the pro-life movement which exist for the purpose of offering alternative help to young women who otherwise may seek an abortion. These agencies offer care for young single mothers with pregnancy services who thus avoid the abortion but who then go on to raise their child (and their later children, many with other fathers) and become dependent on welfare. Unfortunately, this crisis mentality of the pro-life movement envisions only two alternative outcomes for each applicant: that the girl will have an abortion or that she will keep the baby—as a single mother on welfare. Of these births, only two percent of such children in the past have been placed for adoption.[4] Fredrica Matthews Green indicates that if the pregnancy-care movement could find effective ways to encourage women to choose adoption, they could help give these children a two-parent home and offer both the women and the children greater opportunity. "By thinking beyond merely 'saving the baby' and building another welfare family, they could serve the children and mothers better by helping the mother accept adoption as a solution. This, of course, is a heavy assignment—to encourage a child-woman to give up a biological and emotionally immediate gratification in order to ensure that her child will have the benefits of a productive life in an intact family as well as to leave her free to complete her education and to grow into productive adulthood. This is a call for a very unselfish act. If placement into the adoptive home is made early enough after the child's birth, the success of the placement and adoption is more likely." (See endnotes 4 & 5) And the young mothers possibilities of building an occupation and future for herself are stronger.

Adoption placement as an alternative to failed attempts at meaningful life at home with a welfare mother or in foster homes can be further encouraged by tax relief for adoptive parents. A five thousand dollars tax credit, available to all adoptive parents as well as natural parents in the upper levels of the working population and even at lower levels of the middle class is a logical step in making adoption and committed parenting affordable to the less affluent and in encouraging the practice for all levels of the society. Such an arrangement would be not only democratic in effect but it would also be "a bargain," according to Patrick F. Fagan of the Heritage Foundation.[6] This would require national legislation as well as state installation efforts. Fagin shows how these tax credits for adoptive families would result in a considerable savings for the state and federal governments and would cost much less than is currently being spent on foster care.

In developing a plan for the care of children it should be remembered that promises and hopes of young pregnant teenage women are hardly comparable to the substantive and legal undertaking of adoptive parents. Judges of appropriate local courts need to be trained to understand that few of the promises of childish young pregnant women usually amount to anything but mere words. The standards by which judges accept the promises of young pregnant girls are hardly comparable to the standards set for adoptive couples. It is almost as if the program was designed to promote the failure of child rearing, using the least able parents available. Only if the vast overload and confusion of bureaucratic social service rules and regulations now in force are voided by the government at all levels, and only if the local courts are able to relieve themselves of conflicting procedures and decisions can the problem be resolved. The current laws, regulations, and procedures require redesign in order to promote responsible parenting. The purposes related to the best interests of the children and the society need to become the ethos of child welfare staffs, institutions and courts.

Placement for Children Who Are Not Adoptable

Some children have become so traumatized by multiple foster-home failure experience that they have become un-placeable in foster homes. Some children also need care for only a temporary period, because it has been determined that their parents will be able and appropriate parents by a time certain. These children should not be placed in foster homes where their loyalty to their parents might be threatened.[7] Other children who are older and unadoptable for reasons of their family situation or other conditions might be accommodated in appropriate institutions for children. For such children the possibility of one of the newer types of children's residential homes is appropriate. Richard Mackenzie indicates that orphanages, especially those under sectarian and religious auspices have developed to such an extent as to offer the kind of care which provides a success rate far better than a life in a series of foster homes.[8] The success rate of institutional child rearing now approaches the level of achievement shown by adoptive and natural homes where both parents are active with the children, based on rates of social pathology and other life difficulties.

The revision of the welfare and foster home system would require that the states and provinces effect a number of changes in their policies, including the dropping of anti-adoption bias in pregnancy counseling, and the discontinuance of using the foster care system and the welfare system for promotion of the failing single-parent family. Foster care should only used with a goal of short-time family reunification. If the probabilities of providing children with a two-parent self-sufficient home are very limited, then rapid adoption processing must be considered in the best interests of the children. The expressed promises of parents need to be very carefully considered in comparison with their past behavior and handling of their children. David Genders, in a chapter in this book, presents us with a description and general evaluation of such institutions. David Liederman and Mary Liepold also deal with such institutions in their chapter in this volume.

The critical factor of such institutional effectiveness rests very much on the quality and extent of motivation of the staff for the children's best interest. Still another view of institutional child care is presented by Hans Goldsmith. He describes the network of 70 children and youth villages in Israel with over 50 or more years experience, in which about seven percent of the nation's children are reared, at a cost of $5,000-$9,000 per year. These villages began in 1933 and were modeled to fit into the Kibbutz movement which needed at that time a program to care for the children of very busy parents involved in critical settlement development. This was followed by the responsibility of these agencies for care of thousands of post-Holocaust children, most of them traumatized orphans. The program has been adjusted to the changing demographics and the needs of many immigrant youths in Israel. Also there were the special needs of neglected and abused Israeli children; and children from Soviet lands with cultures strange to other youth. These villages have proven, by and large, to have been successful in rearing children for self-sufficient and responsible citizenship in Israel. These residential schools use young adults for staff rather than older, trained social workers, and the staff to residents to population is kept limited to 10:1, rather than the American rate of 4:1. By and large the staff is selected to provide appropriate role models rather than for counseling training. The program is operated on a voucher system with a means test to determine how much the child's parents shall pay toward the village fees.[9]

The Training of the Humane Professions

The various humane professions derive their authority from state licensing boards made up of the professions—namely Psychiatry, Psychology, Social Work, Marriage, Family and Child Counselors, etc. Similarly, the teaching profession is licensed by state boards of teachers in all the states of the United States. Similar arrangements are in existence in most other Western nations. In most of these states, the legislature authorizes a licensing procedure with boards of professionals specifying the requirements for its professions.

Until the 1960s, these boards were, by and large, a reflection of the culture of the time, as they related to the norms and values of the society. In the matter of the family, these professions supported the general understanding of respect and authority as an ally of the state and as having priority over all the personal concerns of the individuals in the family and society. Thus most family counselors, social workers and such, when confronted with an individual personal problem in his or her client-families, would usually seek to determine what could be done to preserve the family. Beginning with the late 1960's, this orientation of the professions changed. The new orientation was one of promotion of the individual and egalitarianism, rather than the family. This trend developed in great part due to a supposedly "new" professional conclusion that any family where differences and conflict occurred was unhealthy for its members and should be dissolved. (This view was only much later faulted by the accumulated research which revealed that even a conflict-ridden family was preferable over divorce and life for most children with a single parent; a subject which we have already presented.)[10]

Another reason this orientation became a common pattern was the growth of health insurance provided mainly by employers with "mental health" benefits for the covered employees and the individuals in their families. It became an accepted pattern for such health reimbursements to relate to individual rather than family problems. Fees based on services to current clients were responded to in a manner which would be most likely to keep the client coming back. If the clients' immediate concern was how he or she could achieve personal desires in a difficult marriage, it was unlikely that the professional would offer the more difficult but appropriate task of working at keeping the marriage together. In such settings, the professional would be reluctant to focus on discussion of a subject which would be uncomfortable for the client even though that was what was probably best for the client in the long run. In a sense, in playing to the less mature, non-committal desires of the client the professional probably did much harm. To press the client to analyze his relative desire for immature gratification at the expense of losing his ties to his or her children and family, might result in his seeking other professionals, whose ranks were by now replete with clinicians who were more ready to play the self-gratification game. Those professionals who were on the staffs of public welfare and other agencies whose assignments were related to management and distribution of public largesse, with huge case loads to manage were usually focused on the mechanical process of providing for individual clients rather than to seek family cohesion, stability and rehabilitation. In their professional meetings, however, these professionals in welfare agencies would usually support the comfortable position adopted by their clinical peers.

Thus the ethos of the clients "choice" above almost all other goals norms and values became the standard. In the process these professions were thus no longer allies of the family and the society.

Presenting an ethos based on client goals without equal emphasis on the interests and needs of the client family, community, employer, and neighbors makes the professional ethics code counterproductive to the obvious long range resolutions of client problems. Additionally, providing for confidential help which the client needs without careful examination, analysis, and help with the dynamics of the clients problems merely postpones and spreads the pathogenic processes.

Those who would wish to save and reclaim the family are perhaps no longer able to depend on the professional staffs of psychiatry, psychology and social work (depending on their orientation).[11] The issues of confidentiality and clients rights, particularly for immature clients, usually results in extension of immature client choices without consideration of theother individuals affected by the problem

It would be a real omission, in discussion of the government and the family to omit consideration of governmental actions and their actual destructive effects on the family. Kay James states that "Big Government has engaged in massive intrusion into the family with disastrous consequences."[12] James notes that among other actions, government maintains a tax system which punishes two-parent families and forces both parents to work. It maintains a welfare system which rewards parental illegitimacy and punishes women who get married. Its laws promote a culture of divorce and illegitimacy. In a Supreme Court action a century ago, the family was described as "the sure foundation that all that is stable and noble in our civilization; the best guarantee of the reverent morality which is the source of all beneficent progress in social and political improvement."[13] The Princeton Economic Institute notes that the American "income tax chains mothers to a job," pointing out that in 1940, those with an annual income of $5 million were defined by the tax office as "rich." By 1992, this definition was set at $52,500 annually for tax purposes. "It now takes two incomes to support a family at a standard which once required only one income 30 years ago. The government now takes nearly 40 percent of the income from the average American family, up from 25 percent in 1960." It states that "many women today are chained to their jobs because they lost their economic freedom to stay home and raise their children during their [important] formative years."[14] Kay James' caution to government "to do no harm" is necessary for a government which has financed, for more than a half century welfare programs which have made the economic role of the father irrelevant to millions of families and in the process, has spawned its own problems of social pathology and civil disorder. It was also this government program which sponsored pressures of paternal economic demands without protecting the position of the responsible family father.

Actions Possible at the Local Level

The Religious Institutions

There are many opportunities for people who get together in local communities to promote the reclaiming of the family. The first avenue is the churches, synagogues and related community institutions. The reason these institutions may provide a ready receptivity to programs for reclaiming the family lies in their basic religious system.

Basics of a Religious System in Any Population

The basics of a religious system in a small population group, such as a local community usually include the following:

- Central to any religion is a shared commitment to a jointly held accepted set of principles of faith and belief beyond self.
- There is also a commitment to uphold these beliefs and faith by celebrating life through delayed gratification for agreed-upon goals.
- There is also a shared commitment with fellow members of the religion to pursue a life pattern based on the articles of faith and belief.
- The shared commitment requires all members of the religion to deal with the members of their families and of their religious organization and their sub-group in a mutually responsible manner. The com-

mitment also requires care for their children in such a manner as to make them responsible to each other and to the religious and other legitimate authorities and usually in a socially responsible manner. Such a commitment almost always carries with it the emotional dynamics of parents concern for the best interests of their children and family. The commitment also entails the acceptance of a set of norms and moral rules, the acceptance of supervision by others in their religion, not only by their religious authorities but also by their religious peers. Most religious groups also involve a respect for wisdom, learning and authority, which provides for them the benefits of the group experience.

The ritual, activities and prescribed lifestyle and behavioral pattern contained in the commitment serve not only to reinforce the hold of membership but also to isolate and distinguish the members from others who are not so committed. This reinforces the authority of parents over children and reinforce the responsibility of parents for their children before God and their community. This is also important in that it restrains adolescents and young adults when they most need such limits.

It is probably through the instrument of the religious institution that a redefinition of marriage can be achieved as is necessary if the family is to be reclaimed. For centuries it was the religious institution which defined marriage and the family, and the unit of membership in these institutions was always the individual family. Under the religious definition, marriage was a covenant.[15] It was only as a result of the growth of secular humanism that the parameters of marriage were chipped away, bit by bit. At first, marriage as adapted from the church in its move to city hall was related to the concept of an inviolate contract, meaning that the contract was a permanent agreement between two eligible people, and that it could be voided by agreement of both partners only under special circumstances, or could be voided for cause if a partner were to violate his or her responsibilities. It was only under the influence of secular humanism that divorce in a number of states became possible if moved by either partner. In effect, no-fault divorce made marriage an equitable contract. In fact, as no-fault divorce is now defined, it is probably less of an assurance to its partners and dependents than is that of the common commercial contract dealing with property or material goods.

Another reason religious institutions are probably the most likely ally for those seeking reclamation of the family is in the nature of the interaction between marriage and religion.[16]

Religion and The Family: Interaction Effect and The Family

Involvement in religion has been found by Fagan to provide evidence that the strength of the family unit is intertwined with the practice of religion: Who are more likely to be married, less likely to be divorced or single, and to manifest high levels of marriage satisfaction. Fagan found that religious service attendance is the most important predictor of marital status and happiness. The regular practice of a religion apparently helps people in poverty to move out of poverty. Religious beliefs and practice contribute substantially to the formation of personal moral criteria and sound moral judgment. Regular religious practice has been found by Fagan to generally inoculate individuals against social pathologies and disorders such as suicide, drug abuse, out of wedlock births, crime and divorce. Regular religious practice apparently promotes beneficial mental health, less depression, increased self esteem and greater family and marital happiness. As a support system religious involvement presumably helps repair damage caused by alcoholism, drug addiction and marital breakdown. Its regular practice has been found to be a positive support of longevity for personal physical health, longevity, and prevention of diseases and health problem. Considerable evidence exists to indicate that religious involvement reduces the extent of such problems as sexual permissiveness, teen pregnancy, suicide, drug abuse, alcoholism and to a considerable extent deviant and delinquent acts. It increases family cohesiveness and family protections from deleterious forces.[17]

It is in the religious institutions that some steps toward marriage protection, divorce prevention and reclamation are already being demonstrated.

The first of these actions is a program in which the churches, synagogues and other religious institutions arrive at a compact on a marriage policy requiring a wait of at least 30 days before a marriage can be conducted in the institution or the involvement of religious functionaries. During this waiting period the couple must attend and participate in a marriage preparation course covering such subjects as a jointly understood and accepted definition of the intended marriage (as a covenant, not a limited contract). Also, there is a required discussion of the way in which children are to be reared, and the applicants' agreement as to what each partner expects in their responsibilities to each other, to their children, and to their extended families. The question of how the new family is to handle issues such as the promotion of each others careers, the expectations which each partner has for the others action under various conditions and in various situations is thoroughly discussed. If these issues cannot be resolved by agreement during this period of preparation then the couple is encouraged not to marry and to wait until they can reach a lasting agreement. Where these community compacts have been established, follow up research has shown that the marriages in such cities have proven to have far fewer divorce and separation experience. This is a proven and effective divorce prevention mechanism.

Another program sponsored by individual churches and synagogues is based on having an annual family retreat for families, usually held over one or more weekends. The retreats are conducted at a facility at some distance from the institution at which child care and teenage activities are available. The couples are grouped according to age ranges and/or the number of years of marriage. Sometimes a group of such institutions send their couples to a joint retreat center. The theme of the retreats may involve discussions of ways in which the marriage can be helped, ways in which problems can be recognized and resolved, and how to better manage the children. Such family retreats are highly effective in helping families to develop the "CEO function" in families especially in families without fathers and husbands. Another important topic is the effective use of parental time, especially if both parents are employed full time. The children also attend youth group meetings where family problems are discussed with other youths under adult direction. The adults also discuss the need for "time off" for each of the parents and how this can be arranged. How to deal with peer culture problems is also discussed, and how to help the children fend off the youth counterculture pressures are also dealt with.[18] The role of fathers in the family in such discussions is dealt with in the notes.

Another program conducted by many religious groups, either alone or in joint sponsorship is the operation of a marriage and family clinic, employing psychotherapists who are in agreement with a policy developed by the institution and in line with a program carefully prepared and seriously entered into marriages, full commitment, and agreement on critical issues, etc. In these clinics families with serious problems seek help. The difference, however, between other publicly available clinics and the church and synagogues sponsored agencies is that in the latter the referrals are made by church pastors and ministers, and the practitioners give assistance in line with a pro-family religious policy.

Some suburban religious institutions also sponsor programs to serve their sister institutions in the inner city, helping conduct projects for multi-problem families. The goals for these services are the same as for families in the suburbs but the nature of the relationships between the inner city families and those who come to help them are quite different. One of the fortunate aspects of the age demographics power is in the number of potentially helpful and mature people who will be available in the coming years. This number is very large, in the form of the "baby boom" generation who are now entering the retirement period of their lives.[19] These helpers from the suburban religious groups to the inner cities and to single parent families everywhere will, of course require intensive training. A full discussion of the project goals would have to be conducted, followed by supervision by periodic group conferences for analysis of progress and problem resolution.[19]

Many of these religious congregations have made a shift from the broad and distant overseas and social justice goals to the more surgent goals of reclaiming the family in their own communities and in their city environment. This has required a shift not only in fund expenditure but also in human resources. This shift will probably become more evident as their institutions come closer to the realization that without families their congregations will shrink as the baby boomers reach retirement. The future of the religious institutions and the society in which they can persist requires a pro-active shift in their agendas.[20] They can only ignore this task at their peril.

The thousands of agencies available in the family service and children's protection field can well serve to support the "repair and re-modeling" of families under stress. Unfortunately, there is often a dearth of values and morality in many such agencies. Whether the psycho-therapeutic orientations of their staffs and whether their professional-ism is offset with a sincere concern may differ from agency to agency and therapist to therapist. Similarly, the religiously oriented premarital counseling and the "marriage menders" programs sponsored by many churches may be successful to the degree that these workers can suc-ceed in reaching their clientele as adequately concerned and competent people. (See Judith S. Wallerstein and Sandra Blakeslee; *The Good Marriage: How and Why Love Lasts*, Houghton-Miffin, New York, 1996.) These authors studied some fifty "happy" marriages and based on their findings and Wallerstein's forty years of family therapy practice, they outline their definitions of good marriages and their development. The researchers have indicated a number of types of marriage and have indi-cated the problems that each type of family faces. They indicate that marriage is a transforming experience, something which cannot occur in anyone who sees himself or herself as the main major focus of their life, ahead of the marriage and family concerns. In each of the success-ful marriages, happiness meant feeling respected and cherished by their partner. Mutual respect for family members was based on integrity—a partner was cherished for his or her honesty, compassion, generosity of spirit, decency, loyalty to the family and fairness. Also important was admiration of the partner as a sensitive and conscientious parent and as a moral person. Such partners may have experienced serious difficulties and conflicts with one another, but they were ready to deal with frustra-tions and disagreements in realistic ways which indicated continued respect for one another. The struggles and problems over "equality" in an "equalitarian era" were met by most of these couples with a mutual willingness to change as long as the best interests of their family and children came first. In the researchers view, these families early on created a firm understanding for their relationship and continued to build it together. The successful families regarded their marriages as a "work in progress" which needed continued attention and mutual involvement in the marriage and family developmental tasks outlined by the researchers. These tasks, in a sense, can be seen as a match for the similar individual developmental tasks as outlined by Eric Erikson. The failure to overcome a task in marriage is similar in effect to the failure of a person to deal with an individual development task of Erikson.[20]

The Need for a Pro-Family Community Policy

The adoption of a pro-family policy by the religious institutions would most likely be insufficient for building a family support culture in the communities of the Western world nations. This is because there are too many antagonistic familial effects occurring day-by-day in the numerous activities of the various non-religious agencies of the communities. The police department, the universities and schools, and the courts are only a few of the agencies that may operate counter to family cohesion and stability. Thus it is important that pro-familial policies be examined and supported actively by the government and non-governmental agencies of community life at all levels. It is important that each agency and organization in community life examine its actions at all levels and seek to determine how each of these activities affect family life, and seek to promote pro-familial supportive services.

The Public Schools

In the public schools system, the promotion of programs which help parents to reachieve the authority, bonding, control and responsibility over their children and their children's lives is critically important. Reclaiming this responsibility of the schools is necessary if only to keep order among the children. Without it learning is impossible. The schools also have to reclaim the responsibility to teach the children to become competent in the basic subjects, without which the children cannot become responsible citizens, employable workers and adequate family members. The schools owe the parents an adequate performance of their children in scholastic achievement. As long as the students demonstrate a competence gain and advancement in the basic subjects, as measured by standardized objective tests, parents have little to be concerned. But, when such achievements are not demonstrated, then parents and the polity may justly seek empowerment over their children's destiny by selecting an alternative to the schools which they have been funding. Thus the right of a parents group to establish a charter school or to demand the right to transfer their child's portion of the school funds into private schools or other public schools is a logical conclusion.[21] It must be noted that the excellent academic performance of the public schools of the past, as is evident now primarily in the current performance of the private and public schools of the suburbs were not and are not the product only of the schools alone. Where the children's learning success is demonstrated one can find considerable cooperation between parents and schools in shaping and monitoring the youth peer culture, in promoting a culture of school attendance and academic achievement in setting limits for child behavior and decorum, and in setting and monitoring expectations for student performance. This kind of joint school/parent cooperation and stimulation require leadership by the schools for parent involvement in the joint interests of parents and children. For this, a shift in the defensive stance of public school bureaucracy probably is required. It is obvious that something like the competition of open market (vouchers) may be required. In the meanwhile, individual families may necessarily have to find adequate resources for their children in suburban schools, and even pay the expense of private school tuition.[21]

It is important for the religiously oriented community institutions to make their goals and purposes known to the civil personnel, including the judges in juvenile courts, domestic relations courts, child and spousal abuse, neglect agencies and adoption courts. The people working in these programs have a constant crisis of time in which to determine the facts, problems and the dynamic family factors which occur in the lives of those for whom they make lasting judgmental decisions. Many of these programs are no longer operated according to the values and norms of the pre-1960 years. Because the personnel of these programs were reared in the years which followed the 1960s, many of them no longer understand and utilize the value system of the community culture which supported parental control, responsibility and family cohesion. Instead, in an age of increased client rights without responsibility, these institutions frequently relied on a complex of rules and procedures which often did not focus on issues important to the families in the proceedings. All too often family processes critically necessary for family functioning were interfered with, and, in some instances, action was frequently taken which was counterproductive to the child's best interest and the courts purposes. What is needed now is an interaction between civic minded, pro-family religious community members and community agencies in order to promote family development and cohesion, so that these agencies may be enabled to function in the best interests of the children and their parents and their parent-surrogates. The goals of these agencies are deeply tied to the issue of child rescue which are critical to the rehabilitative deliverance for children. These agencies also need an understanding of behavior in the "culture of poverty." Rector describes the cognition of many of these families as behavioral poverty he refers not to a lack of protein, minerals, vitamins, calories or nutrients, shelter and facilities.[22] Rector states that those defined as "poor" by the U.S. Government have almost the same life standards as people in the upper middle-class. "Behavioral poverty" is a breakdown in conduct that is necessary for the formation of healthy families, stable personalities and self-sufficiency. He specifies behavioral poverty as a cluster of social pathologies including aspiration and achievement inabilities, unwillingness to control ones children, increased single parenthood and illegitimacy, criminal activity and drug and alcohol abuse. A simplification of the terms of illegitimacy and often single parenthood might be described as irresponsible sexual activity on the part of men and women and adolescent boys and girls.

One of the most respected Western sociologists, James Q. Wilson describes the devastating life of children raised in the clientele of these agencies.[23] The only current answer to this problem is to place young unmarried pregnant girls in a social structure without moral supervision. This is important in teaching adolescent and young to be good parents and to protect them and their children, from the influence of gangs, drugs and crime. Any young unmarried pregnant woman who wishes to establish an independent household at public expense would be given such support only if she lives in some kind of family shelter or group home managed under adult private auspices, including appropriate religious groups accepted by local authorities. He proposes that such girls would be given a check which has to be countersigned by an adult supervisor of the setting. Wilson suggests a retention of the welfare system for women who need it as a temporary bridge to get through a death, desertion or divorce in the family but only if this dependence lasts less than two or three years. If it takes longer, then a work program should be individually worked out so that the mother can become a self-sufficient adult. For the young mothers he proposes an entirely separate system for those girls who are now raising the next generation of our children.

The removal of legal barriers which interfere with the adoption process, such as the restriction of adoptions on the basis of race are a necessary legislative goal for each state or provincial legislature. The anomaly of having no adoption placements for new babies other than a return to their crack-addicted or otherwise incompetent single mothers is representative of an inhumane society in the light of the huge list of appropriate adoptive applicants hungry for a child. The child's best interests should be paramount even at the expense of matters of race or tribe.

The Welfare System, Family Life, and the Foster Home Maelstrom

Illegitimacy and single parenting is probably the most serious social problem in the United States. This illegitimacy is more important than other social pathologies because it is the nexus of where many families fail the children. Single parenting can be directly related to the breakdown of the family and sets a negative norm for many people in the society. Directly related to the causes of illegitimacy is the effect of a welfare system that rewards non-work, unemployability, irresponsible sexual activity and promotes a lowest common denominator for academic performance, among other ills. It promotes the prevention of family formation and punishes marriages and work by reductions in welfare when they are reported to the authorities. It helps create a foster care system which destroys thousands of children for wholesome involvement in the mainstream of society and prevents adoption of children by thousands of alternative couples and families willing and even "hungry" to provide a life for them. This structure of welfare and foster care law is based on theoretical rights and programs, the purposes of which have long since been lost or forgotten.

According to Fleming, the federal welfare system has created a mother-state-child family system which acts to discourage young men from marrying, supporting and becoming fathers to children.[23]

Revision of welfare and foster care law needs to occur not only at national levels which are distant from local application but also at provincial, state, county and even lower levels. At best, national policy only creates millions of pages of regulations and exceptions which usually make the law inapplicable locally. Such national policy formulations only serve to perpetuate central bureaucracy and to promote more state and county bureaucracy to offset and interpret them. Instead of tinkering with national social policy, what needs to be done about welfare is the development of a national set of objective principles for the purposes and goals of welfare and child support, with at least for the present, a set of block grants from national to local and regional communities. A planned "phase out" of such block grants should be planned to follow in ten to twenty years, during which time communities and regions would be expected to find and develop alternatives to the welfare programs, based on local, state, and national interests.

Welfare as a Family Destroyer

Welfare presents a particularly aggravating factor in the pressure against the family as an institution. Because welfare has the unintended consequence of subsidizing inadequate motherhood, it makes fatherhood unnecessary for women who want to have their own home and financial security. In some Western nations, the combination of welfare grants, housing allowances, medical care, food stamps and women's and children's nutritional allowance—none of which are taxable—adds up to an amount which surpasses the after tax income of any job the mother could find in the marketplace. Neither could any wage after taxes earned by a low level male worker match the total welfare related tax exempt income of an unmarried mother with two or more children. Thus, not only is the income of a wage earning husband made irrelevant, but so is the need for schooling and vocational training for employment made irrelevant for the parents and the children in the family. Thus welfare and related grants make possible a culture of dependency which is transgenerational in effect—a culture where the government makes employment and involvement in the mainstream marketplace unnecessary. This system of subsidy for the elimination of economic fatherhood and which, in the process by de facto effect eliminates the need for a legitimate father in the home, has many destructive effects on the family and the society. The figure of the father in these families is replaced most often by a boy friend in control, but whose responsibility and concern for the children's best interest is usually absent. Control and monitoring of the children by their own welfare mothers usually disappears as soon as the children become stronger than their mother or as soon as they can run faster than she. A kind of "culture of pseudo poverty" develops in such a family. It is usually surrounded by other mother-headed families, where men do not marry their conjugal girl friends, where men are indirect beneficiaries of the welfare subsidies, where the mothers' only obligation to the welfare system is not to marry, and where the mother can only lose her income by being charged with felony child abuse or neglect, a seldom occurring complicated court action. We label it "pseudo poverty" because the total welfare benefit, which in a comparable non-developed nation would be considered affluence. Even in the developed nations the total welfare package usually amounts to much more than what has been described as the income level of the "working poor," whose children attend school regularly, whose fathers work hard, often on more than one job and whose parents press their children to move upward in the society by working up a set of good references from jobs which are considered as "dead end" by others in the "culture of poverty." Many immigrant families, particularly from Asian countries, are among the "working poor" and moving rapidly up the socio-economic ladder in the Western world. On the other hand, it must be noted that there is a sizable labor underground economy in most welfare states on which taxes are not paid and which is also available to the population involved in the "culture of pseudo-poverty." That serves as an additional incentive to promote the welfare population in continuance and growth. This means that this culture is growing in the society. Having involved a sizable population among Black and Latin population, it is fast expanding into what Charles Murray describes as the "white underclass." His opinion is that in the most Western societies, operating welfare states will eventually be made up of two social classes: (1) the underclass with weaker family structure, severe social pathology including crime, drug addiction etc.., and with an underground economy; and (2) the rest of the society, complete with strong families, communities, and so forth, who will live in "gated cities, towns, and neighborhood, protected from the external population, and highly taxed for protection and in providing subsistence resources to the underclass. Whether the underclass will surround the gated communities or vice versa, with the underclass in walled off reservations as is now provided to the native Indian population (as predicted by Murray) is not clear. Such a society where few can have the opportunity to have a family and a chance to move upward if they have the desire and ability, presents us with a dreary and conflicted future. It is because of this prospect that it becomes clear that welfare as a way of life is destructive both to individuals and the prospects of a democratic society.

The resolution of the problem is related to the situation of the single parent family. The resolution of these problems rests primarily on the growth and revitalization of the religious and voluntary institutions in the local communities, in the suburbs, and in the inner cities, and in the resumption of these institutions of the moral leadership of Western communities.[24]

Involving the Fathers

One of the most serious problems relating to the reclamation of the families in the Western world is that of involving the fathers in the lives of their children, present and future. We have already commented on the problems of the non-custodial father earlier in this paper, who, whether for good reason or not, have been motivated and perhaps encouraged to drop out of the lives of their children.

For those fathers so separated from their children it would be salutary for local religious organizations and voluntary social service agencies to help rebuild the father/child relationships. For this they need trained volunteers who can be helpful in mediating the reunion of fathers and their children. Many of these fathers now have to take their children to shopping malls because they have no proper home where they might bring their children without excessive expenditures. It might also be helpful to provide some family reunion facilities where fathers and children might spend some time together, under the aegis of sponsoring local religious or voluntary organizations. In any case, it is important that "parents without partners," whether fathers or mothers have group settings available to them where they might have help in resolving their day-to-day problems. Separated and divorced fathers and mothers need an accepting setting where parents are secure in their roles as parents, and will be helped with the children if they need it. It is also quite possible that local religious and voluntary agencies might more easily fill the role of "go-between" in getting the divorced spouses to resume their roles as joint parents even though their marriage has ended.

A pro-family policy is important for the local community on a number of issues, each of which could well be initiated, supported and carried out under the sponsorship of a community pro-family council made up of the religious and voluntary agencies. Policies could be designed for the promotion of children staying in school, for career planning, and for helping the children to postpone or overcome destructive immediate gratification, and to avoid problem behaviors for the sake of a desired future. Carefully designed vocational planning programs may succeed in delaying sexual diversional experiences and in avoidance of destructive drug or alcohol peer activities. Similarly, pro-family councils might also succeed in establishing community programs which honor the local mother of the year, the local father of the year and the parents of the year, and note the achievement of chosen families which have held together and supported the rearing of children under difficult circumstances. Similarly, pro-life councils could be helpful in encouraging and honoring self-help and mutual aid organizations of families facing special problems. Similarly pro-family councils might be helpful in honoring the teachers who have most helped children learn the familial settings and the roles of parents, or who have most helped bring parents and schools together in terms of promoting learning by the children. Similarly the pro-family councils might help honor those community leaders who have promoted the ideals of moral behavior. An example is Dr. Laura Schlessinger in Los Angeles who has promoted in her radio program responsible parenting and adoption of children needing homes. Similarly pro-family councils could promote the work of those who support responsible dealing among people in the community. Dennis Praeger, also of Los Angeles radio fame, is another such example of someone promoting the principles of honesty, family life loyalty and stability, self-responsibility, the building of social and human capital by education and training, the principle of postponed gratification in the building for future, self-reliance, community service, anti-promiscuity, the renewal of requirements for public servants to maintain a moral life in public and private and the rebuilding of a value system for families, institutions and community and for the promotion of these virtues.

Conclusion

A number of scholars have indicated the depth of the relationship between the traditional family and civilization.

Dench[24] believes that the improbable viability of a culture involving millions of unattached males has not yet sunk into the public consciousness. When the true state of this demographic problem becomes clear to most of the society he believes that most of the people in the Western nations will become concerned and seek for a change in the way in which society operates, and will press for a serious change in the culture.

Similarly Adelson,[25] a noted Michigan psychologist indicates that "there is a very high price to be paid for the individualism that is so central to the American (and Western) ethos of individualism which involves childlessness, a lack of commitment to family life and a low investment of self in the rearing of children."

Apparently, once the true costs of this style of life become clear, especially to the women of the Western nations, it is probably only a matter of time before the relationships of courtship and marriage will be sharply changed.

Carlson indicates that the "family renewal (will) come only as certain family tasks or functions become protected from immersion with industry and deindustrialized and then returned to the household. Under these models, the measure of economic success will be found in the *formation* of marriages, the *birth of children* and the solidarity of the household group."[26]

Midge Decter believes that many family and related problems of the society can be resolved only when "assuming responsibility for one's life, for one's everyday choices as well as for one's moral conduct" is resumed in the modern society. These standards have been brooding in America for a long, long time. Every private weakness is by now regarded as a legacy of potential misbehavior, every discomfort as an injustice, every wrong turn as an enforced imposition from outside, every defeat as a malfunction of "the system." "The slightest suggestion that the consequence might be connected with one's own behavior has become anathema."[27]

Yet another facet of the problems of the Western family is found in the financial parameters of the institutions. Lester C. Thurow, a noted American economist believes that the contemporary one-earner family is now extinct under capitalism, because it takes more than one earner to provide for the needs of the modern family.[28]

Now that the two or more earner family becomes clearly necessary from an economic view, a simultaneous finding among psychologists and child development experts reveals that every child needs the full attention of at least one parent during the first year of life, if he or she is to become fully developed from an intellectual point of view. Unless the economic resources of the society provide generous earned income tax credits or some other reverse income tax for such families, then these two constraints on the family will have to be brought into congruency. That, or perhaps a huge differential tax on single-earners and couple's without children could make it possible for families with both parents and children to survive economically. This would have to be arranged in such a manner that the extra income to child rearing families is arranged as a strong co-incentive for stable, complete families where the children are in school and the extra income carries no stigma.

Another problem frequently occurs in families with working mothers, especially where both parents are being pressed or encouraged to put in extra hours at work away from home. In some instances mothers find themselves drawn to the job because it is intellectually more fulfilling for them (than staying at home with the children.) Brownlee and Miller indicate that both parents say they work for a variety of reasons. These are:

- We both work because we need the money.
- It's OK for both of us to work because our child is in good day care.
- If only companies were more flexible, I would spend more time with the kids.
- I'd be happy to stay home with the kids if my wife earned more money.
- If taxes were lower, one of us could stay home with the children.

These authors believe that these reasons are "lies told by parents to themselves and each other because they believe that they need all of the money they earn despite the room for discretionary expenditures which they might do without if they really had to." These authors believe that few topics are as important and involve as much self-deception and dishonesty as finding the proper balance between child-rearing and work. William Bennett[30] believes that the need for the two-earner claim on the family is a "cop-out" especially for the middle-class who blame family problems on the economy or insufficient help from the government: "If a couple really makes children a priority, they will find jobs that allow them more time with their kids, even if that means making less money and living somewhere less expensive." Thus, it is a possibility that Thurow may be proven wrong, and that those families which have the will to focus on adequate child rearing may find a way to accomplish it.

One more helpful note is offered by Murray[31] and Thomas.[32] Murray indicates that "communities survive by socializing their young to certain norms of behavior. They believe that socialization is achieved with the help of realities to which parents can point: 'you have to work, or you won't eat,' 'If you don't have a husband, you won't be able to take care of your children.' 'If you commit crimes you will go to jail.' From this raw material communities fashion the gentler rewards and penalties of social life that constrain unwanted behaviors and foster desired ones. Outside the inner city, we are busily reconstructing the damage done to the social fabric (which suffered trauma from the 1960s activities), with considerable success. Inside the inner city, that fabric has become so tattered that it is difficult to see any external means of restoration." Thomas says that it remains to be seen whether small towns (and suburbs) will absorb (the) newcomers "graduating" from the inner city who have earned their way into these small towns and enclaves of the middle class. Whether these towns can absorb them and retain their stability and integrity is to be seen. These who would move from our dysfunctional big cities to small towns, thinking they can thereby escape all their problems without taking a hard look at their own lives and thoughts, make a fundamental miscalculation. They bring themselves and their problem folkways with them. Carlson[33] indicates that we have always developed a compromise as the new and old towns and suburbs have adjusted to newcomers from the inner city or the immigrant neighborhoods as they gained steady jobs and better education for their children, when they were in time welcomed into local community groups and churches. The problem is whether such assimilation will occur before too many boundary lines and freeway fences are developed between the middle class and the people from the inner city.

Western society is fast moving toward a separation of those who have been socialized and who make up the mainstream of society and those who are on the margins or who make up a counter society. A variety of walls are being established between them whether they are those of the gated communities, police lines between areas, prison walls, community watch programs and other mechanisms of apartheid. This, plus the continued efforts of multicultural and racial seclusions now being emphasized in the schools is fast moving them toward a split society. These are two separate cultures. Those on the fast track where children are effectively reared by their parents and surrogates to move upward on the socioeconomic ladder, and those who are on the insulated reservations of problem populations served as social victims needing subsidized housing, subsidized jobs, day care, subsidized peace programs, special youth services to keep gangs under control and other special policing. Those in the gated communities and protected condominia will continue to pay heavy taxes to subsidize the apartheid reservations and program devised by the "new class" and operated by government to separate the inhabitants of the reservations. In this kind of social scenario it is obvious that there would be no integrated society. The product of such social planning would obviously produce two separated enclaves: One would be made up of intact families trying hard to rear and protect their children with the parents making every effort to monitor their children's lives, to protect their children's learning either at private or select suburban schools, to keep close ties to their church or synagogue, and to help their children to build lives of positive morality and stability. The other enclave would be increasing populations of single parent families, many of them at-risk of falling further and deeper into their inner city culture and population and at the mercy of the anti-social elements about them.

David Popenoe presented a keynote statement at the World Congress of Families at Prague on March 22, 1997. In this paper which was titled "How to Restore the Nuclear Family in Modern Society" he presented a number of conclusions on the subject.[34] He listed reasons why the two-parent family is far more important to children and to society than ever before in history. He presents a note of hope based on the fact that the family is a continuing fundamental and psychological product of humankind which hasn't changed over the years. The reason for that is that human beings are a pair-bonding species. He suggests that the leadership of Western societies follow a number of strategies to restore the nuclear family. They are:

- *Dampen the Sexual Revolution* by promoting sexual abstinence through the high school years, by encouraging women to become more sexually reticent and reserved prior to marriage and by reining in the organized entertainment industry. Many adolescent girls express a need to learn how to be interesting to adolescent and young men without being sexually available to them.
- The second strategy of Popenoe is to *Promote Marriage* by getting the word out about the emotional, economic and health benefits of lifelong monogamy, by educating people about the nature of modern marriage; noting that it is more than a life of passion and romance, that it is a long-term friendship between a man and women that requires constant effort and care to build and maintain plus a strong moral commitment to the institution, as well as to each other and those about them; by casting shame and stigma on those childbearing couples who unreasonably divorce or have children out of wedlock and by promulgating widely the findings about how divorce damages children.
- Popenoe's third strategy is to *Renew a Cultural Focus on Children* by emphasizing that children are our future, and which will perceive that life as an adult is incomplete without children who have the best of their parents invested in them.

Brad Stone believes that the emphasis on individualism is "cancerous." He believes that "Ours is a culture in which the natural end of marriage, the rearing of children to maturity, has been replaced by the emotional and sexual gratification of adults...where a natural division of labor and gender have been replaced by an androgynous ideal buoyed by avarice." He believes that we have somehow convinced ourselves of a woman's exclusive right to choose but in which we are surprised to find that men often refuse to shoulder responsibility for women's choices. He states ours is a culture in which marriage is deemed just one among many equal "life-style options" (and where) volitional fatherlessness has become routine." It is important to note that the positions listed by those supporting this ethos in most instances are self-serving and promote a policy of irresponsibility for both women and men, and the family responsibility for its children are, in most instances, considered only after the interests and rights of the parents have been served. The ethos of personal individuation has outcomes related to single parent families, absent or missing fathers, legitimization of sexual promiscuity among adults, and weak social outcomes for children.

This ethos is promoted by the people whose ages are such that many of them are either childless or among the parent population of multiple divorces and much de facto child neglect. This population congerie is, by and large strongly influential on the shape of the general culture, on the determination of who shall be stigmatized in the society and what the social rules should be. With the shape of family policy as enshrined in the intellectual elite and their followers, the relationship of many adults to their children is identical to colonization, an offset with a bit of "quality time."

If it were not for the fact that so many accept this dysfunctional ethos, some of us might begin to believe that this is really a con-artist's alibi for manipulating people, or perhaps it is the psychological rationale found among the mentally ill, or perhaps this is a child trying to explain that his urges got the better of him. This countercultural ethos tied to irrational behavior is hardly the policy for a self-respecting society. It is time that we begin to label it what it is. We need to reshape our definitions of what is good and bad for children and families in the mainstream of our society.

ENDNOTES

[1] John Ashcroft, David Blankenhorn, James Dobson, John Engler, William Galston, Kay James, Dr. John Kennedy, Steve Largent, Dan Quayle and Paul Weyrich, "Can Government Save the Family?," *Policy Review*, Sept/Oct 1996, no. 79, pp. 43-47.

[2] Fagan, Patrick F. and Wade F. Horn, "How Congress can Protect the Rights of Parents to Raise their Children," *Issue Bulletin no. 227*, Heritage Foundation, Washington, DC, July 23, 1996.

[3] Yoest Charmaine Crouse, "State Group that Fight for Mom and Dad," *Policy Re-*

view, Nov/Dec 1996, pp.17-19. She lists the Michigan Family Council Report by Brian Willats, "Breaking Up is Easy to Do: A Look at No-Fault Divorce in Michigan" as continuing research on the subject of No-Fault law.

[4] Fredrica Mathews-Green, "Pro-Life Dilemma: Pregnancy Centers and the Welfare Trap," *Policy Review*, July/August 1996, pp. 40-43.

[5] One of the first requirements in taking a child into care should be the determination of the birth parents. Then each (the father as well as the mother) should be interviewed and required to have their interest in the child, and competence and potentiality and intentions for the child be clarified. If they are not interested in the child or if their potential as parents is too limited, then their close relatives should be interviewed. If no adoption parents are found among relatives, and if the biological parents sign off, then an adoption by a non-relative should be made. Every effort should be made immediately after acceptance of the pregnant girl or women has been accepted for care. If adoption is decided on, then the mother should be given every possible preparation to plan her life without the child, and she should have help in understanding that she is doing this in the child's and her best interests. In every instance, the child's best interests should assured and enforced. In some instances close relatives or friends might be willing to provide an appropriate foster home, suitable for the child and amenable to his best interests. If so, this kind of foster home should be accepted.

[6] Fagin indicates that each foster child costs the government an average $13,000 annually, and a tax credit of $5,000 is the equivalent of a loss of $1,000, to the government thus each adoption is worth $12,000 annually to the society. In addition, the high probability of the adoptive child growing up to be a self-sufficient person is a savings in cost to the tax payer, and the increased probability of his becoming an annual tax payer for his entire adult life means that such a policy of encouraged adoptions may well have such an impact in terms of cost-benefits as to have a permanent effect on the national deficit of many western nations. Fagin Patrick, *Promoting Adoption Reform: Congress Can Give Children Another Chance, Backgrounder #1080*, Heritage Foundation, May 6, 1996. Yet another aspect of the adoptive alternatives is to be considered. Numerous families which are currently offering foster care, or which have served as foster homes in the past have indicated their readiness to be adoptive homes, according to Fagin. Thus administrative costs processing many of the adoptive homes are also likely to be saved.

[7] McKenzie, Richard B., *The Home: A Memoir of Growing Up in an Orphanage*, Basic Books, NY, 1966 McKenzie, Richard B., "Review the Orphanage, but Don't Expect Help from Child-Care Professionals," *American Enterprise*, May/June 1996. Also see Genders, David M., "Program of Traditional Agencies for Families," (chapter contained in this Volume), and Liederman, David S. and Mary Liepold, "Signs of Hope in Troubled Times: US Programs that Work for

Children and Families, (chapter contained in this volume).

[8] The reason for this degree of success in institutions is that many of the house parents in institutions of voluntary and religious see their work as a mission rather than a job. For a child whose own parents have forfeited their rights, the devotion of a religiously motivated parent surrogate is far better housing and rearing than to play what McKenzie called "Foster care roulette."

[9] Goldsmith, Heidi, "Shalom for At-Risk Youth," (Letters from Abroad) *Policy Review*, Nov - Dec, 1996, no. 80, p. 7. Cost per child per annum in these villages is $6,500 - $9,000 per year as compared to American rates of $26,000. Israel's federal requirements and standards for these residential institutions are, of course, much less onerous than American institutions, but observers believe that Israeli institutions are adequately safe, healthy and psychically wholesome.

[10] See endnote 5 and 16 and textual material listed on "The Legacy of the Single Parent Family."

[11] A noted pro-family professional psychologist recently described a training session required by his state professional board for annual renewal of his license. In this session there was discussion of a particular client who made her living as a sex-prostitute. The psychological trainer insisted that the prostitute be referred to as "sexual service practitioner or sex worker," because the term "prostitute" was demeaning and expressed a moral value which professionals should not use. The fact that the prostitute was spreading a sexually transmitted disease to her clientele, and thus damaging numerous families, was apparently considered irrelevant to this professional. In the new professional code one may only promote and teach protection (safe sex) and safety in sexual encounters and that the stability and safety of affected families is a value issue on which psychologists must remain neutral.

Yet another aspect of psychotherapy relates to family cohesion. This is the fact that, according to Finola Bruton "Any undue emphasis on individualism is detrimental to the cohesion of the (family and in turn) society". It is true, she states, that an important value of all family life must be support for individual growth and development. But, she states, individual rights must always be anchored by duties and responsibilities. According to Bruton without family and society human existence is empty and without meaning. Because the emphasis of most psychotherapy service in contemporary times is on helping the client to achieve his or her individuals rights without too much concern for responsibilities for others, this creates a tension contemporary psychotherapy overall promotes family dissolution.

[12] James, Kay, "Do No Harm," *Policy Review*, Sept/Oct 1996, p. 47.

[13] See Murphy v. Ramsey, 1995.

[14] "Our Income Tax Chains Mothers to a Job," Pacific Economics Institute, *The Weekly Standard*, Oct 28, 1996, p. 10.

[15] Jonathan Sacks, (in his article on "Social Contract Covenant" in *Policy Review*,

July/Aug 1996, pp. 54-57 states that the historical and traditional formulation of marriage has always been the covenant, and has never been limited to the secular and lesser formulation of the contract. He states that "What binds Society is not a contract but a covenant." The difference is that parties can disengage from a contract when it is no longer in their interest to continue with it but a covenant binds them. A covenant is predicated not on interest but rather on loyalty and fidelity. Sacks, who is the chief Rabbi of Britain and a recognized theological historian indicates that the difference between the two terms is in the religious concept of Emanuel, which is often wrongly translated by some as "faith," which is not a cognitive but a moral term. It means willingness to enter into and stand by a long-term, open-ended commitment. It means "faithfulness."

Sacks states that a social contract is maintained by the threat of external force, in the case of a marriage this would be the state. A covenant leads us on to families, communities and associations of civil society. The first term is political, the second is social and human. Sacks emphasizes that the first has a materialistic dimension but the latter has a spiritual dimension involving the grace of human relation, loyalty, fidelity, responsibility, integrity. The first is a transitory pattern. The latter has eternal dimensions.

[16] Fagin (Religious and Family Life), report #1064, Heritage.

[17]How do religions have this effect? Fagin cites a number of authorities on the differences between "healthy religious practice" and "unhealthy religious practice." The latter has been generally viewed by Americans of religious faith as the "mispractice of religion." Apparently, the difference between the two forms of religion relate to the intrinsic and extrinsic of religious practice. Those who follow the intrinsics of a religion have a greater sense of responsibility and greater internal control, are more self-motivated and among children, do better in their studies. The extrinsic, on the other hand are more likely to be dogmatic, authoritarian and less responsible; to take less internal control, to be less self-directed, and (among children) do less well in their studies. The intrinsics are usually more concerned with moral standards, conscientiousness, discipline, responsibility and consistency. Extrinsics are more self-ndulgent, indolent and likely to lack dependability. The extrinsic practice of religion is characterized by self orientation, outward observance and little inner orientation of the religious principles as a guide to behavior. A simple way to describe the difference is that the intrinsic member of the religion is involved in it because it gives meaning to his life, it helps him understand who he is in relation to the eternal verities of life, to his brothers and sisters, parents and other humans and how he can control his actions in fairness to all other humans. The extrinsic member doesn't care where he fits into the eternal scheme. He is only concerned with what the religious movement can do for him and what he wants for himself. The extrinsic seeks a religion which gives him status and advantage, and which makes him more comfortable with the "goodies" he has gathered. He wants religion to help

him deal with guilt if he has any. The intrinsic member wants religion to help him be more worthy of the benefits he seeks, to be more acceptable in the eternal scheme of things and to better understand how he can become a more worthy member of the religion and mankind. Fagin emphasizes that it is intrinsic members of religions who provide strength to the development and strengthening of the family. It is the family and the community of humans which intrinsic religion supports and defends, institutions which the extrinsic frequently write off.

[18] Reuven Bar Levav, in his book *Every Family Needs a Chief Executive Officer: What Mothers and Fathers Can Do About Our Deteriorating Families and Values* (New York, Fathering Inc., 1995) emphasizes the need for every family to have clear direction, and not the confusion which comes from not knowing who is really in charge. In the CEO families, the mother and father usually determine the policies of how the family will operate, and as the children grow up, the parents will usually consult with the children on their preferences, recommendations and reasons. When the parents have reached a position on issues, they will usually be made known to the children with the reasons.

These policies, however, are worthless unless they are congruent with the day-by-day behavior of the parents. Otherwise they will either be ignored by the children or they will be accepted on the level of "saying one thing and then doing something else"–a hypocritical stance. Children learn not only from what their parents say but most importantly from what they do. Values are best taught by parents through personal demonstration in their day-to-day activities and choices. Bar-Levav indicates that more often than not, the loss of the father represents not only a personal loss to the children and the wife but also a loss of leadership in the family. A mother who has lost her husband through divorce finds that there is no one to share the important familial decisions, because she loses her own leadership qualities in the process of the divorce conflict that follows. This process of dissolution of the family creates an atmosphere where no one seems to be in charge. So many other things demand attention that in fighting the war the qualities being fought over are often lost as well. Bar Levav indicates that in the absence of consistent fathering children often fail to become civilized beings. The basic sense of compassion does not come in mother's milk. Growing children do not become self-disciplined unless they have been disciplined first by consistent "fathering," often carried out by their mother with the very young. But, Bar Levav emphasizes that no fathering will take place except on a firm bedrock of mothering. Bar Levav indicates that missing fathers aren't really happy in their life in the "wilderness,"—they are, more often then not, the victims of their own selfishness. And those men who stay on as husbands, but who withdraw into themselves and keep quiet and inactive, leaving their wives to take over as matriarch, usually end up as suffering from their own authority vacuum. Their wives carry the burden and they are as unhappy as their sisters who have mated into the reverse mode of authoritarianism. Incidentally, in the process of the divorce, not only do fathers lose family leadership by their absence, but mothers lose family leadership as well. Under these conditions the family is left without leadership.

Bar Levav states that homosexuality in men can also be destructive of the fathering process. He believes that it makes no sense to celebrate homosexuality any more than it does to condemn it. He recommends instead that we guard against the confusion or roles in the next generation by better mothering and fathering. Bar Levav does not accept the genetic basis of homosexuality.

Bar Levav believes that human problems will abound unless and until each of us learns to be responsible for our behavior. All relationships stand on mutual respect, including those between parents and children and need to be worked at. To really succeed as a father one must be seen by the child as a strong pillar of security. Sons particularly fear weaknesses and inconsistencies in their fathers. It is the fathers role to pull their children away from adhering to the mother when they no longer have an objective need for it. Otherwise the children experience difficulty in becoming self-sufficient. This may explain why so many children without fathers extend their dependence on their mothers or others available in their life. Among women this is evidenced by the ubiquitous patterns of dependent child pregnancies. Without fathers, families and societies fail in the absence of self-restraint. Fathers who instill self-restraint in their children are in very real sense the trustees of civilization. Even very good mothering does not often establish self-control or self-discipline. These qualities usually develop only in a crucible of no-choice where unruly behavior is controlled by competent fathering.

The development of reasonable beings under competent fathering requires that all of us, as children and later as adults accept the bitter fact that forces more powerful than any of our wishes operate in the universe. Bar Levav emphasizes that reasonableness requires that we need to learn from our fathers that we really do not have the freedom to always have our way. We may protest having limits imposed on us, especially as we as children discover that most children and reasonable adults accept them. Limits are not only reassuring, they lessen anxiety because they imply that someone knows what is safe and good and what is not. Bar Levav believes that good fathering requires challenging the child's false claims of competence and independence. Problems in our society are in great part related to too many in a generation of children whose claims of independence has not been challenged and taught self-restraint in their early development. Thus our society experiences high rates of crime and delinquency and many young people have particular difficulty in fitting their behavior to the expected behavior in marriage. As unmarried and even as married partners, too many in the society exhibit sexual irresponsibility or to familial irresponsibility. Bar Levav believes that "feelings push children and adults away from reason, and the result is often self-defeating and/or destructive to others." It is the lack of self-discipline in control of these feelings which underlay much of the anti-familial effects of the common culture. Neither love nor hate need be the basis for the important life choices. It is really the father's responsibility to support the children in not yielding to the anti-social values of the neighborhood and street culture. Being labeled as "square" is much less damaging to the personality in the long run than growing up in emotional confusion without sufficient clarity about right and wrong behavior.

[19] A very interesting sidelight on the matter of family rehabilitation appears in an family service agency journal by Carol H. Meyer, titled "Individualizing the Multi-Problem Family" (*Social Casework*, vol. XLIV, no. 5, May 1963, pp. 267-272). In this article Carol Meyer, a professor at the Columbia University School of Social Work, described a ten-year project undertaken in St. Paul, Minnesota which sought to help multi-problem families solve their difficulties. In this respect there were many failures of relationship with these families. Meyer indicated a number of phenomena about these families which made them hard to reach and hard to help in the resolution of their problems. Most of these phenomena would probably be recognized by an objective observer as within the culture of poverty (see Segalman, Ralph and Asoke Basu, *Poverty in America: The Welfare Dilemma*, Greenwood Press, Westport, Connecticut, 1981, pp. 5, 6, 9, 12, 14). This surprising aspect of this culture of poverty seen some 33 years ago in the inner city is that it is still observed in the present-day inner city. This culture is now reflected in many of the families of the present. One may conclude that the social disorganization of the past and present failing population is now becoming a major cultural pattern of the rest of the population.

In the St. Paul study of single parent families in the sixties researchers found that a special approach to the clientele was required if the intervention was to have any effect. This was because the family culture of poverty lacks both an understanding of institutional models and the communication processes of a business-like relationship. Thus the social worker who introduced herself to the client as a worker from the family agency got "nowhere" with the client, but the social worker who introduced herself by her own first name and said that "I'm here to help you" did develop a relationship with the client, especially if she pitched in and helped with the accumulated pile of dishes. Those who demonstrate their helpfulness succeeded in teaching competency as a mother as she worked alongside of the client. Similarly, the worker who talked about how to better control the children or the best way to budget family money did develop a relationship as she worked, helped and taught these skills to the client. The social work role here was probably the same as an elderly grandmother or aunt did as in families still equipped with extended available relatives. Social workers who sent someone to "stand in" for her, found that the substitute had difficulties. Only where the "first name" worker brought her substitute in as a "friend" was the substitute able to make any headway. It is no surprise that the St. Paul demonstration project foundered after the first set of devoted workers were followed by replacements who were less able to become "friends" rather than professional workers.

A useful source of help in familial preservation is the May/June 1996 issue of *The American Enterprise* which is entirely devoted to marriage and family life. Particularly interesting sections include "The Marriage Savers," pp. 28-34, Gertrude Himmelfarb's "Beware the Child Raising Manual" (pp. 50-51) warns "that an expert is sometimes the worst person to ask" under the editorial titled "Marriage Matters," pp. 4-6.

Marriages can be repaired and family life can be improved as long as the tie to the children is paramount in the parents. Richard B. McKenzie in his work *The Home: A Memoir of Growing Up in an Orphanage* (Basic Books, NY 1996) states that "A Good Orphanage Is Better Than Bad Foster Care." Various observers such as Christopher Laseh arrive at the conclusion that the idea of love as self-sacrifice and submission to a higher loyalty was too much for the psychotherapeutic sensibility to accept. The mission of the post Freudian therapists and their professionals had become the gratification of every client impulse. For selfish therapists there seems to be no required duties, denials, inhibitions or restraint for their clients, only rights and opportunities for change. Paul Vitz in *The Psychology of Religion: The Cult of Self-Worship* (W. B. Eerdmans Pub. Co., New York, 1996) indicates that self-theory in psychotherapy promotes the view that loving and trusting yourself and "doing your own thing" leads to achievement of the highest states of individual adjustment. Under selfish therapeutic theory there are few duties or restraints on the client and the goals of this theory become closely related to dissolution of marital and family ties in the name of personal growth and autonomy. A person who lives by such philosophy would hardly present a suitable altruistic and responsible role for his or her children.

[20] There are voluntary organizations at national, state, regional and local levels which offer mentoring services for girls and young women in an attempt to provide the socialization that many have missed in their earlier family life. Unfortunately neither motherhood or fatherhood can be taught. Those who have studied the way in which their mothers have mothered and fathers have fathered children know that it is not like plumbing or carpentering. There may be techniques which are more successful than others, but the skills are frequently not as important as the intent, the motivation and continued concern exhibited by the player of the role. In a sense, the skills of parenting and child development without the personal intent and concern are often found in the professional day care or homemaker. These skilled persons have the "words" but may lack the "music" of parenting. What the paid worker has may be less important than what the sincere parent may offer given the time, opportunity, and motivation. Parenting apparently develops out of a selflessness about the child which cannot

be purchased. The parent, the concerned relative, the sincere friend and the willing volunteer with the time, stability and opportunity have much to offer the child. It all seems to revolve around the willingness to put the child first ahead of all other values in one's life. Often this willingness to parent other peoples children is found in religiously motivated people, and in religious institutions which are part of the local community scene.

This human concern makes the difference between the paid day care worker and the concerned family relative or willing friend. Because of this, a child often can successfully be raised in a family supported by a collection of neighbors in a village. But this is not a "village of government workers." It is also because of the lack of this quality that makes for the failure of some institutionally raised children to become part of the social mainstream, and why others succeed so well. Some programs as Head Start, Upward Bound, and other efforts of the War on Poverty in the United States had great success with children, especially in their first phases, and others failed miserably. For some of the workers in the program it was a "calling," a matter of personal life purpose, and for others it was "just a job" or a "career." For those for whom parenting or surrogate parenting is a life-purpose, the skills and processes can be taught, but for those who see it as a duty to be performed, the skills become irrelevant.

It must be emphasized that the skills of parenting are important. In the past, and in many of the currently effective families, individuals were taught to be parents by members of their extended family or by older family friends and relatives. These skills are also taught in small communities and in friendship interethnic and some church groups. A version of these skills have been made available through what the editors of the *Policy Review* (March/April 1996, pp.12-14) call the "Marriage Menders." Most of these parenting skills have been passed on by the grandmothers and grandfathers from generation to generation. Many of these skills are also taught by independent family and child therapists and agencies and some educational institutions as well. We need to emphasize that not all licensed therapists and agencies are equipped to provide the necessary skills, because many of these agencies and therapists tend to emphasize therapeutic goals which are counterproductive for family rehabilitation and cohesion.

Religious institutions have a long experience in caring for their members and in the process they have achieved a proven loyalty and adherence to their principles including familial responsibility on the part of the members. These religions include the Mormons, the Amish, the Mennonites, Orthodox Jews, the Seventh Day Adventists, some of the Evangelical Protestant Christians, and some of the Catholic churches. A number of Evangelical African American churches have already demonstrated a functional pattern of life style, virtue and morality. These cohesive religious groups have a familial life pattern devoid of many of the social problems experienced in other populations. Many of these religious groups, in the process of emphasizing these precepts, may in the process require the surrender of individual freedoms cherished by many in the contemporary society.

See: Kephart William H. in *Extraordinary Groups: An Examination of Unconventional Life Styles* Ed., St. Martins, 1986.

[21] The responsibility of the schools to the parents and the tax paying public is one which has been little discussed in recent decades. It is important to note the dismal level of performance of the public schools particularly in the inner city. The policies of these schools in these settings remind one of the definition of a fanatic–"someone having lost sight of his goals who now redoubles his effort." We offer here a comparison of many of the public schools of the past and those of the present (other than suburban public schools and private programs in chart III.)

Charles Murray in his recent analysis titled "A Stroll through the Income Spectrum," *The American Enterprise*, July/Aug 1996, (pp. 40-41) indicates that the problem of the imploding school system is not uniform and universal. He tells us that "one of the best-kept secrets about public schools is that, outside the major cities they're often very fine." He says that "the working stiff" (his name for the family father whose family doesn't live downtown in a big city) and who doesn't have a high income "and doesn't have to spend several thousands dollars on annual tuition." The bottom line is that tens of millions of Americans in the second and third fifth of incomes have a higher standard of living than a larger proportion of the Americans with income in the top fifth."

What really are the problems of the public schools? William F. Jasper in "The State of Our Decline: A Post-Mortem on Public Education," *The New American*, Aug 8, 1994, pp. 5-9, indicates that there is a difference of meaning of terms when used by educational bureaucrats at the city, state and national level and when used by ordinary people. When school bureaucrats say that something "positive" needs to be done in the public schools, their purpose is to aggressively and unconstitutionally expand the reach and control of the federal government and the administrative school bureaucracy. "Positive" means "more legislation, more statist nostrums, more educational fads and more money under the shop worn banner of "reforms," Jasper quotes Myron Lieberman in that "the American school system is in irreversible and terminal decline."

The American school system, says Jasper, has conned the American public with the 1983 report *A Nation at Risk* which indicated that "educational foundations of our society are being eroded by a rising tide of mediocrity that threatens our very future as a nation". The claim may be true, but we note, but the mediocrity was, at least in part the result of an anti-elitist, anti-excellence policy promoted by the same organizations of education. It was dishonest as well, from Jasper's viewpoint because the agenda promoted by the report was based on reforms which were responsible for much of the chaos and decline of the school.

Among the commission report findings were the concern that on nineteen academic tests, international comparisons by Americans were never first or second and were last seven times. Average achievement of high school students on most standardized tests was lower than it had been 26 years before. Between 1975-1980 remedial mathematics in public four years colleges were necessarily increased by 72 percent because of the inadequate competency of entrants. The Scholastic Aptitude Tests demonstrated an unbroken decline from 1963 to 1980.

So after ten years of "positive reform" costing a few trillion dollars, with invasion of federal investments and controls installed by increased governmental staffs, what was the outcome? By every conceivable measure academic, social, moral, spiritual and economic Jasper concludes that "the public school system in the US remains a colossal disaster."

There are a number of indices which are evidence of the failure. These include the findings that ninety million American adults cannot write a letter, figure out a bus schedule or comprehend jury instructions. Twenty-six percent of U.S. children in public schools are in special education classes compared to the one to three percent norm for other countries. SAT scores may have regained minuscule improvement but are still lower than 1960s level. American students in public schools spend only 41 percent of school time on basic subjects of math, science, history, English, and the rest of their time is spent on ancillary studies of sex education, drivers training, multiculturalism, consumer affairs and skewed versions of family life discussion, etc. The result is that 21 percent of college entries require remedial math courses, and 16 percent remedial writing and remedial reading. Over 2,000 major corporations had to provide basic remedial work for their new employees, 22 percent in reading, 41 percent in writing and 31 percent in math. And over a quarter of high school students drop out or fail to graduate (see Jasper as cited and Allyson Tucker "The Dismal State of Public Education," *The World and I*, October 1994, pp. 32-36).

And the American public school system's funding over the past decade increased from 108 billion to about 210 billion dollars by 1991-2, while falling even further in its achievement with little change in the number of children attending. Tucker (above) finds that reforms based on increased spending, higher teachers salaries, smaller classes and similar changes do not work because these factors are not related to school performance or student achievement. Tucker believes that only fundamental reforms including parental choice, school autonomy and deregulation can reverse the deteriorating performance of the public schools. Tucker (above) finds that the huge labor unions including the National Education Association, the American Federation of Teachers, the school janitors unions and their affiliates raise millions of dollars for legislative pressure to insure that their jobs are made adequately remunerative and secure, with feather bedding where feasible. When reforms are proposed they are either rejected or so amended as to be meaningless. Studies by various states indicate that less than 40 percent of all funding actually reaches the teacher or the classroom. The balance is diverted to administrative and supervisory staff who often work to dilute the teaching process.

The power of the teachers unions in the United States is so great as to be the second largest fund raising organization for the party of the current presidency. (See Jeffrey Bell, Populism and Elitism: Politics in the Age of Equality, Regency Gateway, New York, 1993.) The teachers unions and through them the public schools have thus become politicized and rather than supporting the children's learning needs the schools seem to exist for the accommodation and convenience of the educational monopoly.

The dismal conditions in American public schools are matched by public education in England, Australia and elsewhere in the Western world. We have devoted much space to the subject of schools because of their importance to family reclamation. Until the parents and localities regain some control over their children's classrooms, the resolution of anti-familial sex-education and other curricular matters may require community pro-familial pressure by parents.

[22] Rector, Richard, "Requiem for the War on Poverty," *Policy Review*, Summer 1992.

[23] Fleming, Thomas "The Truth About Patria Potestas," *The Family in America*, Rockford Institute, Rockford, Il, vol 10, no 11, Nov 1996, pp. 2-7. Wilson, James Q., "No More Home Alone," *Policy Review*, March/April 1996.

[24] How can We Resolve the Problem of Welfare? An intensive study of the welfare state indicates that part of its dysfunctionality derives from the problems of the massive centralized governmentally directed structure which is basic to the welfare state. To promote the family life of dependent populations requires "retail" rather than "wholesale" management of the welfare process. This is a practical matter. There is also a political science concern in that the principle of subsidiary is a clearly necessary basis for most governmental operation. When the principle of subsidiary is ignored, a government becomes laden with the over regulation by a centrality seeking to install one of a few molds on the intricacies of a complex nation of many cultures and populations. Because welfare is currently centralized in most welfare states, and because this central model is at the core of welfare's dysfunctionality, it would probably be preferable for retention of central funding, and for release of the administration of welfare to the states or provinces in the form of block welfare grants. The development, enactment, and operation of such a welfare-reform program is basic to the preservation and rehabilitation of the family in the western world. Robert Rector has made it clear that the family in general, in the developed nations cannot be rescued unless a complete change of welfare direction is brought about. Either the growing population of single parent families and their progeny are to be supported in subsidized poverty along with their pathogenic chaotic patterns, or the reverse shall have to occur, including the diminution of welfare; the enactment of work

as an important critical part of daily life for everyone, and the promotion of self-reliance and self-sufficiency for all. Because the family life of welfare dependent families is dependent on their self-sufficiency, increased pressure on absent fathers for child support will probably be tied to local welfare control, but hopefully this will be accompanied with involvement of these fathers in the lives of their children, and increased employment aid to help those families develop a parent model of self-sufficiency for the children. The removal of the welfare model of family life is necessary if the family is to be reclaimed in the industrialized nations.

[24] Dench, Geoff, *Transforming Men: Changing Patterns of Dependency and Dominance in Gender Relations*, New Brunswick, New Jersey, Transaction Publishers, 1996.

[25] Adelson, Joseph, "Splitting Up," *Commentary*, vol. 102, no. 3, Sept 1996, pp 63-66.

[26] Carlson, Allan, "Toward the Virtuous Economy," Keynote Address at The World Congress of Families, Prague, The Czech Republic, March 22, 1997. Mr. Carlson's paper can be secured at the Congress American Office, care of The Rockford Institute, Rockford, Illinois.

[27] Dichter, Midge, "How the Rioter Won," *Commentary*, vol. 94, no. 1, July 1992, pp.19-22.

[28] Thurow, Lester C., "Changes in Capitalism Render One-Earner Families Extinct," *USA Today*, January 27, 1997, p.17A

[29] Brownlee, Shannon & Miller, Matthew, "Families Tell Themselves Why They Work," *US News and World Reports*, May 12, 1997, pp. 58-73

[30] Goodfame, Dan "The Chairman of Virtue, Inc," *Time*, Sept 16, 1996, pp. 46-49. (An overview of William Bennett and his ethos.)

[31] Murray, Charles "The Legacy of the 60s" *Commentary*, vol. 94, no. 1, July 1992, pp. 23-30.

[32] Thomas, Andrew Peyton "The Death of Jeffersonian America?" *The Weekly Standard*, Aug 26, 1996, pp. 26-29.

[33] Carlson, Allan, "Toward the Virtuous Economy," Keynote Address at The World Congress of Families, Prague, The Czech Republic, March 22, 1997. Mr. Carlson's paper can be secured at the Congress American Office, care of The Rockford Institute, Rockford, Illinois, and Carlson Allan, "Two Cheers for the Suburbs," *The American Enterprise*, Nov/Dec 1996.

[34] Popenoe, David, "How to Restore the Nuclear Family in Modern Societies," World Congress of Families, Prague, The Czech Republic, March 22, 1997. The Popenoe paper is available as part of the proceedings of the Congress through The Rockford Institute, Rockford, Illinois.

ABOUT THE AUTHORS

David M. Genders is President & CEO, Pacific Lodge Youth Services and Foster Family Agency, Woodland Hills, California. B.S., Butler University, M.S., Southern Connecticut State University and doctoral studies at Brigham Young University. He has taught Special Education teacher training at Southern Connecticut State University, Pepperdine University, California State University—Northridge, Wisconsin State University—Steven's Point and National University. He has been directly involved in residential treatment services for severely disturbed, neglected and abused children since 1973. The past seven years have focused on restructuring the lives of juvenile offenders. Throughout his involvement with children, he has emphasized the importance of facilitating and encouraging family participation in the education, care, and treatment of children.

David S. Liederman, as the Chief Executive Officer of the Child Welfare League of America (CWLA) since 1984, heads the oldest and largest voluntary organization in the United States concerned with developing and improving services to abused, neglected and deprived children and their families. His nearly forty-year career in human services includes ten years in the Massachusetts state government as an elected member of the House of Representatives, the first Commissioner of the Office for Children, and the Chief of Staff to the Governor. Mr. Liederman earned his bachelor's degree at the University of Massachusetts in Amherst and his Master of Social Work at the University of Pittsburgh where he was honored with a distinguished alumni award. In addition to his numerous awards and acknowledgments, he was recently honored with The National Assembly of National Voluntary Health and Social Welfare Organizations' 1996 National Executive Leadership Award the National Association of Social Worker 1997 National Lifetime Achievement Award.

Mary Liston Liepold is Director of Program Resources at the Child Welfare League of America (CWLA), Washington, DC, where she is primarily responsible for foundation fundraising. From 1991 through 1996 she was editor of *Children's Voice*, the CWLA magazine. Child well-being is her central concern, but in 20 years as a writer and editor, she has developed materials in areas ranging from poetry to volcanology and from international relations to rock and roll. Her most recent publication is "Parenting without Punishing," in the May, 1998, issue of *Mothering* magazine. She holds a doctorate in American Literature from the Catholic University of America.

David Marsland (MA, Ph.D.FRSH) is Professor of Health Informatics and Director of the Centre for Epidemiological Research at Brunel University, London, UK. He was educated at Watford Grammar School; at Cambridge University, where he was Classics Scholar of Christ's College; and at the London School of Economics, where he undertook postgraduate studies in sociology and held a Morris Ginsberg Fellowship. His teaching and research focuses on social policy, social theory, research methods, and epidemiology. He has been an Advisor to the Parliamentary Social Security Committee, and in 1991 he won the first Thatcher Award for contributions to the analysis of freedom. The latest of his more than twenty books was *Welfare or Welfare State*, published by Macmillan in 1996.

Dennis O'Keeffe is Senior Lecturer in the Sociology of Education at the University of North London. He has lectured widely in the United States, Canada, and Australia, as well as extensively in Eastern Europe. He has been visiting professor of education at Brigham Young University, Utah. He has coordinated extensive research into the problem of school truancy and is the author of many books and articles on education and social science. His most recent book is *Issues in School Attendance and Truancy*. He is currently writing a book on political correctness and engaged in a translation of Benjamin Constant's *Principes de Polititique*.

Geoffrey Partington gained honors degrees at Bristol University in history and London University in sociology and economics, and higher degrees in education in Bristol University and his doctorate in politics at the University of Adelaide. In England he was a history teacher, headmaster and inspector of schools. He is currently a Visiting Scholar in the Flinders University of South Australia, where he taught after emigrating from Britain in 1976. He has taught in the University of the South pacific in Fiji and has recently carried out consultancies into teacher education in New Zealand and the United Kingdom. His books include *Women Teachers in the Twentieth Century* (1976), *The Idea of an Historical Education* (1980), *The Australian Nation: Its British and Irish Roots* (1994) and *Teacher Education and Training in New Zealand* (1997).

Ralph Segalman is a professor of sociology (Emeritus) at California State University at Northridge. His experience includes over 25 years as a practicing social worker and community organizer, and also about 25 years as a professor in sociology and social work. His education includes a bachelors and masters degree at the University of Michigan and a Ph.D. in social Psychology at New York University. He has done field work in sociology in Israel, Morocco, and many European countries. His writings include academic works on *Poverty in America: The Welfare Dilemma* (with Asoke Basu); *The Swiss Way of Welfare: Lessons for the Developed Nations; Conflicting Rights: Social Legislation and Policy, Social Insurance and Public Assistance; The Deviant, the Society and the Law; Dynamics of Social Behavior and Development: A Symbolic Interactionist Integration of Theories; Cradle to Grave: Comparative Perspectives of the State of Welfare* (with David Marsland), and chapters in *Leadership: Theory and Practice; Work and Employment in Liberal Democratic Societies; Children and Families: Abuse and Endangerment;* and others. He also has presented major articles including "The Family: Past, Present, and Future" (with Alfred Himelson), "The Politics of Poverty" (with Alfred Himelson), and others.

Robert L. Woodson, Sr. is founder and president of the National Center for Neighborhood Enterprise (NCNE), a nonprofit research and demonstration organization that was created in 1981 to support grassroots initiatives which are addressing such societal problems as family dissolution, youth violence, and substance abuse, engendering social and economic revitalization in their communities. A strong proponent of strategies of self-help and empowerment, Woodson is frequently featured as a social commentator in the print and on-air media. He received a B.S. from Cheyney University and a M.S.W. from the University of Pennsylvania. Among the many awards he has received is the prestigious John D. and Catherine T. MacArthur Fellowship. His publications include *Youth Crime and Urban Policy, A View from the Inner City* (1981), *On the Road to Economic Freedom: An Agenda for Black Progress* (1987), *A Summons to Life, Mediating Structures and the Prevention of Youth Crime* (1988) and most recently, *The Triumphs of Joseph: How Today's Community Healers are Reviving Our Streets and Neighborhoods* (1998).